HUMAN ACTIVITY PATTERNS
IN THE CITY

WILEY SERIES IN URBAN RESEARCH

TERRY N. CLARK, EDITOR

Resources for Social Change: Race in the United States
James S. Coleman

City Classification Handbook: Methods and Applications
Brian J. L. Berry, Editor

Bonds of Pluralism: The Form and Substance of Urban Social Networks
Edward O. Laumann

Nonpartisan Elections and the Case for Party Politics
Willis D. Hawley

Politics and Poverty: Modernization and Response in Five Poor Neighborhoods
Stanley B. Greenberg

Education, Opportunity, and Social Inequality: Changing Prospects in Western Society
Raymond Boudon

Guerrillas in the Bureaucracy: The Community Planning Experiment in the United States
Martin L. Needleman and Carolyn Emerson Needleman

The Roots of Urban Discontent: Public Policy, Municipal Institutions, and the Ghetto
Peter H. Rossi, Richard A. Berk, and Bettye K. Eidson

Ethnicity in the United States: A Preliminary Reconnaissance
Andrew M. Greeley

Mayors in Action: Five Approaches to Urban Governance
John P. Kotter and Paul R. Lawrence

Leadership and Power in the Bos-Wash Megalopolis: Environment, Ecology, and Urban Organization
Delbert C. Miller

Human Activity Patterns in the City: Things People Do in Time and in Space
F. Stuart Chapin, Jr.

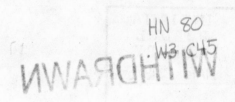
HUMAN ACTIVITY PATTERNS
IN THE CITY

Things People Do
in Time and in Space

F. STUART CHAPIN, Jr.

A WILEY-INTERSCIENCE PUBLICATION

JOHN WILEY & SONS, New York · London · Sydney · Toronto

Copyright © 1974, by John Wiley & Sons, Inc.

Library of Congress Cataloging in Publication Data:

Chapin, Francis Stuart, Jr., 1916-
   Human activity patterns in the city.

  (Wiley series in urban research)
  "A Wiley-Interscience publication."
  Bibliography: p.
  1. Time allocation surveys—Washington metropolitan
area. 2. Social surveys. I. Title.

HN80.W3C45   301.5   74-5364
ISBN 0-471-14563-7

Printed in the United States of America

10 9 8 7 6 5 4 3 2 1

The Wiley Series in Urban Research

Cities, especially American cities, are attracting more public attention and scholarly concern than at perhaps any other time in history. Traditional structures have been seriously questioned and sweeping changes proposed; simultaneously, efforts are being made to penetrate the fundamental processes by which cities operate. This effort calls for marshaling knowledge from a number of substantive areas. Sociologists, political scientists, economists, geographers, planners, historians, anthropologists, and others have turned to urban questions; interdisciplinary projects involving scholars and activists are groping with fundamental issues.

The Wiley series in Urban Research has been created to encourage the publication of works bearing on urban questions. It seeks to publish studies from different fields that help to illuminate urban processes. It is addressed to scholars as well as to planners, administrators, and others concerned with a more analytical understanding of things urban.

TERRY N. CLARK

PREFACE

This book is about living patterns of city residents—the way they allocate their time to different activities in the course of a day, the rhythm of these activities around the clock, and the locus of these pursuits in city space. It looks into variations in activity patterns among subsocietal segments in the population, and it explores postulated antecedent ties these patterns may have with felt needs and preferences. Thus these may be more clearly understood and taken into account in planning and policy decisions on public investments in community facilities and on the delivery of services to residents of the city.

The origins of this volume go back to the late fifties, to some earlier work on the growth and development processes of cities. This line of work brought out how public investment decisions on the locations of thoroughfare improvements, utility extensions and schools, and private investment and zoning decisions on the locations of industrial areas and shopping centers, triggered residential development and influenced its direction and intensity. In later stages of this work, a model was developed which could simulate the growth of cities for short periods into the future, given information on these key public and private investment decisions. Such models serve a purpose in evaluating the implications of investment decisions before they are implemented and set in brick and mortar.

Although our model could achieve fair accuracy in estimating the pattern of residential development for the short term, beyond a three- to five-year growth period results were less impressive. For longer periods, the unknown and slower-acting "residual factors" begin to exert a cumulative influence and can no longer be treated in the model as constants in the development process. Some of my colleagues moved on to explore decision factors on the supply side of land development in greater detail, seeking to determine more precisely how decisions are made, and with what effects on the land development process. My own work became more and more concerned with the people who reside in the areas created by this process, an aspect of the demand side of the picture. For this kind of emphasis, not only is there a concern about residential preference and consumer behavior in the housing market, but today living quality and social equity have become policy issues in public and private investment decisions. Thus such questions as these are now becoming more relevant: how do facility and service systems supplied through such public and private investments affect the living patterns of those who live in the areas thus created? How do these decisions modify or shape the life systems not only for those who may live there for the period in which housing and many of the other investments are amortized, but for those who under present national housing policies will be second- or third-round users of the space during the "trickle down" period when the housing shifts to successively lower-income groups? In brief, what can we say about the fit of these investments to the living patterns of those destined to reside there for the full life of these investments?

At this time there are no studied approaches to questions of this kind, nor does the line of work reported in this volume provide any immediate answers. The concern here is with outlining an approach to the study of lifeways of people who live in the metropolitan area—identifying differences in living patterns for various segments of the population, especially for those aspects of everyday life which relate to the living qualities of the city, and determining what kinds of factors are associated with these living patterns. In short, the concern of this volume is with an approach to understanding the diversity of living patterns to be found in a city, with the notion of subsequently bringing this knowledge to bear in investment decisions. Given this kind of approach, the next step would thus be the development of measures of user demand as it differs from the investor's perception of user demand. But since user demand and, more specifically, user satisfaction with present opportunities and user preferences and expectations about changes in the future can be expected to vary with the life style, the first step involves the development of a base of understanding about life systems in the city. The work outlined here is designed to provide a beginning in developing such a base of understanding.

To bring out another way of thinking about the purpose of this volume, let me focus more directly on recent urban planning emphases and be more pointed about what I see to be a glaring omission in the practice of planning. An inspection of the output from city planning agencies across the country under the so-called "701 Program" of the National Housing Act of 1954 (a program designed to financially assist local planning agencies develop general plans for growth and development) indicates a strong preoccupation with the supply side of the picture and a relative insensitivity to users of space whom this planning is in part intended to serve. Although there has been a long tradition of dedication to the "public interest," and much is being said these days about community goals and citizen participation, these emphases appear to project a perspective about residents of a metropolitan area as though they were homogeneous in their lifeways and value orientations. To the extent that plans sought to meet minimum standards of health, safety, and general welfare, there was no occasion to question such a homogeneity assumption. So long as minimal standards were involved, the public interest was cloaked in a kind of axiomatic immunity. But with the rise of affluency in the post-World War II era, when attention has shifted increasingly from minimal to more optimal standards, the cloak of immunity has worn somewhat thin. Moreover, with the social ferment of recent years, the accompanying assertion of group identity, and pressures for civil rights and "a share in the pie" by previously silent segments of the population, it has become increasingly clear that investment decisions can no longer ignore the fact that the general public is made up of a number of publics and the public interest, a number of interests.

These themes indicate *why* the line of work reported here was undertaken. Let me now briefly sketch out *what* this line of work consists of and how this volume is organized. There are essentially two thrusts to the work presented here. One develops the underlying rationale for the study of activity patterns in a city, translates this conceptual view into an analysis strategy, and examines field techniques used and problems encountered in making this approach operational. The other focuses on the nature of these activity patterns, and makes some tentative statements about city life in the American scene as determined from applications of this strategy.

Work of this kind is heavily reliant on the behavioral sciences for its theoretical base. Although not included within the scope of the work presented here, in this respect the allocation of time by households to different activities can be approached in the traditions of economic theory. However, when the emphasis is on the social construction of human activity, as it is here, theoretical work from the other behavioral sciences is more relevant, particularly psychology, social psychology, sociology, and anthropology. Yet because activity systems as behavioral phenomena must eventually be juxtaposed with another set of phenomena concerned with development processes and the spatial organization of the physical environment, an aggregative level of study and analysis somewhat outside the main-line empirical traditions of these fields is required. Moreover, such an aggregative level of analysis lends itself well to the possibilities of using a systems approach in the analysis of the interface between activities and the physical organization of space in the city, an emphasis which is also somewhat outside the traditional empirical orientations of these fields. So in these respects, this volume approaches human activity with somewhat different ends in view and along lines that may lead to analytical emphases different from those customarily pursued in social and psychological research.

In line with the first thrust mentioned above, Chapter I reviews work on time allocation and indicates the scope of our work in this connection, and Chapter II sets forth the conceptual framework for the study of human activity systems in the urban scene. Chapter III is concerned with making these concepts operational in ways that planning agencies might use in getting a line on the living patterns in their jurisdictions. The succeeding chapters present results from applications of this research to a large metropolitan area and two of its submetropolitan communities in which our methods of study evolved. As a backdrop, a sample of residents from metropolitan areas in the 48-state portion of the American scene is used to bring the results into a more general perspective. Chapter IV is descriptive in its emphasis and indicates just how people of a metropolitan area allocate their time, where they spend it, and something of the temporal rhythm and the spatial locus of their activities. Chapter V describes the diversity of activity choices among people of differing ethnic and socioeconomic makeup, and Chapter VI seeks some explanation for patterns of activity choice in an exploratory application of a model developed in Chapter II. Chapter VII reviews selected results of Chapters IV through VI in terms of their promise for planning- and policy-related applications, and it comments on research and development emphases with a view to extending the work presented in Chapter II.

To the reader interested in the theoretical aspects of human activity the first two chapters and the last part of Chapter VII will be of primary interest. To those concerned with field techniques, Chapter III and Appendix I will be of special interest. Finally, to those desiring insights into urban living patterns that can be gained from analysis of activity data, Chapters IV through VI and Appendix II will be of particular interest.

Special acknowledgment is due The Ford Foundation and The John Simon Guggenheim Memorial Foundation for support during the academic year 1972–1973, when this series of studies was brought together into one focus. Acknowledgment is also due the Center for Studies of Metropolitan Problems of the National Institute of Mental Health for support during the summer of 1973 when the work on Chapter VI was undertaken. Much of the computer work in reanalysis of the data was supported by the University Research Council and the Computation Center of the University of North Carolina at Chapel Hill; throughout this and earlier stages of the work the University's Center for Urban and Regional Studies was of inestimable assistance as sponsoring agent of the research.

A special note of appreciation is due a number of colleagues who, unknowingly perhaps, have made contributions to what is set forth in this volume: Richard K. Brail, Edgar W. Butler, Asta C. Cooper, Linda A. Fischer, Philip G. Hammer, Jr., Henry C. Hightower, John R. Hitchcock, Joseph T. Howell, Maury D. Klein, Cris R. Kukuk, Frederick C. Patten, John L. Robson, and Robert B. Zehner.

F. STUART CHAPIN, JR.

University of North Carolina
Chapel Hill
December 1973

CONTENTS

TABLES

FIGURES

HUMAN ACTIVITY PATTERNS IN THE CITY

CHAPTER ONE

INTRODUCTION

A momentary pause on a street corner in the heart of a city never fails to fascinate, whether in the thick of the rush hour, the dawning of a day, the late evening hours, a Saturday, a Sunday, or a holiday occasion. People coming from somewhere, going somewhere. Persons in motion, repose, or conversation—each with a home address, most with a family, a circle of relatives, friends, neighbors, and acquaintances, and some with a web of affiliations extending to church, clubs, and other groups. Each individual possessing a network of ties in space—ties to different places in the city, but sometimes to other cities or places—business contacts, vacations, visits, and the like. Each individual also possessing a network of ties back in time—ties that take him back to prior events in the day, the week, or the year, to earlier years here in town, to other cities or places, and finally, to a homeplace.

Such a street corner glimpse, with all its richness of life, its humdrum, or its isolation—real or imagined—is but a sampled impression of one moment in time and at one point in one particular metropolitan area. How to capture the essence of this life in synoptic fact? How to extend one's grasp from a single street corner to all the byways of the city, and from a single instant to all those before and after? In short, how to describe the living patterns of a city—how people play out different routines, assume different roles, and possess different predispositions to do things in particular ways? This is what the study of human activity patterns seeks to do. It is a noble purpose, one fraught with many difficulties, yet one that is slowly being implemented and with improving success.

1

The critical dimensions in describing activity involve observations of the things people do in time and space. Time allocation has been a source of interest and a medium for social surveys for half a century at least, but spatial analysis of activity, especially as a measure coordinated with time allocation, has been pursued only relatively recently. Whether or not both dimensions are part of a study is of course a function of the purposes to be served by the study in the first place.

As spelled out below, the orientations of the work described in this book have an eventual concern with the interface between human activity and the organization of space in the city. There is therefore an interest in both time and space dimensions. The underlying assumption here is that activity and environment each influences the other. If the interdependencies between living patterns and spatial structure in the living environment are to be traced, not only is a theoretical construct that conceives of activity in time and space a requisite; an empirical capability for tracing these interdependencies in the urban scene is no less a requisite.

To introduce our approach and place it in the context of other work in progress, we first review the historical development of interest in time allocation and briefly identify the mainstreams of recent work. We then outline the general directions in which our own work is moving, preparatory to developing the conceptual framework outlined in Chapter II.

TIME ALLOCATION STUDIES

Time has been a source of speculation for centuries. Its meaning in a philosophical sense dates back at least to the pre-Socratic age of Greece in the sixth century B.C. at the time that Heraclitus speculated about the rhythm of events and the order in change as the reason of the universe. As a discipline concerned with interpreting the affairs of mankind, history certainly organizes what transpires in terms of time and the chronology of human events. A recent cooperative survey by scholars from a variety of fields under the editorship of Fraser (1966) makes it quite clear that time enters into the concepts of most sciences. The importance of the time cycles of day and night and of seasons as regulated by the sun have a fundamental significance for plant life and animal and human behavior. The human perception of time—its subjective and objective aspects—is studied in psychology. In the physical sciences, time has an instrumental significance in many forms of scientific inquiry; even relatively recently, it has had great theoretical importance in physics, as demonstrated in concepts of relativity and light velocity postulated by Einstein. Indeed, Fraser suggests the possibility of a new discipline, *chronosophy,* developed around the interdisciplinary and normative pursuit of knowledge across a range of fields including philosophy, the social sciences, and the natural sciences.

The Historical Roots of Time Studies

The use of time as a basis for studying social behavior is a relatively recent development in the social sciences. Its theoretical significance centers around notions of the allocation of time as a resource. But the earliest interest in time was more as an accounting device for the study of social behavior. Even so, in this usage time is not entirely divorced from notions of resource allocation, for the statistical form of time allocation records is certainly reminiscent of monetary accounts. Indeed, time studies probably grew out of the first family income and expenditure studies. A student of time studies in the international social science community, Szalai (1966) not only attributes the usage of the term "time budgets" in sociological literature to budgetary concepts in family expenditure studies, but sees interest in both as having grown out of conditions of poverty in cities in England and France in the eighteenth century. As early as 1797, Sir Frederick Morton Eden's *State of the Poor* study made use of family budget information in reporting on the depressed state of living conditions of the laboring classes of England. Frederic Le Play's descriptive case studies of working-class families in Europe, published over a period of years beginning in the 1850s, also used family budget information in recording deprivation experienced by the families chosen for study. Drawn by Le Play's work into a similar career, Ernst Engel, however, gave more attention to family budget statistics and incentives for work and buying, an emphasis that grew out of his studies of various segments of the German population. From this work came Engel's Law on the inverse relationship between income and the proportion taken up in food expenditures. In this connection, Szalai (1966, p. 3) points out that Engel's work marked a distinct beginning point when "the family budget no longer represented an economic situation but in a certain sense a report of economic activities from which conclusions could be drawn regarding the behavior pattern and motivation behind the activity."

The use of time in household studies first emerged in the twentieth century. In his survey of time-budget work, Szalai reports that the first studies in Europe were those undertaken in the early years of Soviet

Union economic planning. In this connection, he reproduces 24-hour time budgets of men and women workers in Moscow, comparing results from S. G. Strumilin's 1924 study with G. A. Prudensky's replicating study in 1959, and points out potentialities of time data for studies of social change. Among the early post-World War II developments in France cited in his survey are Jean Stoetzel's study of the impact of urbanization on living patterns of women, and Chombart de Lauwe's work examining time use in a family context where both spouses work. Szalai reports a veritable explosion of studies in the early sixties in both Eastern and Western Europe. These include in his own country a large-scale time-budget study of the Hungarian Central Statistical Office (1965) and his own work (Szalai, 1964) on leisure time and shift work under the auspices of the Hungarian Academy of Sciences.

In the United States, some of the earliest experience in using time allocation as a basis for studying human effort comes from studies of factory management by Frederick W. Taylor (1911) in the early 1900s. He first introduced the "time and motion" study, sometimes alluded to as the beginning of what is known today as the management sciences. Sorokin and Berger (1939), who reviewed the state of the art on the American scene at the time they were making their time allocation studies, cite a study published in 1913 which appears to be the first instance when the focus was on the worker's spare time rather than on his working time. Their survey also carries references to a host of studies, beginning in 1927 and extending into the thirties, undertaken as Agricultural Experiment Station projects for the study of the housewife's use of time on the farm.[1] Probably the study by Lundberg et al. (1934) of the use of leisure time in suburban Westchester County and Sorokin and Berger's own studies in the Boston area could be considered the forerunners of contemporary studies. The former made use of time-study techniques in a community context, and the latter is most significant for its treatment of methodological issues. Undoubtedly the reason for a lapse of interest in time studies that followed was the inordinate amount of detail involved in compiling information and the expense of analyzing vast quantities of data.

With the development of computer technology, however, and the great savings in time devoted to data handling that this meant, in the fifties there was a revival of interest. Among the first to recognize these opportunities, Foote, who had interests in research on labor-saving electrical appliances, and Meyersohn, who had been working on leisure-time behavior, combined forces and set out in their Tarrytown study to improve techniques.[2] The Foote-Meyersohn report (1959) presented at the World

Congress of Sociology at Stresa served to rekindle interest in the international social science community in time-budget studies. As a result, under Szalai's leadership, one of the most extensive cross-national cooperative social science ventures ever attempted was launched in 1964 in 12 countries in both the East and the West. Using standardized survey techniques and following common sampling and coding rules, Szalai (1972) and his colleagues brought together in one encyclopedic volume the results of this effort, including papers on a wide variety of methodological issues by participants in this enterprise. This study is notable for its richness in comparative cross-national descriptive perspectives. Although not a part of this consortium, the studies undertaken in Japan by Nakanishi (1966, 1970) for the NHK Public Opinion Research Institute provide insights into changes in Japanese leisure-time patterns associated with the introduction of television.

Another line of development, somewhat independent of the above beginnings in the use of time in social analysis, is the work done in the transportation field beginning in the early forties. Much of it came out of research sponsored by the U.S. Bureau of Public Roads, but the work of Kate Liepmann (1944) focusing on the time absorbed in commuting to work contributed to the momentum of interest in time and transportation which continues unabated to this day. The institutionalization of this interest is exemplified in the Public Roads-sponsored "origin and destination surveys" conducted experimentally before World War II but introduced on a mass basis in the years following.

Time-Space Emphases in Recent Work

Much of the more recent work follows the lead of these transportation studies and joins time allocation with spatial concepts of human activity. Along with a continuing use of time in various kinds of investigations as an accounting device, the more recent work also turns attention to the theoretical significance of time allocation and its temporal-spatial aspects. Much of it also reflects a strong interest in the potential of time-use studies for policy analysis. The seminal work of Meier (1959, 1962) in communications theory and the growth of cities served to focus attention on the potential of time allocation studies in policy analysis. In 1959, he proposed the application of time accounts in the evaluation of the social efficiency of planned improvements to cities.

Although it is not within the scope of this summary to take note of all the great variety of work in progress at this writing, it is useful to cite some of the main lines of research emerging and to cite developments which relate more directly to the emphases of this book.[3] There appear to be at least two classes of recent work in the behavioral sciences, one interpreting time allocation in the context of economic behavior and the other in terms of social behavior.

If the time and motion work of industrial efficiency studies and the more recent applications of this primarily tool-oriented kind of analysis to the operations of governments, hospitals, universities, and military commands are disregarded, what remains in the realm of economic behavior studies has to do primarily with household time allocation. The work of Becker (1965) suggests that by treating time as a resource that can be traded off with money, some fruitful insights can be gained in household activity choices. Treating the household as though it were a small factory, he examines its choices of activities on the basis of utility-maximizing behavior. For off-work periods of the day, the members of the household are seen to combine time with capital goods, raw materials, and labor in the production of "commodities" such as, say, going to the theater or watching television, with the actual choice of activity subject to resource and time constraints. Choice is examined first under conditions where time and goods are treated in fixed proportions and then under conditions where substitutions are made between time and goods. Following a similar direction of thought, Linder (1970) reasons through the household choice of goods and services of the "harried leisure class" under differing constraints of income and time. Viewing money and time as related resources involved in the choice process, Linder shows how choices in the expenditure of money for consumer goods also lock the individual into the expenditure of time in maintenance, repairs, and "down time."

Although not radically different from the view taken by the economist, the alternative view is concerned with choice in a social context. As in the work from economics, this stream of thought concentrates on household activities, with particular attention given to nonobligatory forms of activity where the individual is presumed to have more latitude in the exercise of choice. Some of it views activity choice as a function of the individual's satisfaction-seeking behavior in the fulfillment of certain needs, and some of it views activity choice as a function of tradeoffs among constraints.

Among the emphases evolving from this stream of work, we refer to three lines of development to indicate something of the range of orientations in the work in progress in which time and spatial aspects are examined as joint considerations in human effort. Using essentially a constraint-preference approach to human activity, the first work cited below follows a sample of mover households from the place of original residence to their new surroundings, observing how their selection of residential environments affects their daily activity patterns from the time the old routines are disrupted until the time an equilibrium is achieved in the new location. The second line of work focuses primarily on the constraints imposed on a person's activities. It views constraints as the negative determinants of choice and develops a conceptual view of the way in which constraints affect choice in time and space as a person moves through different stages of the life cycle. Also concerned with the constraints rather than the incentives of behavior, the third research group focuses on stress arising out of constraints as a basis for studying activity choice.

At this writing, the first work cited here is perhaps more involved in an empirical exploration of some of the theoretical issues surrounding human activity choice than are the other two lines of work. Although we have ascribed to it a constraint-preference emphasis, Michelson (1972, 1973) characterizes his work in somewhat different terms. Concentrating on movers in the Toronto metropolitan area and one subset among moving families, he utilizes activity choices as a medium for studying (1) the way these families select themselves for different residential environments as they perceive their life styles, and (2) the adjustive capacity of the family for achieving a new equilibrium in daily routines, including adjustment to stress-producing constraints that sociophysical surroundings impose on activity choices. His subjects are complete families in the child-rearing stage of the life cycle not constrained by income in the exercise of residential preferences, and his residential environments are single-family or high-rise housing and center-city or suburban locations, a two by two set of options in living environments before and after the move.

Michelson (1973) postulates a pattern to moving behavior that can be conceived in terms of stages in the sequence of family moves evolving through the life cycle. This sequence begins with a base-line stage, progressing through a stage of successive incremental adjustments, and eventually reaching an approximation of the family's ideal residential environment. The beginning stage is either when the family is formed or when it arrives in the metropolitan area, with the initial settling-in move largely set by income constraints, prior social contacts, and location factors such as access to the chief wage earner's place of employment. The second stage occurs generally in the child-rearing period of the life cycle and may consist of a series of moves in incremental response to successive strains, which may continue indefinitely or eventually converge on a final move. This move, which he sees as an effort to approximate an ideal environment, is the third stage in the sequence. In this framework, moves are seen to be a compensating process for deficits in the sociophysical environment as they are perceived or encountered over a period of time by the family. In a sense, the "push" part of residential moves thus derives from constraints, but Michelson's notions suggest that once the compensating aspects of the move have been accounted for, the "pull" part can be examined from a preference viewpoint.

His current work will not be able to test the full sequence of the staging of moves, but it will enable him to make an analysis of push-pull factors in one move based on direct interrogation about sociophysical features that are a source of irritation in the place being vacated in relation to features that are cited as a reason for selecting the new place; through follow-up interviews it will enable him to establish the success in overcoming sources of stress in the original sociophysical environment. However, more directly relevant to interests here is the opportunity that Michelson's longitudinal study affords for examining the new patterns of activity choice, both those attributable to overcoming the original constraints and the residue choices that might be attributable to preference. Such an approach would seem to view the individual as exercising a preference only after certain other constraining conditions are eliminated or otherwise taken into account.

The second line of work, dating from 1964, is based on studies in Lund, Sweden by Hägerstrand, who came to study human activity systems from a concern with the physical organization of the urban community. The extensive work undertaken in the development of study methods, particularly in the development of a time and space notation system for comparing household activity sequences, has yet to appear in English language print. However, a distillation of this exploratory work (Hägerstrand, 1969) suggests that human activity may best be understood in terms of the constraints rather than the incentives of activity. Hägerstrand postulates the activity sequence of the individual in terms of time-space life paths for a day, a week, or even a lifetime, where the probabilities of an activity being chosen can be viewed as a function of tradeoffs between three kinds of constraints. One kind relates to the physiological capability and access to the means of engaging in an activity. A second relates to the time schedules and spatial paths of other people or those set by institutions with the tools and materials required in production, consumption, or transactions. A third relates to custom, law, and various hierarchical systems of authority in the society. He suggests that in planning for a city systematic study of human activity in these terms might well provide a basis for a more direct consideration of the requisites of human activity, that is, the complementarity in timing and the coordination in space necessary for residents to pursue the most elemental tasks of everyday life.

Taking the Hägerstrand view that choice is primarily a function of constraints, the third line of work moves off in a different direction. Again drawing on extensive exploratory work, in this case centering on a university community in London, Cullen (1972) and his colleagues note that since much of the average weekday is tied up in routines over which people have little day-to-day control, the sequence of a day's activities in the life of an individual is "pegged" round key structuring episodes (work, homemaking, eating, sleeping, etc.) that are interspersed with "relaxed forms of behavior" which serve to give the day's events balance and continuity. Cullen sees both practicalities and conceptual problems standing in the way of applying utility-maximizing concepts or in explaining behavior in terms of preference analysis of the kind used in social research. He sees these interspersed forms of activity being shaped by the individual's experience with his environment and the disruptions or disturbance encountered in the daily sequence of all forms of activity. He emphasizes the importance of "stress links" between activity and environment, postulating that the interspersed activities in the average weekday, instead of being based on choice, may be the result of stress responses encountered in a loosely woven workday. This emphasis is reminiscent of the traditions of psychology focusing on conditioned response to environmental stimuli—in this work, conditioned response to negative stimuli in the sociophysical environment.

THE ORIENTATION OF THIS STUDY

As in the foregoing work, this study has an underlying focus on behavior-environment dynamics. It does not take an environmental determinism view of behavior, any more than it takes a rationalistic thought-controlled view of behavior. Rather it conceives of a person's activities in the urban scene as the result of a complex and variable mix of incentives and constraints serving to mediate choice, often functioning in differentially lagged combinations, with some activities directly traceable to positive choices, and some attributable to negative choices in the sense that constraints overshadow opportunities for choice.

In some respects, the view taken here runs counter to the reductionism bias in much of present-day scientific inquiry. But this view is not so much in reaction to these biases as it is a bias in the opposite direction, a strong belief in the necessity of a combinatorial emphasis or "whole cloth" view which defines the contingencies of human activity in terms policy makers can recognize, evaluate, and project into the realm where they must make tradeoffs and reach decisions.

In presenting the conceptual view described in Chapter II, we can lay no claims to sifting through the vast amount of work that must be subsumed in a combinatorial approach. Rather the strategy has been to enter upon an intermediate level of conceptualization based on general drifts of thought as they have been synthesized in the literature by those who are monitoring many specialized areas of scientific investigation. This strategy has distinct risks. However, we believe that if "whole cloth" approaches of the kind we are advocating are made contingent on continuous reexamination, a valid case can be made for working at this level of generalization.

This kind of emphasis places a premium on studying human behavior in much more aggregate forms than those customarily examined by behavioral scientists. In conceiving of the scale at which we approach human activity, it may be useful to think of the empirical work that provides the reference material for our studies as falling into classes of behavior arranged in an ascending scale from a micro to a macro level of emphasis. At the most micro level, the emphasis is on personal behavior—the individual acting in response to felt needs in the context of a defined environment of other individuals, institutions, conditions, and physical surroundings. Also at the micro level but somewhat more extensive in scope, a second kind of emphasis is on group behavior, say, behavior of the family, a clique, a gang, a committee, or possibly a coalition—a group of individuals forming a socially integrated entity and functioning through informal group-sanctioned actions in some defined environmental context. Still at the micro level but still more extensive in scope, a third emphasis is on firms, governments, hospitals, prisons, military commands, or other complex organizations—combinations of individuals and groups functioning as institutionalized entities and operating in formalized routines under explicit policies, laws, or practices within their defined corporate or institutionalized settings. Finally at a macro level, the emphasis may focus on societal behavior—collectivities of people, small groups, and complex organizations functioning in patterned ways in relation to various social systems and the cultural environment of the larger society.

The amalgam of these various scales of viewing behavior of greatest relevance to policy analysis encompasses what might be called a "small society" or, for our purposes here, the segment of the larger society that is represented by a metropolitan community. For policy purposes, the population units of interest are the subsocietal segments which reflect a relatively homogeneous life situation in terms of economic circumstances, ethnicity, stage in the life cycle, and other life style criteria, but which also reflect the characteristics of a political constituency, potential or existent. But to understand behavior patterns of such segments of a metropolitan community, it is necessary to conceive of these patterns in terms of the behavior of individuals. Since individuals relate their activities to those of groups and institutional entities, however, in the process of aggregating individual activities into activity patterns for entire population segments, indirectly the study is taking into account behaviors of entities at all of the above-noted scales of human behavior. Thus when the term "human activity patterns" is used, this refers to patterned ways aggregates of residents in the metropolitan community go about their daily affairs, that is, how archetypical persons (statistical means) from key socioeconomic segments of this small society pursue their rounds of daily activity. This community could be a Standard Metropolitan Statistical Area (as used in later chapters and widely used in census summaries), or it could be the "daily urban system" as proposed by Berry (1972), the "urban field" as conceived by Friedmann (1973), or the "urban realm" as described by Webber (1964).[4]

Research and development focused on human activity systems in the metropolitan community are viewed here as offering an important approach to the study of urban structure, certainly in a spatial sense but possibly in a social sense as well. An R & D effort of this kind might be conceived in four phases: an initial phase of *description,* that is, a study of patterned ways different subsocietal segments of the metropolitan community use the city, its facilities, and its services; next, an *explanation* phase, that is, a study of the factors that appear to regulate activity patterns thus described; then a *simulation* phase, that is, the development of a model capable of reproducing activity patterns, incorporating these explanatory factors; and finally, an *evaluation* phase, in which the simulation model is used to investigate the likely impacts on human activity of the implementation of various alternative plans and policies. In this frame of reference, the work reported here properly falls into the first two phases.

There are applications to urban planning and policy studies that go with each phase. As is brought out more fully in later chapters, the descriptive and explanatory phases provide the urban planner with a means for understanding the way people use a city; they give a synoptic view of the rhythm and the spatial locus of life in the city. They provide a basis for identifying and understanding the diversity in activity patterns to be found among segments of the population representing different life styles in the metropolitan community. These will be discussed more fully later.

Beyond what is covered in the work reported here, there is a key area of application that comes directly out of the first two phases and is concerned with the development of models of urban spatial structure and studies of the dynamics of change in the spatial organization of the city. A second area of application comes out of the next phases of an R & D effort and is concerned with simulation, then the application of time allocation in the evaluation of the social efficiency of planned changes in the spatial organization of a city. In the remainder of the chapter, we consider briefly each of these two areas of application.

Applications in Spatial Structure

Human behavior at this aggregate level can be examined in several time scales: in terms of a 24-hour day, a week, a season, or a lifetime. Most of the analysis in succeeding chapters focuses on the weekday, although Saturday and Sunday data are introduced to give insights into weekly patterns of activity. But in order to bring out the relationships between daily activity patterns and urban spatial structure, it is useful to examine briefly a form of behavior that assumes meaning primarily in the lifetime of the individual. We call this "moving behavior." In his study of moving stages of a family, Michelson (1973) demonstrates the interdependencies between moving behavior on the life time scale and the routines of a household on the daily time scale.

In our work, we postulate the connection between daily activity and spatial structure via two ongoing processes set forth in Figure I-1. The left-hand flows in this process are seen to be energized through a continuous process of conscious or subconscious evaluation the members of the urban household make with respect to two aspects of the "activity space": (1) their satisfaction with their day-to-day activity routines in social and geographic space, and (2) their satisfaction with the amenities of their social and physical surroundings. In a geographic and physical sense, members of the household are continuously assessing activity opportunities with respect to both the mix available to them and the pleasantness that this mix involves in getting to and from activity centers (home to work, home to shopping, home to schools, home to relatives, home to friends, home to preferred forms of recreation, and so on). With respect

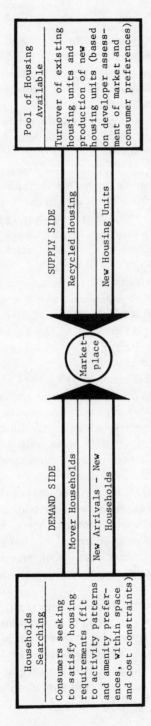

Figure I-1. The housing market process through which household activity systems and preferences on amenities influences urban spatial structure.

to amenities, there is an ever-present sensitivity to the adequacy of the dwelling (its space, layout, facilities, and the yard) and the neighborhood (the kind of neighbors, the attention they give to maintaining their homes and yards, the extent of traffic and inimical land uses in the area, the safety and social compatibility of the environs for rearing children, and so on). Often triggered by a change of family size, a change in family economic circumstances, or some crisis in the household, a time comes when the dissatisfactions with the present situation *pushes* the household into a search for housing.

The upper flow in the diagram represents the movers who experience both a "push," that is, a tipping-point dissatisfaction with an old residential environment, and a "pull," that is, a tipping-point attraction to another residential environment sufficient to decide to move. These are the households in the upper flow of the moving stream. The lower flow depends on in-migration and the rate at which new families are forming. In national studies from which came the activity data used in later chapters, it was found that in a three-year period 45 percent of the households in the sample moved (Butler et al., 1973). It might therefore be reasonable to estimate that roughly 15 percent of the households of a metropolitan community are likely to be in the two streams on the left-hand side of the diagram in any one year.

The right-hand side of the diagram shows one of the key processes by which residential areas change in a physical and spatial sense, in part as a result of lagged effects of the left-hand side (housing units becoming available when vacated by movers) and in part the result of land developers anticipating a market (new housing units being added to the housing supply). The upper flow of recycled housing and the lower flow of new housing generated by the land development process thus represent the sources of housing supply.[5] Under classical land rent theory, the marketplace strikes an equilibrium between the two, and in the dynamic view, the spatial structure of the city is constantly responding, the amount of space converted to new housing being a reflection of developers' estimates of the residue of demand not taken up by recycled housing. It is through this process that human activity influences the spatial structure of the city.

Though indirect and involving processes that extend over a time period more commensurate with the life cycle than the daily or weekly time scale, the moves people make provide the connection between daily activity patterns and the changing patterns of residential land use in urban spatial structure. The day-in and day-out experience of households in the pursuit of their out-of-home activities and the cumulative levels of dissatisfaction with access to their places of out-of-home activity become one source for triggering the push part of the moving decision. The other source derives from levels of dissatisfaction with amenities of the living environs of the kind Wilson (1962), Butler et al. (1969), and Lansing et al. (1970) have sought to measure in their work. Activity and the residential livability studies thus provide a basis for estimating the push forces underlying moving behavior.

The reciprocal of these forces, that is, the mix of accessibilities and amenities that constitute the pull forces of moving behavior, is generally part of the same investigative studies in which push factors are examined. However, the pull aspect, which has to do with prospective choices, is somewhat more difficult to measure. It faces some of the same difficulties that preference analysis has encountered in many other predictive studies. Not only do unpredictable situational factors enter into choices at the moment they are made, but rarely do preference studies present choice alternatives in the framework of constraints under which choices must be made. In study after study where preferences are followed up in an investigation of actual behavior, the correspondence between stated preferences and eventual behavior has been of relatively low order. Although not designed to study moving behavior, the "game" Wilson (1962) introduced into his interviews about living qualities of the city gives explicit consideration to cost constraints that subjects take into account in the course of indicating preferred choices in residential features. The "game" on activity choices in the use of leisure time reproduced in Chapter III (also not specifically designed for mover studies) in effect approaches accessibility considerations in the same kind of constraint-preference framework. These illustrate directions for improvement of preference studies in both the amenity and accessibility dimensions of the pull aspect of the move. Conceivably instruments of this kind, carefully designed around the major contingencies that enter into the choice of new residence, can improve on the success of conventional preference studies.

Activity Analysis in Simulation-Evaluation Studies

In applying time allocation to evaluation studies as proposed by Meier (1959), time is used as a medium for assessing the social impact of planned improvements. It can be used to test the social efficiency of a particular part of a plan, or it can be used to examine alternative plans for the total transportation and land use configuration of a metropolitan area. Thus in reaching a decision among alternative general plans, in effect Meier proposes evaluation of social efficiency in terms of two questions. (1) With respect to the land use and transportation systems proposed, how much more time does one particular arrangement free up for residents than do the others? (2) How much more variety in activity opportunities for the use of this freed time does one alternative land development scheme offer than do the others? Meier sees the combination of two such tests as a measure of the richness of life that any particular plan offers with resepect to all the others.

This approach was used in the analysis of our Washington data in comparing the quality of life there with the national scene. In this kind of application, instead of asking the above questions, we put it this way:

1. Within the various income and racial categories, how much relatively free time do Washingtonians have in comparison with levels of free time to be found in Standard Metropolitan Statistical Areas in the nation as a whole?
2. Given the relative differences in levels of discretionary time available to residents within the different income-race groups, what diversity of activity do Washingtonians have relative to the range found in the nation as a whole?[6] (Chapin, 1971)

The results showed that for all income categories Washingtonians, especially whites, ranked above their national counterparts in the amount and diversity of free time, but within the Washington scene there were pronounced disparities among income and racial categories.

In applying Meier's richness-of-life criteria to alternative transportation and land development plans, it is obvious that a simulation capacity is required. The methodological approaches have been under study for several years. Brail (1969) has outlined both a transitional matrix and a computer simulation approach to time and spatial patterns of activity,[7] and Tomlinson et al. (1973) use an entropy-maximizing type of model in predicting the distribution of subjects engaging in different activities in time and location (types of location as opposed to geographic location).

Nevertheless, simulation encounters formidable problems in projecting activities into the future. Even simply redistributing the present population to a rearranged spatial structure of a city poses some of the same kinds of uncertainties discussed above in connection with moving behavior. To anticipate activity configurations involves a high order of sophistication in probing choice probabilities under fairly clearly defined contingencies of the kind subjects make in real-world tradeoffs of their choices. However, even though there are some serious problems in projecting activity patterns into the future, simulation models can be expected to serve a useful purpose in the analysis of existing spatial structure and in evaluating the social efficiency of one change introduced in the existing order of things over other alternative changes. Given sensitivity analysis of such models and longitudinal information on activity response to physical changes in spatial organization, it can be anticipated that the simulation-evaluation stages of this research will yield a method of making "social impact" studies.

The foregoing discussion gives a general framework of how our studies of human activity patterns in the metropolitan community fit into broader studies concerned with the dynamics of man-environment relationships. The next chapter focuses on the human part of such a framework; it develops a conceptual approach to human activity followed in the empirical work described in subsequent chapters.

NOTES

1. The modern-day counterpart in the urban scene has come a long way in theoretical and empirical development as exemplified in Walker and Gauger (1973).

2. Their work gave special attention to the development of diary techniques in recording the use of time and the use of content analysis in time allocation. The extension of their work to the use of computer technology in content analysis of diary data is reported by Kranz (1970).

3. Anderson (1971) and Ottensmann (1972) provide some indication of the range of emphases to recent allocation research, including spatial analyses.

4. Berry's "daily urban system" and Friedmann's "urban field" are both based on the notion of the "commutershed" of employed persons in a central city, and Webber's "urban realm" is an aspatial concept that encompasses intercity contact patterns characteristic of businessmen, professionals, and academicians.

5. Clawson (1971), Kaiser and Weiss (1970), and Wheaton (1964) spell out the decision process and the actors involved in this process.

6. Reprinted by permission of the *Journal of the American Institute of Planners*, **37**:6, November 1971.

7. See note 15 in Chapter III.

REFERENCES

Anderson, James (1971). "Space-Time Budgets and Activity Studies in Urban Geography and Planning," *Environment and Planning*, **3**:4.

Becker, Gary S. (1965). "A Theory of the Allocation of Time," *The Economic Journal*, **75**:299.

Berry, Brian J. L. (1972). "Population Growth in the Daily Urban Systems of the United States," Chapter 6 in Sara Mills Mazie, ed., *Population Distribution and Policy*, Vol. V of research reports of U.S. Commission on Population Growth and the American Future (Washington, D.C.: U.S. Government Printing Office).

Brail, Richard K. (1969). *Activity System Investigations: Strategy for Model Design*, Ph.D. dissertation, University of North Carolina (Ann Arbor: University Microfilms).

Butler, Edgar W., F. Stuart Chapin, Jr., George C. Hemmens, Edward J. Kaiser, Michael A. Stegman, and Shirley F. Weiss (1969). *Moving Behavior and Residental Choice*, NCHRP Report 81 (Washington, D.C.: Highway Research Board, National Academy of Sciences).

————, Ronald J. McAllister, and Edward J. Kaiser (1973). "The Effects of Voluntary and Involuntary Residential Mobility on Females and Males," *Journal of Marriage and Family*, **32**:5.

Chapin, F. Stuart, Jr. (1971). "Free Time Activities and Quality of Urban Life," *Journal of the American Institute of Planners*, **37**:6.

Clawson, Marion (1971). *Suburban Land Conversion in the United States* (Baltimore: The Johns Hopkins Press).

Cullen, Ian G. (1972). "Space, Time, and the Disruption of Behavior in Cities," paper presented to the Research Group on Time Budgets, Brussels.

Foote, Nelson N., and Rolf Meyersohn (1959). "Allocations of Time Among Family Activities," paper presented at the Fourth World Congress of Sociology, Stresa. For some of the methodological issues, see Foote in Robert W. Kleemeier, ed. (1961). *Aging and Leisure* (New York: Oxford University Press).

Fraser, J. T., ed. (1966). *The Voices of Time* (New York: George Braziller).

Friedmann, John (1973). "The Future of the Urban Habitat," Chapter 3 in Donald M. McAllister, ed., *Environment: A New Focus for Land-Use Planning* (Washington D.C.: U.S. Government Printing Office). See also Friedmann and John Miller (1965). "The Urban Field, "*Journal of the American Institute of Planners*, **31**:4.

Hägerstrand, Torsten (1969). "What About People in Regional Science," *Papers of the Regional Science Association*, **24**.

Hungarian Central Statistical Office (1965). *The Twenty-Four Hours of the Day*, An Analysis of 12,000 Time-Budgets, Budapest.

Kaiser, Edward J., and Shirley F. Weiss (1970). "Public Policy and the Residential Development Process," *Journal of the American Institute of Planners*, **36**:1.

Kranz, Peter (1970). "What Do People Do All Day?" *Behavioral Science*, **15**:3.

Lansing, John B., Robert W. Marans, and Robert B. Zehner (1970). *Planned Residential Environments* (Ann Arbor: Institute for Social Research, University of Michigan).

Liepmann, Kate K. (1944). *The Journey to Work* (London: The Oxford University Press).

Linder, Staffan B. (1970). *The Harried Leisure Class* (New York: Columbia University Press).

Lundberg, George A., Mirra Komarovsky, and Mary Alice McInerny (1934). *Leisure: A Suburban Study* (New York: Columbia University Press).

Meier, Richard L. (1959). "Human Time Allocation: A Basis for Social Accounts," *Journal of the American Institute of Planners*, **25**:1.

———— (1962). *A Communications Theory of Urban Growth* (Cambridge Mass.: The M.I.T. Press).

Michelson, William (1972). "Environmental Choice: A Draft Report on the Social Basis of Family Decisions on Housing Type and Location in Greater Toronto," discussion paper (Ottawa: Ministry of State for Urban Affairs).

—— (1973). "Residential Mobility as a Deficit Compensating Process," paper presented at the Canadian Sociology and Anthropology Association Meetings, Kingston, Ontario, May 29, 1973.

Nakanishi, Naomichi (1966). *A Report on the How Do People Spend Their Time Survey* (Tokyo: NHK Public Opinion Research Institute).

—— (1970). *TV Audience Today* (Tokyo: NHK Public Opinion Research Institute).

Ottensmann, John R. (1972). *Systems of Urban Activities and Time: An Interpretative Review of the Literature*, An Urban Studies Research Paper (Chapel Hill: Center for Urban and Regional Studies, University of North Carolina)

Sorokin, Pitirim A., and Clarence Q. Berger (1939). *Time Budgets of Human Behavior* (Cambridge, Mass.: Harvard University Press).

Szalai, Alexander (1964). "Differential Work and Leisure Time-Budgets," *The New Hungarian Quarterly*, **5**:16.

—— (1966). "Trends in Comparative Time-Budget Research," *The American Behavioral Scientist*, **9**:9.

——, ed. (1972). *The Use of Time* (The Hague: Mouton).

Taylor, Frederick W. (1911). *The Principles of Scientific Management* (New York: Harper and Brothers).

Tomlinson, Janet, N. Bullock, P. Dickens, P. Steadman, and E. Taylor (1973). "A Model of Students' Daily Activity Patterns," *Environment and Planning*, **5**:2.

Walker, Kathryn E. and William Gauger (1973). "Time and Its Monetary Values in Household Work," *Farm Economics Review*, **65**:7.

Webber, Melvin M. (1964). "The Urban Place and the Nonplace Urban Realm," in Webber et al., *Explorations into Urban Structure* (Philadelphia: University of Pennsylvania Press).

Wheaton, William L. C. (1964). "Public and Private Agents of Change in Urban Expansion," in Melvin M. Webber et al., *Explorations into Urban Structure* (Philadelphia: University of Pennsylvania Press).

Wilson, Robert L. (1962). "Livability of the City: Attitudes and Urban Development," in F. Stuart Chapin, Jr. and Shirley F. Weiss, eds., *Urban Growth Dynamics* (New York: John Wiley & Sons).

CHAPTER TWO

A CONCEPTUAL APPROACH

TO THE STUDY OF

HUMAN ACTIVITY SYSTEMS

Over the years cities have been described in many ways, depending on the beholder and his or her particular interests. This book describes a city in terms of how people allocate their time to different activities and where activities take place. In the usage here, "activities" are classifiable acts or behavior of persons or households which, used as building blocks, permit us to study the living patterns or lifeways of socially cohesive segments of metropolitan area society. The approach taken here seeks a level of conceptualization that has meaning not only in interpreting the social construction of a metropolitan community, but eventually also in examining interrelationships between activity systems and the spatial organization of the city—its land use systems, its community facilities, and its service systems.

In this respect, the rationale sketched out in this chapter carries a caveat. This asserts that to be fruitful for planning and policy analysis, the conceptualization of activity systems, though requiring a sensitivity to the micro level world of the individual person, must nevertheless be designed primarily around lifeways and thoughtways at the level at which political constituencies or publics form and assert themselves. Thus conceptually the focus is on activity systems of the population as a whole and, in particular, of different segments of the population that possess group identity and potential for response in the political arena.

Although our approach is conceived broadly in terms of life systems of the metropolitan community and its subpopulations, the emphasis throughout is on the activity outcomes of these life systems, that is, the recognizable public behavior of people in the community as a whole and in its several segments. In the broadest context, this approach must allow us to conceive of how activities of individuals and households relate to activities of such institutional entities as firms, labor unions, churches, philanthropic groups, and myriad other forms of complex organizations man has created to deal with his needs. But for purposes of exploratory investigations reported here, particular attention is given to conceptualizing human activity in terms of archetypes in the population[1]—how and why persons of different sex, from households at different stages in the life cycle, and from societal segments of different ethnic and socioeconomic composition allocate time to different pursuits in their day-to-day affairs.

Some students approach this kind of task deductively. They might approach the metropolitan community as a social system, positing certain structure-function constructs, then deriving thoughtways and lifeways in the context of such constructs, and finally testing what is observed in reality against these concepts. Others approach such a task inductively. With respect to phenomena under study here, they might approach the metropolitan community in terms of the outcomes of the "sifting and sorting process" by which society becomes stratified, positing a societal structure from the analysis of the thoughtways and lifeways of man as observed in reality. A combination option is to approach the phenomena "transductively."[2] In this approach, *a trial statement of concepts* concerning the cause and effect relations that follow from this structure are drawn from deductive origins to provide an initial organizing framework; then within this context, *empirical observations and analyses* are undertaken in inductive traditions to supply feedback to the general model. Then a new but refined trial statement of the model is used for another round of the transductive process and another round of empirical observations and analyses.

This approach of merging theory building with empirical research on a round-by-round basis has been the one by which the conceptual framework presented in this chapter has evolved. No attempt is made to reconstruct the development of this schema round-by-round, nor is any attempt made to present the framework in a formal statement. Rather, I present the concepts in general summary form at their present stage of development and then discuss the empirical approach followed in this work.

The first section below is definitional in the sense of forming a general perspective about urban activity systems and indicating how human activity systems fit into this larger picture. The second section is definitional in a more specific sense and introduces concepts of time and activity relative to the individual person. Drawing on these concepts of the individual's behavior and sociological concepts of stratification, the third and final section outlines the rationale for examining activity patterns for various population strata in the metropolitan community and presents the research strategy followed in later chapters.

URBAN ACTIVITY SYSTEMS

"Urban activity systems" is an umbrella kind of term for the patterned ways in which individuals, households, institutions, and firms pursue their day-in and day-out affairs in a metropolitan community and interact with one another in time and space. The routines of these entities and the web of relations with one another are clearly very complex. As brought out by Webber (1964) these relations are both spatial and aspatial, some with a focus in a place-community and some extending into a boundaryless societal community which may be regionwide, nationwide, or worldwide. For place-communities, the systems perspective offers possibilities not only for identifying interrelations among systems by tracing how the activities of residents of a city and such institutional entities as firms, unions, churches, and various other formal organizations and informal groups relate to one another, but also for tracing interrelations between urban activity systems and ecosystems in nature, and between each of these and the systems in man's built environment—systems of land use, utilities, and community facilities

Although it is beyond the scope of this effort to go into the ramifications of such a general systems perspective, we may note the opportunities that this method of thought offers for studying the complex phenomena: in posing and testing different concepts of order among sets of phenomena, in identifying relationships among the parts within ordered sets, and in tracing the dynamics of interaction among the parts and the ordered sets. But even the task of delving into urban activity systems as one of these sets, seeking to determine order and relations and to develop a clear picture of the functioning of these systems, is beyond the scope of this effort.[3] Indeed, as will become evident in subsequent sections of this chapter, to deal with the complexities of human activity patterns alone requires a number of simplifying assumptions that place some limitations, under our present state of knowledge, on the interpretation of results.

To construct a general systems model requires submodels that not only accurately simulate real-world processes of each component system but also utilize a common denominator unit for measuring interaction among these systems. The more inclusive the system, the more universal the unit of measure must be. Thus for systems of the scope involved in investigating interactions among urban activity systems, ecosystems, and land use systems of the kind suggested above, a likely unit would be a measure of energy transfer as proposed by Odum (1971). If the system is somewhat less inclusive, as would be the case in modeling the functioning of urban activity systems, Meier's suggested approach (1962) of bringing concepts of communications theory to bear in the study of urban phenomena may someday offer the most appropriate line of research and development. By this approach, the emphasis would be on measuring and monitoring information flows.

In each of the three component systems to urban activity systems (human, economic, and institutional), there are of course long-established traditions of thought for conceptualizing the organization and functioning of each. Such work is certainly basic to exploring the possibilities of developing a systems approach to urban activity systems. For the human activity component, particularly in the study of broad societal aggregates, one can bring to bear sociological concepts of stratification and social structure to determine the nature of the social environment that conditions behavior in various strata of society. One also can draw on concepts of psychology to examine behavior of the individual, and on concepts of social psychology to gain understanding of behavior patterns of groups of people in these strata. For the economic activity component, the theory of the firm and equilibrium theory provide insights into the organization of firms and in understanding their transaction patterns, which in turn provide a basis for establishing networks of economic interaction in a metropolitan area. By the same token organizational theory and work on complex organizations and formal groups provide a basis for the study of institutional entities as these pursue lives of their own but also function with ancillary ties to the other two activity systems.

Yet even if a systems approach were to concentrate only on urban activity systems, there is as yet no operationally feasible common denominator unit of measure that works equally well within each of the urban activity systems and at the same time provides a means for examining interaction between these systems. Although Meier has suggested one basis for investigating this level of interaction, there are some substantial problems of obtaining data in the forms needed if this approach is to be used. To date, the effort that goes into the study of intersystem relations consists of extensions of models within the various component systems. For example, economists go to some lengths to take account of social behavior as it intrudes on otherwise "pure" economic behavior, including its effects in the pricing system of the market as "social costs." By the same token, sociologists and psychologists following their own traditions of theory freely extend their systems of thought to take in economic phenomena when they become important in rounding out a particular line of thought.

Certainly using time allocation as a basis of monitoring human effort, which is involved in this work, offers no more promise of capturing all considerations of consequence in studying interactions between entities in the various urban activity systems. Yet it takes no stretch of the imagination to see that these systems have interrelationships in a time sense. For example, the daily and weekly routines of individuals are affected by the schedules various institutional entities follow: shift schedules of factories, store hours, office hours of doctors and other professionals, times and lengths of theatrical and musical offerings, the hours schools are in session, and the meeting dates of clubs. Moreover, each institutional entity has its own schedules, for example, the factory has schedules for acquisition of raw materials and processed inputs, for production, for maintenance of equipment, for delivery of finished products, and so on.

Although time has a bearing on such schedules and in the coordination of relations between entities, time of course gives no measure of the substantive nature of interaction. Perhaps the most that can be said about the use of time as a medium for defining interaction among the subsystems of urban activity systems is that all activities can be expressed in clock or calendar time, and that when a meaningful base measure emerges, time will have a use in the computation of rates and intensity of interaction and in establishing sequence to interaction.

A MICROANALYTIC VIEW OF HUMAN ACTIVITY

With the foregoing general introduction to urban activity systems, we now turn to developing a conceptual perspective of human activity. In this section the behavior of the individual is the focus of interest; the next section turns to behavior patterns of entire aggregates of population in the metropolitan community.

At a very elemental level, human activity consists of physiologically regulated behavior and learned behavior. The former has to do with such basic functions as sleep and intake of food. These can be postponed by the individual to some extent but only within limits. Experiments indicate that physiological functions of the human being are closely attuned to day and night cycles of the earth's movement in relation to the sun.[4] So it makes a great deal of sense to think of regularities in human activity in terms of these time concepts. There are activity variations by seasons which are part of an annual time cycle, and there are variations by years which are part of the life cycle of an individual. Like the lenses of a microscope that can be used interchangeably, different time scales can be used to probe differences in activity by time spans—by the day, the week, the season, or in the life cycle. In a very fundamental way properties of physiologically regulated activity set the temporal rhythm of the individual's activity routine and influence the scheduling of all other activity.

Conceptual Approaches to Learned Behavior

Learned acts of an individual have been conceptualized in two ways. In the main-line traditions of social psychology, exemplified here in the ideas of George Herbert Mead, an act is "the ongoing behavior of an individual initiated by a want and directed to the end of satisfying that want through the use of suitable elements in the environment" (Lee, 1945, p. 12). The explanation of an act is to be found in an impulse-stimulus-response sequence. The act involves first experiencing a want, then an arousal of interest in doing something about the want, and finally a satisfaction (or dissatisfaction) from having done something about it. The impulse-stimulus-response sequence is ongoing and can be repeated or it can subside, depending on the level of satisfaction. In short, the learning process produces a readiness to engage in the act or to turn away from it. This propensity of the individual to act in order to satisfy a want is referred to as "motivated behavior."

In the second, more recent Skinnerian view, thought-initiating behavior is considered to be irrelevant, and the act is seen to be controlled by elements in the "operant conditioning" context, not by "autonomous man" (Skinner, 1971). Operant conditioning is the introduction of positive or negative reinforcement in the environment.

In both views, environment is considered to be everything that has an effect on man's behavior, including his own behavior which preceded the act. In the first and longer established school of thought in psychology, the environment provides the opportunity for the act but does not initiate it; in the Skinner view, the environment not only provides the opportunity for the act but also conditions the act through its consequences. Thus instead of an act being described in terms of the thought processes of a person, it is described in terms of manipulated environmental contingencies external to these processes. It does not deny the existence of thought processes, but because the way in which these processes function cannot be scientifically proved, it defines acts entirely in the controllable elements in the environment where proof can be supplied.

Time is an element in both schemas for explaining human behavior. In the Skinnerian view it is concerned with structured behavior in an experiment and is used to establish sequence to sets of acts, to monitor speed and delay, and to record durations. In the traditional view, time can be construed in two ways. In the first, time offers a means for analyzing the pattern or structure to human activity as observed in the present. Here time is used to record when an act occurred, its duration, and the sequence of an act in relation to a series of different acts. In the second usage, however, it is concerned with life processes. In some respects, the process emphasis draws on interpretations of time within the person, what psychologists call "subjective time," whereas the time patterns derived from environmental contingencies make use of the concept of "objective time" (Doob, 1971, p. 8). In a process sense, time enters into human consciousness in a subjective way, with part of the sense of time being embedded in the past, part embodied in the present, and part of it ongoing into the future. Thus if we were to trace an act of learned behavior in an individual, we would seek the meaning of that act in the context of its before and after significance as well as its meaning of the moment. In this view, even trivial acts are conditioned by what has gone on before in the life process and what is perceived as consequences that follow. In the structure emphasis, time is instrumental to defining patterned activities of individuals and to studying the structured lifeways of entire segments of a population.

Applications of Behavior Concepts to Urban Planning

Both approaches have applications to urban planning. The underlying principles of Skinnerian behavior modification can be illustrated in transportation behavior. Thus if the objective of a transportation improvement is to induce people to change from the practice of each person driving his own car in rush hours to a car-pooling or bus-riding practice, one approach that can be used is the rationing of gasoline, as was done in World War II and as tried in a confusion of different plans in the seventies. Another might be to use an approach followed in a San Francisco Bay Area experiment. In this example, traffic lanes on the Bay Bridge were assigned in such a way that those who drove in car pools or took the bus had the time advantage—their vehicles had access to especially controlled express lanes whereas those who persisted in driving alone were forced into a reduced number of lanes of slow-moving traffic.

Here a reward (positive reinforcement) is offered to the traveler who conforms and punishment (negative reinforcement) to the traveler who does not. It is not difficult to conceive of applying these principles to moving behavior of families in the reordering of life in the city in order to integrate (or segregate) neighborhoods or to mix (or concentrate) economic groups; nor is it farfetched to conceive of modifying real estate development behavior by presenting or withdrawing reinforcing or aversive stimuli, for example, by selective programming of public works or by changes in regulatory measures.

The more traditional school of thought on human behavior is no less applicable to urban planning and, indeed, is perhaps more congenial to the vagaries of democratic political processes as we know them today. In western political traditions, the objectives in the development of the metropolitan area and in the delivery of services theoretically are defined in consultation with citizen constituenices (instead of being developed and supplied by autonomous political decision-makers). Thus behavioral analyses that take into account felt needs of different constituencies would seem to be an important technical input not only in specifying objectives but also in defining the environmental contingencies for political decisions. As noted earlier, planning analyses have often emphasized the supply side more than the demand side. Assuming this imbalance is remedied, however, the broadened analyses not only would draw on conventional investigations of land use, community facilities, and public services, but also would be concerned with the felt needs of user groups in the community, the facilities and services available to take care of these needs, their use of them, their satisfactions (or dissatisfactions) in using them, and the intensity of feelings about their unmet wants. From these investigations, cues for the definition of community objectives can be found, planning criteria established, and alternative ways of providing for facilities and services explored with more direct consideration of the way in which these changes match up with felt needs of user groups and their living patterns. Moreover, benefit and cost estimation in planning analyses can reflect more focused concern for the human side of the ledger. In brief, when objectives and alternative plans considering all the interest groups involved are finally moved into the political decision-making arena, deliberations on public improvement programming, regulatory measures, and the like will be based on more complete information about the constituencies they are presumed to serve.

Since the traditional school of thought gives some recognition to person-wants as these relate to behavior, this view, then, has something to say on the formulation of objectives for planning. In the operant conditioning school of thought, objectives concerning change in the environment are supplied external to the preference formulation, and the concern is with achievement of change by manipulating the reinforcement contingencies. This view has something to say about carrying out plans. It must be clear by now that both approaches are relevant to urban planning. The traditional view with its sensitivity to understanding want-related bases of behavior surely fits into the plan-preparation phases of urban planning. But the plan-execution phases can certainly draw on Skinnerian principles of reinforcement; indeed, the notion of a guidance system in the effectuation of a plan is quite compatible with this approach. In short, the strategic aspects of arriving at a plan belong with the first approach, and the tactics of plan execution belong with the second.

Since we are concerned in this book with bringing into urban planning more direct consideration of the way in which people in a metropolitan community go about their round of activities on a day-to-day basis and how variations in these activity patterns call for differing emphases in planning for facilities and services, the first model described above on thought-directed behavior will be of primary interest.

A Model for Interpreting the Individual's Behavior

In its most skeletal form, the behavioral sequence adapted from this model states that the act consists of a motivational component, a choice component, and an outcome component. For purposes of heightening the dynamic aspect of this behavioral sequence, the rational aspect of an act is given more emphasis here than can be demonstrated empirically in everyday life.

The motivation part of this model derives from a felt need or want of the individual directed toward one or more goals; the choice component is the phase of the act devoted to considering alternative ways of satisfying the need or want and making a selection from among these alternatives; and the outcome component consists of the overt stage of the act—a recognizable action or series of actions selected by the individual as offering the best feasible way of satisfying the need or want. According to the level of satisfaction or dissatisfaction experienced previously, these three components of an act can be spoken of as predisposing a person to engage in an act when an opportunity arises, or not to engage in it. The energizing element in this model is the individual's ongoing drive to satisfy his or her wants, with the feedback of satisfaction-dissatisfaction levels of a previous experience in seeking to satisfy these wants regulating the intensity of the drive to engage in the behavior again.

The "want" aspect of motivation is sometimes characterized in terms of levels that are graded from physiological needs to what are called self-actualizing needs (Maslow, 1970). The hierarchical ordering of needs runs something like this: (1) need for food, water, etc.; (2) need for safety, security, stability, order, etc.; (3) need for companionship, affection, identification, etc.; (4) need for esteem, prestige, success, etc.; and (5) a need for achievement or the fulfillment of the individual's potential. This hierarchy appears to span physiological, sociocultural, and personality bases of motivation. In relating needs to an act, the life-sustaining needs of a physiological nature produce what may be regarded as compulsory acts. In this work we are concerned primarily with sociocultural bases of need which produce acts of a more voluntary nature. For purposes of exploring this hierarchy, we use at least one example from each of three of Maslow's need levels (second, fourth, and fifth)—(1) security, (2) status, and (3) achievement—with the expectation that other wants, including simply personal enjoyment (a third-level need), will be introduced in later extensions of the work (Chapin, 1968).

Security has to do with both personal safety (for example, safety on the streets of a city) and mental well-being. Status derives from concepts the individual acquires from the larger culture, the person's assessment of his position in the social structure, and his drive to move up the status hierarchy (getting ahead). Achievement is a drive for personal fulfillment and recognition such as success on the job and in responsibilities a person assumes in the church and in political and other organizational activity. In contrast to these three kinds of felt need, the "enjoyment" basis of an activity, which must eventually be incorporated more directly into the framework, would relate to personality and the individual's tastes, talents, and other capacities for responding to a situation.

The choice component of the model is used here in the context of choice theory (Ackoff, 1962, Chapter 3). A choice is seen to be made in relation to one or more wants, a set of perceived and feasible alternatives for achieving these wants, and the perceived cultural and social context for making the choice, that is, the contingencies concerning the environment of choice. These contingencies include conclusions reached from an assessment of the probable consequences of each alternative and its potential for satisfying the one or more wants and conclusions from taking into account the behavior of others and the choices they make. The results of these assessments are seen to produce a choice.

The action component has to do with the outcome of the choice, the visible behavior resulting from the thought process posited above. Since no means has yet been devised to trace the stimulus-response sequence from motivation to choice to action, it is necessary to infer the thought processes connecting wants with acts (which can be recorded empirically).

AN AGGREGATIVE MODEL OF HUMAN ACTIVITY IN THE CITY

In shifting the focus from the behavior of the individual to the patterned forms of behavior of entire aggregates of individuals, the sociocultural dimensions of human activity assume more meaning. In the schema concerned with individual behavior, at least two of the motivational bases for an act have a clearly indicated sociocultural context. Satisfaction of the status-seeking need is dependent on the social structure of the community, its stratification into subsocietal segments, and the opportunities for according status to the individual thus provided. The need for achievement is not fully satisfied without the opportunity for recognition that reference groups in the larger community affords. The third, the felt need for security, especially the need for security in the achievement of a sense of mental well-being within the community environment, also has a social dimension, although the personality aspect is usually stronger.

In the model of individual behavior, opportunities for satisfying a felt need must be specified in the form of situational contingencies in the environment. According to this rationale, a person in appraising these contingencies is motivated to act (or not to act) by the anticipated satisfaction (or dissatisfaction) that is likely to be experienced from engaging in that act, after considering the constraints involved and after considering other perceived alternatives and their constraints. Since each subsocietal segment and the status hierarchy of all segments in the metropolitan community in effect supply the social milieu required for the fulfillment of status-, achievement-, and to some extent, security-based motivations, the aggregate model can give explicit and more meaningful attention to environmental contingencies. Also there are other elements that are more readily recognized and can be given explicit consideration. One of these has to do with roles assigned to individual members of families or households by the society at large and by the subsociety. Still another factor is the spatial aspect of an activity. This gets at the availability of facilities or services, that is, physical access opportunities of following through on motivations to act.

Of course, in moving to a more aggregative approach, the potential exists for the design and development of a general systems approach. Conceivably the *motivation→choice→action* sequence could be incorporated into such a systems framework. For example, needs introduced "by hand" in setting environmental contingencies mentioned above conceivably might be generated within the general system. But the design of such a model is enormously complex, indeed, in many respects as complex as the metropolitan community itself. Obviously simplifications would be essential, and with simplication the risks of error increase. To design such systems would require an order of commitment and work across discipline lines we have yet to witness, and to apply such an approach would require access to data in forms and at a scale that would require some major changes in existing information-gathering systems. For these reasons this approach, though appealing, has not been considered seriously in the present effort. Turning now to a model of very simple design, it will soon become clear that even this effort needs further refinement, further rounds in the R & D process.

The General Framework

As a beginning, Figure II-1 is a way of representing the behavioral sequence that has been under discussion up to this point, but adapted to apply to aggregates of population.[5] With respect to the empirical work to follow, it serves as a point of departure in developing the analysis format for the research summarized in this book. Although some changes in terminology are introduced, it should be noted that the same behavioral sequence developed in the preceding section is incorporated in the uppermost branches of Figure II-1.

The new features in Figure II-1 are not only necessary if the behavior sequence is to be applied to population aggregates, but also essential in bringing the framework nearer to being useful for urban planning. First of all, the output of the model now refers to "activity pattern," which signifies a tendency for a population to behave similarly. In the model of

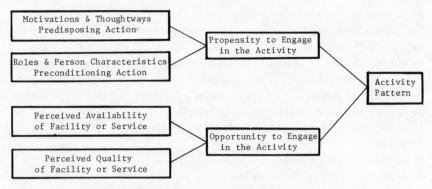

Figure II-1. General model for explaining activity patterns.

individual behavior "an act" is an episode of behavior discrete to an individual. To examine behaviors of population aggregates, it is necessary to simplify by combining acts of a similar functional nature into more general categories. In doing this there are losses and gains involved. The motivations attributable to an act of individual behavior tend to become less salient when acts are grouped into activity classes, but by grouping acts and dealing with more generic forms of activity, it is possible to begin to define behavior patterns that are common to whole groups of people. This is necessary for urban planning applications of the model because the provision of facilities and services is based on having a clientele of sufficient size to warrant the costs of supplying them. Moreover, according to the constituency caveat cited above, we have an interest in groups with existent or potential political identity.

A second feature has to do with the availability of a situation, facility, or service requisite for the performance of an activity. Instead of viewing the behavioral sequence entirely as a "demand" phenomenon, the consummation of an activity is seen to be dependent on a "supply" consideration as well. In other words, reading from right to left, the diagram in Figure II-1 states that an activity pattern is contingent not only on a propensity or readiness to engage in the activity, but also on there being an opportunity to engage in that activity in the sense that a facility, service, or other instrumental means is available which permits the activity to take place.

Further toward the left of Figure II-1, the framework posits for each of these two requisites at least two antecedent sets of factors. In the upper branch, the diagram signifies that the propensity to engage in an activity is determined by a set of energizing factors (motivations and thoughtways predisposing action) and a set of constraining factors (roles and personal characteristics preconditioning action). Following the lower branch of Figure II-1, the opportunity to engage in the activity is seen to be a function of the existence of a favorable situation for the activity to occur. In other words, it is a function of access to the requiste facilities or services in sufficient quantity and in locations sufficiently convenient to permit the level of use indicated by the propensity to engage in the activity reflected in the upper branch of the diagram. However, it is also dependent upon a quality of facility or service of sufficient acceptability so as not to discourage that level of use.

In brief, then, each stage in the sequence of the earlier model of individual behavior has been modified. Instead of motivation alone, thought-ways of people of different social background, role factors, and personal characteristics have been introduced as additional considerations. At the choice stage, not only must there be a propensity to act, but this must be accompanied by acceptable opportunities to act. And the act itself is now expressed generically as an activity which must be generalizable to a large enough proportion of the population so as to constitute a "class action" or activity pattern.

In broad outlines, then, Figure II-1 indicates the contingencies that lead to an activity pattern. In order for a mix of needs common to a particular segment of the population to generate an activity pattern, it must be compatible with role concepts of that segment of society and satisfy such other preconditions as stage in the life cycle (and/or age level) and health status that serve as constraints, but there must also be opportunities in terms of institutions, social organizations and facilities, and/or services in order to satisfy the felt needs in the form of an activity. When the appropriate conditions are met, the circuit switches can be thought of as being closed, connecting the various branches in Figure II-1 and allowing the energized needs to generate the activity within limits set by constraints.

Not shown in Figure II-1 are the resultant satisfaction (or dissatisfaction) that materializes and the feedback to the motivational and thought-way component that affects the predisposition of the population segment to continue or discontinue the activity (as reflected in later rounds at the same, greater, or lower intensity levels). Also not shown is the larger general systems context that affects the opportunity circuit—the existence of economic, social, and political institutions necessary to supply the opportunities; the existence of organizations with a disposition to provide these opportunities; and the general compatibility of a facility or service thus supplied with the felt need for access and quality of service. Also not shown are the external influences (technological change, cultural change, and so on) that go with an open-system view of the functioning of such a model. All the influences explicitly indicated or implicit to the functioning of the model shown in Figure II-1 are indicative of the complexity of human activity systems and suggest why a systems approach to monitoring interactions among these sets of influences will eventually be needed in sorting out all the separate effects.

The Research Strategy

The Figure II-1 schema suggests the general scope of an approach to the study of human activity systems. Although it aims to serve as a beginning in the development of a theoretical framework for understanding and interpreting these activity systems in terms useful for planning and policy formulation, it serves an immediate purpose of providing guidelines for the series of empirical studies taken up in ensuing chapters. These studies fall into the description and explanation phases of an R & D thrust outlined in Chapter I for human activity.

In the descriptive kind of investigation, attention is directed toward identifying similarities and differences in activity patterns exhibited by a population under study and among various subsocietal segments in this population. In the explanatory type of investigation, the concern is with factors postulated as having an influence in shaping these activity patterns. In this second kind of investigation, attention will focus here on one branch of the sequence represented in Figure II-1, as follows:

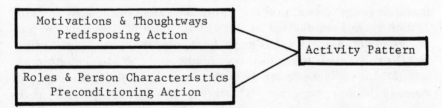

Data limitations do not permit exploration of other components contained in the more inclusive framework.

Before we take up the elements in this truncated version of the explanatory schema, it may be helpful to consider the descriptive phase as one which deals with the assumptions that go with the explanatory phase represented in this diagram. Although not stated above, there are two basic assumptions: first, activity patterns of the metropolitan community vary with the cultural makeup of the community; and second, they vary with the social structural context of the community and its subcultural spheres of influence. For purposes here, the cultural makeup of the community is defined in terms of ethnic concentrations which show a strong sense of group identity and cohesion. The social structural context is defined in terms of status concepts that apply within the large community and within the various ethnic groups. Variations in activity patterns from both sources are presumed to be most marked in discretionary forms of activity.

Given these systemic influences on modes of behavior, the explanatory phase, then, is concerned with determining the diversity of activity within these subsegments of the community and exploring the influence that role and personal characteristics (preconditioning factors) and motivations and attitudes (predisposing factors) have in explaining activity patterns. In this respect, it is postulated that variation in activity patterns among segments of society, particularly in the relatively more voluntary kinds of activity, will be according to motivation and thoughtway variables and according to role and selected personal characteristics. It is anticipated that because attitudinal dimensions and personality sources of variation within any population segment are not explicitly dealt with in the model, the levels of explanation will be at a relatively modest level.

Activity Patterns (Dependent Variable).   Some further refinement in our definition of activity patterns, the dependent variables, may serve a useful purpose. In the usage here, an "activity" is a classificatory term for a variety of acts grouped together under a more generic category according to some established activity classification system. The nature and the extent of grouping (and thus the nature and extent of the activity classification system) are dictated by the uses to which activity data are put. For example, an activity class might be simply "shopping," but it might be (1) driving from home to the shopping center, (2) buying groceries, and (3) driving home again. It might also consist of (1) driving from home to the shopping center; (2) hunting for a parking space; (3) parking the car; (4) walking from the parking lot to the supermarket; (5) picking up a cart, walking the aisles, and selecting grocery items; (6) going through the check-out line, paying the checker, and waiting for the groceries to be packed in bags; (7) carrying the groceries to the parking lot and loading them into the car; (8) driving home; (9) carrying the grocery bags into the kitchen; and (10) putting the groceries away. If the concern is simply with shopping as a phenomenon of our culture and the gross time allocation involved, then the first definition is adequate;

if the concern is with public transportation planning, the second break-down may be a more logical one. If the concern has to do with studying the supermarket chain's merchandising environment with a view to attracting a larger share of the market, the third breakdown may be the most appropriate.

An activity has a number of properties. It has a duration, a position in time, usually designated by the start time, a place in a sequence of events, and a fixed location or a path in space. The activity may involve only the subject whose actions are being reported, or the activity may be shared with others—family members, relatives, friends, neighbors, business associates, acquaintances, or strangers. An activity has a purpose or character which can be used in establishing the taxonomy of activities in the classification system being used. For the purposes here the activities will be classified at a level of detail that has meaning as an overview, preparatory to planning for facilities and services at a more detailed level of study (see Chapter III for classification system).

It was brought out above that "activity pattern" refers to a tendency for people in a given population to behave in a similar way. More precisely, in the usage here, existence of a "pattern" means that some criterion for the minimum number of persons in a population engaging in the activity has been established (here a minimum proportion of the population as a whole or of some defined subsociety of a specified metropolitan community). Although for purposes of the present discussion activity patterns are measured primarily in mean hours of duration and mean locus of an activity, in passing it might be noted that it is possible to define patterns in other terms, for example, in sequential or cyclical patterns.[6]

As suggested above in references to voluntary-nonvoluntary aspects of activity, there is a variation in freedom of choice among different kinds of activity. In this respect, the activities of an individual or a population of individuals can be conceived as forming a continuum extending from obligatory to discretionary forms of activity. The ordering of activities in this fashion connotes that some are more postponable than others. Stated another way, the ordering suggests that on the average people have more latitude for choice at the discretionary end of the continuum and little or no latitude for choice at the obligatory end. Thus sleep and food intake would be classified as obligatory activities, and watching TV and rest and relaxation would normally be classified as discretionary activities. In between, the assignment of an activity to one or the other category can vary with the person and the circumstances.

As noted earlier, the schedules imposed by institutional entities in connection with their activity patterns (work hours, store hours, doctors' office hours, museum hours, and even TV programming schedules) affect the timing and duration of activities of persons. Such activities as work and going to the doctor's office generally fall in the obligatory classification of activity, and the allocation of time to these activities affects the freedom of choice for individuals in the allocation of time to other activities. These considerations indicate that what is "discretionary" and what is "obligatory" are relative concepts. An activity is "discretionary" if there is a greater degree of choice than constraint, and "obligatory" if there is a greater degree of constraint than choice.[7]

Preconditioning and Predisposing Factors (Independent Variables). Turning to the independent variables, the first set, role and background factors, function as constraints on the performance of various classes of activity. Among the role factors that may precondition people to certain behavior are the decision-making role in the household (usually performed in American society by the head of the household and the spouse of the head) and the mix of sex, breadwinning, and child-care roles. Among the personal characteristics that constrain people to behave in certain ways which might be included here are age, stage in the life cycle, and general level of health.

According to the schema above, once role and personal characteristics are taken into account, the predisposition of the population or any of its subsocietal segments to engage in different kinds of activity is determined to an important degree by a combination of motivations and attitudinal characteristics particular to each such activity. Arranged in order from those of a more compulsory nature to those of a more voluntary nature, the following motivational bases for an activity indicate the range of needs which might be said to have a bearing on activity patterns.

1. *Subsistence needs*
   a. *Basis of motitvation:* need for sleep, food, shelter, clothing and health care.
   b. *Requisite means of satisfying needs* (institutionalized systems for ministering to basic needs): for example, income-earning opportunities from vocational training, education, medical care, social service, etc. (These opportunities presuppose economic organization for production and delivery of goods and services and the organization and delivery of other services implicit in the above listing of basic needs—all supplied by other elements of urban activity systems identified earlier.)

2. *Culturally, socially, and individually defined needs*

   a. *Basis of motivation:* felt needs for security, status, achievement, affection, and social contact; outlets for exercise of personal talents, ingenuity, prowess, and skill; need for mental release, for example, the release of feelings of joy, fear, frustration, or alienation; and need for physical release, for example, physical exercise as well as rest and relaxation.

   b. *Requisite means of satisfying needs:* opportunities for seeing kinsmen, friends, neighbors, and others; opportunities for participation in church, voluntary organizations, and civic activities; opportunities for creative activity, for engaging in recreation and other diversions, and for rest and relaxation.

In the applications of the schema where relatively discretionary activities are of primary interest, the second set of needs is of primary concern.

In the usage here, the thoughtway aspect of the schema refers to "sets of mind" or attitudes of a culture or segment of society which do not clearly derive from motivational bases of action. Operationally, attitudes are grouped with motivations because often they cannot be clearly separated from need or want bases of action. Thus, for example, attitudes concerning racial integration or the mixing of economic groups in residential developments may be associated with feelings of need for status and security. In this connection, it should be noted that a particular set of motivations and attitudes may prompt action to engage in one activity and not in another. Consequently, in the application of the analytical model above, varying combinations of motivations and attitudes will be postulated in explaining actvity choice in each category of discretionary activity examined.

SUMMARY

The model set forth in Figure II-1 has evolved with the expectation that it might be brought into use in a four-stage R & D thrust which is seen to consist of descriptive, explanatory, simulation, and evaluation stages. In keeping with the planning- and policy-oriented caveat set forth at the beginning, the descriptive-explanatory stages, which are the focus of the framework set forth in this chapter, are conceptualized at a level intended to give reality to the metropolitan community and its subsocietal segments both as social constructions and as viable political constituencies, existent or potential. Further, these first two stages are seen as a pre-analysis or preprocessing phase prior to the development of a systems approach, which would come into play in the simulation stage of research and development and eventually in testing planning and policy proposals in the evaluation stage.

As further requisites, it is held that this level of conceptualization, if it is to be compatible with a systems approach and useful in a planning and policy context, must be sufficiently aggregated to interface with processes that govern the spatial organization of the metropolitan area in terms of land use, community facilities, and service delivery systems. At the same time, it is maintained that this level of conceptualization must be sensitive not only to life systems of the individual person and his world of daily pursuits, but also compatible with other activity systems in the urban scene, that is, those of the economic system and other organized systems functioning in the metropolitan area and complexly meshed with the activity systems of persons and households.

With these rather formidable requirements imposed on the schema, a "transductive" approach has been followed in the development of the framework. In pursuance of this kind of framework, initially human activity in the urban scene is conceived in terms of the individual person and his physiologically regulated and learned behavior. From this base of conceptualization, an aggregative model is developed which views human activity patterns in terms of ethnic constituencies of varying socioeconomic status. Then from this model, an abridged version is identified which is intended to serve as a guide in the analyses pursued in later chapters.

Very briefly, in the truncated form of the model, the research strategy sketched out above is concerned with describing activity patterns of a population or various segments of the population and explaining how these patterns come into being. The descriptive aspect of the framework involves establishing what activity patterns are common to the metropolitan community as a whole (Chapter IV) and determining what distinctive differences in activity patterns exist among population segments of different life styles (Chapter V). The explanatory aspect of the research strategy has to do with establishing the relative importance of role and personal background factors that constrain people in the various population segments in their choice of various activities, and the relative importance of motivational and attitudinal factors that predispose these population segments to engage in various activities (Chapter VI).

We turn now to Chapter III where the empirical requirements in pursuance of this conceptual approach are specified preparatory to subsequent discussions of results from our series of activity studies.

NOTES

1.   The notion of an archetype is equivalent to a group statistical mean. Implicit in this notion is the capability of generalizing role, personal, and social characteristics of archetypical persons to the entire subsocietal segment of the metropolitan community from which it is drawn.

2.   This term is borrowed from Britton Harris (1966) whose essay on "The Uses of Theory in the Simulation of Urban Phenomena" presents the common ground on which those who develop theory and those who apply it can communicate effectively.

3.   Some efforts at examining urban systems have already been attempted (Forrester, 1969). This work indicates that technique is available, but that there is some way to go before substantive theory on urban activities is developed and integrated sufficiently to utilize the technique effectively.

4.   A series of experiments by the French speleologist, Michael Siffre, on man's sleep-wakefulness rhythm under conditions when the usual cues are absent suggest that the 24-hour cycle has some fundamental biological importance. See Palmer (1970) and Doob (1972, pp. 68–72).

5.   A first version of this framework was developed in connection with the author's work on activity patterns in an inner-city ghetto community. See Chapin, Butler, and Patten, to be published.

6.   Cyclical patterns have to do with "activity routines." In contrast to "activity pattern," which in the usage here has to do with the extent an activity is typical to an entire population, an "activity routine" refers to the recurrence of a sequence of activities in a person's itinerary, say, in a 24-hour period of a week's time. Clearly, to establish whether a sequence of activities forms a routine requires repeat information on each subject over a period of time. Because the work reported in later chapters does not include repeat data, activity routines are not discussed. However, it might be noted that a routine may take on the characteristics of a pattern if it applies fairly uniformly in a population of some minimum number.

7.   In early pilot studies in Durham, N.C., we experimented with the classification of an activity as discretionary or not directly by the subject, but problems of variability in the way subjects defined what was discretionary made for inconclusive results. Another approach used in the Washington metropolitan area study was based on such predetermined criteria as how long prior to the activity the decision was made to engage in the activity, and what reasons were given for doing so. Unfortunately questions of this kind put to a respondent for all activities over a 24-hour period soon wear out his rapport, undercutting cooperativeness in the listing of activities.

REFERENCES

Ackoff, Russell L. (1962). *Scientific Method: Optimizing Applied Research Decisions* (New York: John Wiley & Sons).

Chapin, F. Stuart, Jr. (1968). "Activity Systems and Urban Structure: A Working Schema," *Journal of the American Institute of Planners*, **34**:1.

Chapin, F. Stuart, Jr., Edgar W. Butler, and Frederick C. Patten (to be published). *Blackways in the Inner City* (Urbana: University of Illinois Press).

Doob, Leonard W. (1971). *Patterning of Time* (New York: Yale University Press).

Forrester, Jay W. (1969). *Urban Dynamics* (Cambridge: The M.I.T. Press).

Harris, Britton (1966). "The Uses of Theory in the Simulation of Urban Phenomena," *Journal of the American Institute of Planners*, **32**:5.

Lee, Grace Chin (1945). *George Herbert Mead: Philosopher of the Social Individual* (New York: King's Crown Press).

Maslow, A. H. (1970). *Motivation and Personality*, second edition (New York: Harper & Row).

Meier, Richard L. (1962). *A Communications Theory of Urban Growth* (Cambridge: The M.I.T. Press).

Odum, Howard T. (1971). *Environment, Power and Society* (New York: John Wiley & Sons).

Palmer, John D. (1970). "The Many Clocks of Man," *Natural History*, **79**:4.

Skinner, B. F. (1971). *Beyond Freedom and Dignity* (New York: Alfred A. Knopf).

Webber, Melvin M. (1964). *Explorations into Urban Structure* (Philadelphia: University of Pennsylvania Press).

CHAPTER THREE

SURVEY APPROACH,
METHODOLOGICAL ISSUES,
AND INTERPRETATION

Before presenting the results of work undertaken in pursuance of the descriptive-explanatory framework developed in the preceding chapter, it may facilitate the interpretation of results to consider briefly the range of the studies and the field methods used. With this end in view, this chapter introduces the various full-scale studies made over a five-year period (as distinct from pilot studies undertaken prior to these); it presents the analytical strategy and discusses survey instruments developed in pursuance of this strategy; and finally it summarizes and interprets some of the problems and issues that have arisen as this work has proceeded.

THE FAMILY OF ACTIVITY STUDIES

Since applications of this framework are made for the most part in the Washington, D.C. metropolitan area (an urban concentration in 1970 of some two and three-quarters million people), the key study in the series is the areawide study of the metropolitan community undertaken in 1968. As a referent for this and other Washington area studies, however, results from two national sampling studies are available, one made in 1966 and the other, a recontact survey, made in 1969. The latter is used as a backdrop for Washington area analyses. All three of these studies were designed for other purposes and, as brought out below, have limitations in following through on various aspects of the conceptual framework. However, two submetropolitan studies provide a richer source of data in this respect, one made in an inner-city black community in 1969, and the other made in a transitional white community in 1971.

Several exploratory studies were undertaken previous to these, as indicated in the chronology in Figure III-1, which shows some of the distinctive features introduced into the activity surveys undertaken over the whole period of this effort. The support for the research in the five basic studies has varied from one study to another, and aspects of all the individual studies have been reported from time to time elsewhere.[1]

Range of Concerns in the Studies

While all five studies have contributed to research on urban activity systems, practical considerations of funding necessitated the alignment of the activity aspect with a variety of other interests. Thus there has been a range of research purposes involved from one study to another, some involving direct use of activity analysis and some making use of it in more peripheral ways. Also, there have been 12 senior research investigators involved in these five studies, and this has meant that many individual research interests came to be accommodated in the designs of the studies. Thus the five studies have had varying purposes to take into account, and the activity aspect has often had strong competition in the allocation of the all-precious contact time in interviews with subjects among these different research purposes.

The basic study in the Washington, D.C. Standard Metropolitan Statistical Area (SMSA) had a primary focus on household use of medical care services and facilities. Nevertheless, from half to two-thirds of the hour's interview time with subjects was taken up in recording the previous day's itinerary of activities and, alternately with each subject, the previous Saturday's or Sunday's round of activities.[2] The primary focus of the 1966 study was on moving behavior of households in SMSA's in the 48-state portion of the United States. Because the activity aspect of this study was a piggyback component to the survey, the activity portion of the schedule was stripped down to a bare-bones listing procedure.[3] The recontact study in 1969 involved revisits to all dwelling units (still standing) that were visited in 1966. Again the emphasis was on residential mobility of households, seeking to establish, for example, how many of

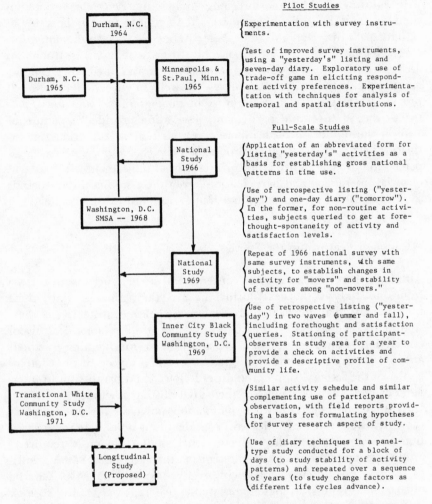

Figure III-1   The chronology of the studies and highlights of methodological changes.

the moves planned in 1966 had actually occurred and to obtain other information on these or future moves. This produced a "nonmover" and "inmover" class of households in the sample, and through a search effort, included a third category of households, "out-movers." Our 1969 activity analyses are based on the nonmovers and out-movers. In other words, activities were recorded for subjects from all households contacted in 1966 which could be located.

In contrast to the three foregoing studies, the two submetropolitan community studies were designed from the outset to feature the study of activity patterns. Not only did these studies obtain a more fine-grain coverage of households for the portions of the Washington metropolitan area selected, but also participant observation was used as a complementary field study method to survey research. In effect, survey research provided a snapshot of a community in photographic detail for a particular day in time, and participant observation provided a picture of "life in the round" through different seasons over a year's time. Nevertheless, having been designed around a variety of other interests (e.g., perception of community problems, residential satisfaction, and patterns of social interaction and participation), even these studies do not permit a full-fledged test of the conceptual framework outlined in Chapter II.

Common Features in the Studies

Although there was a range of concerns and a changing research team from one study to the next during the five-year period in which these five studies were in the field, there were nevertheless consistencies in these studies that enable us to compare results. Among the common features of crucial importance for comparative analyses are the sampling methods and the choice of respondents. But also of importance are the comparability of the activity listing procedures followed and parallelism in interviewer instructions in the use of the activity listing schedule.

As might be expected, when population universes are as diverse as those involved in these studies, cost considerations necessitate some variation in sampling methods.[4] The national studies obviously require a multistage sampling process extending from the selection of SMSA's down to the selection of households within city blocks in SMSA's.[5] On the other hand, in the Washington area studies, where it was feasible to look into patterns in the spatial distribution of activities as well as patterns in time allocation, a simple random sample of households came to be the preferred sampling basis. However, the more diffuse the sample's distribution, the more costly the field operation becomes. As a result of these considerations, in the Washington metropolitan area study 500 sampling points were selected on a simple random sampling basis, and cluster sampling procedures were used for each sampling point. Somewhat comparable procedures were used in the submetropolitan area studies. The basic sampling unit in all the studies was the household (including family and nonfamily households).

The choice of respondent was essentially set in the 1966 national study. Because the primary focus of that study was on residential mobility, there was a particular interest in subjects who had a key role in household moving decisions. For these purposes, the head of the household and the spouse of the head became the prime respondents. Given this commitment, to ensure comparability in all successive studies, the same basis for selecting respondents was followed.[6] This, of course, meant foregoing opportunities for examining activity patterns of other members of the household and studying family networks of activity. Thus in the Washington metropolitan area study where the same basis for selecting the respondents was followed, this happened to be compatible with the medical care focus of the study—here, an interest in the head of the household and the spouse as the members of the household who make decisions on choice of doctor and medical care facility. In the submetropolitan community studies, teenagers were included in the study design along with heads of households and spouses, but other children and nonhead and nonspouse adults in the household were not interviewed.

Of necessity interviewer instructions for the national studies were provided in written form. In the metropolitan Washington area studies, similar instructions on activity listing procedures were included in the interviewer manuals. In addition, special training sessions were given to all interviewers, and several practice interviews were required during the training period. In all five studies, the selection and control of interview days to ensure systematic coverage of all seven days of a week was essential. Although this was handled in a different way from the metropolitan studies, it was a key concession in the organization and conduct of the national studies. In the national surveys, interview days were rotated systematically through the seven days of the week, resulting in one activity schedule per respondent. In the Washington area studies, interview days were systematically rotated to cover the five weekdays, with each respondent providing activity data for one weekday and one weekend day (with Saturdays and Sundays, as brought out above, alternated on a systematic basis).

Table III-1 provides data on completed interviews involved in the five studies, and for the Washington studies compares the sex of heads of households included in our samples with the census findings in 1970. In the last three columns is shown the number of respondents with completed activity listings for weekdays, Saturdays, and Sundays that emerged from our surveys. The smaller numbers of respondents for weekend day activities in the national surveys are attributable to the seven-day basis of rotating interviews described above. The three Washington studies,

Table III-1 Characteristics of Sample Respondents in Five Activity Studies

Study Samples	1970 Census Benchmarks			Year of Activity Survey	Households Sampled			Number of Respondents With Complete Data on All Analysis Variables		
	Number of Households	Sex of Head (%)a/ Male	Female		Number of Households	Sex of Head (%) Male	Female	Weekdays	Sats.	Suns.
National SMSA Sample b/	--	--	--	1966	1,476	85.9	14.1	1,097	139	199
Recontact of Above National Sample b/	--	--	--	1969	1,177	83.9	16.1	905	71	202
Washington, D.C. Metropolitan Area	860,334 c/	76.1	23.9	1968	1,756	79.4	20.6	1,667	807	802
Submetropolitan Inner City Black Community	4,771 d/	62.3	37.7	1969	424	70.5	29.5	382 f/	49 f/	58 f/
Submetropolitan Transitional White Community	3,309 e/	74.9	25.1	1971	708	77.0	23.0	589 g/	277 g/	302 g/

a/ Computed from First Count, File A tapes of the Bureau of the Census.

b/ Consisted of 43 SMSA's drawn from the 48-state portion of the United States. The SMSA list was based on the 1960 Census list.

c/ From Bureau of the Census published reports on General Characteristics of the Population for District of Columbia, Montgomery and Prince Georges Counties in Maryland, and Arlington and Fairfax Counties in Virginia (which made up the SMSA in the 1960 Census).

d/ Black households only. Compiled from Bureau of the Census Report PHC(1)-226 for Census Tracts 0083.01, 0083.02, 0084, and 0085 in the District of Columbia.

e/ White households only. Compiled from Bureau of the Census Report PHC(1)-226 for Census Tracts 8044, 8046 and 8047 in Prince Georges County, Maryland. A part of 8048 which fell within the study area is not included in these figures.

f/ Respondents selected from black households only. The Saturday and Sunday results reflect the exceptionally high refusal rate encountered in listing activities for a second time which was involved in asking a weekday and a weekend day's itinerary from each respondent. Interviewers were given latitude to cut off the second day listings under conditions of hostility.

g/ Respondents selected from white households only.

which systematically rotated interview days among weekdays and between weekend days (resulting in two activity days for each respondent), thus produced roughly half as many returns for each weekend day as obtained for weekdays. As is evident from the table, for different reasons the returns for weekend days in the national studies (relatively small samples) and in the inner-city black study (high refusal rates) present some limitations on carrying through parallel analyses of Saturday and Sunday activities.

ANALYSIS FRAMEWORK AND SURVEY INSTRUMENTS

As indicated in the notes appearing to the right of the diagram in Figure III-1, the analysis strategy and thus the design of survey instruments have been evolving over a period of time. In keeping with the transductive research strategy discussed in the preceding chapter, earlier reports of these studies reflect differing stages in this evolutionary process (and differing research objectives of colleagues associated with me in these studies). Thus earlier reports on the Washington and national studies have been primarily descriptive and exploratory, and it has been only in the submetropolitan community studies that the explanatory model has been introduced.

Although there has thus been an expanding scope to investigations relative to the conceptual framework set forth in Chapter II, in the course of reprogramming analyses for this monograph, gaps in data become greater the farther back we go chronologically in this series of studies. Consequently, though I set forth the overall analysis strategy and introduce an implementing survey instrument below, it must be remembered that these are not fully applicable to the earlier Washington area and the national data sets.

Analysis Framework

According to our conceptual view of activity systems, in the descriptive phase of analysis, the metropolitan community not only is examined for communitywide activity patterns, but it is disaggregated into subsocietal segments for analysis of activity patterns within ethnic and status groups in the population. Under conventional sociological approaches, such segments might be defined on the basis of a single composite measure, for example, the index of social class developed by Hollingshead and Redlich (1958). However, because of the political viability criterion, there are practical advantages in using in these analyses some direct measures of ethnic composition and economic status. In the Washington area, black and nonblack ethnic composition has been chosen as a viable political criterion. Although less easily identified into constituencies, subcategories based on a measure of income per member of household, education level, and occupation level are also examined. The analysis in the description phase indicates for the metropolitan community as a whole and for each subsocietal segment thus formed the numbers engaging in each class of activity and the mean duration for each activity for the activity categories in our 12-category classification system. In such analyses, travel to and from an activity is usually included as part of the activity requiring that travel, but initially it is identified as a separate entry beside the time actually spent on each activity.

According to the schema similarities and differences in activity patterns among subsocietal segments identified in the descriptive phase of analysis can be explained in part by the constraints society imposes on people—a set of factors preconditioning participation in an activity—and in part by the energizers of an activity—a set of factors predisposing participation. Figure III-2 illustrates the kinds of factors that are used in applying this framework; it is a partial version of the general model shown in Figure II-1. In the Washington metropolitan area analyses, primary emphasis is placed on preconditioning factors and the level of explanation

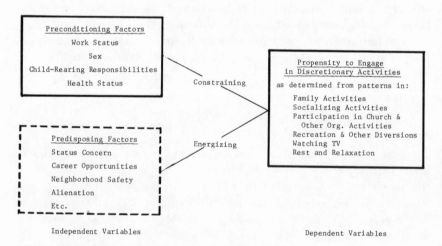

Figure   III-2   Framework for analysis of activity patterns.

they provide within a population group in explaining choices of activity, particularly for discretionary forms of activity. Because predisposing factors are introduced only in exploratory neighborhood studies and thus are not a part of the analyses of all data sets, this box in Figure III-2 is indicated in broken lines. For these submetropolitan area studies, we examine for variations in both preconditioning and predisposing factors, again giving primary attention to discretionary forms of activity.

Survey Methods

There are essentially two approaches to identifying activity patterns in the field. The first is based on survey research methods, and the other on ethnographic study methods. The survey research approach is workable in national, metropolitan-area, and neighborhood-level studies, but for obvious reasons, participant observation by a single observer, the key technique of data collection in ethnographic studies, is normally feasible only in submetropolitan community studies. In the survey research approach, activity data are obtained through structured interviews from a probability sample of persons from some preestablished universe of subjects. This is done in one of three ways: (1) by a check list approach in which subjects identify from a precategorized list of activities those that they engage in on a "typical day" or "typical week" and estimate the proportion of waking time allocated to each activity; (2) by a field listing of "yesterday's" activities in which subjects are asked to list things they actually did the previous day, when they did them, and where they did them; and (3) by a diary approach to "tomorrow's" activities in which subjects keep a diary on the what, when, and where aspects of their activities on the day following the interview.[7] Although some locations such as place of work, shopping place, school, and church can be specified in the first approach, the last two approaches yield more complete results for spatial analyses.

All these forms of studying activity patterns have been used in the course of these studies. The one consistent technique used in the five studies listed in Table III-1 was the retrospective "yesterday" listing approach. Given the constraints (the other purposes served in three of the studies) and the difficulties of diary keeping encountered in pilot studies among illiterate subjects, the elderly, and inner-city black respondents, the retrospective listing became the standard one in the present studies. We turn now to some of the key features of this survey approach (used in all five studies) and of the participant observation

approach (used in the two submetropolitan community studies) for the
background value they may serve in interpreting results in later chapters.

Survey Research Schedule

It may be useful at this juncture to examine briefly an illustrative survey
schedule containing examples of questions that would be needed in pur-
suing the conceptual framework set down in Chapter II. The format reproduced here is an illustrative stripped-down version of the schedule
used in the 1971 submetropolitan study[8]; it is stripped of all experimental and other questions not essential to the kind of analysis outlined
in the previous chapter. This sample format includes questions needed in
defining ethnic groups and in defining socioeconomic strata within each
such group in a metropolitan community for the analysis of variations in
activity patterns by these socioeconomic dimensions. It also includes
questions needed in seeking explanations for activity patterns thus observed, following the model set down in Figure III-2.

Subsocietal Segments and Stratification Variables.   As brought out
above, the subsocietal segments chosen for analysis in later chapters were
based on the ethnic composition of the population (grouped into black
and nonblack segments as determined from Question 33) and the socioeconomic composition of the population as a whole and within each of
the chosen ethnic groups. For purposes of grouping people by socioeconomic status, the illustrative schedule contains three kinds of stratification variables. One is the total household income from all sources
before taxes (Question 32). The population is stratified in various ways
on an income-per-household-member basis as shown in Figure III-3.
Another stratification variable is based on the Duncan occupational index (Reiss, 1961). For the head of the household this is based on Question
17, and for the spouse, on Question 25. In the analyses in Chapter V, the
subject's occupation is classified into one of three categories crudely
labeled "unskilled or semiskilled," "skilled craftsmen and clerical," and
"professional-managerial."[9]

A third stratification variable is the education level of the respondent
(Question 20 in the case of the household head, and Question 27 in the
case where the respondent is the spouse). The categories used in later
analyses are (1) those who did not finish high school, (2) those who have
a high school diploma but no college degree, and (3) those who have a
bachelor's or graduate degree.

Preconditioning Variables. The components of the analytical framework require questions on the subject's sex, work status, child-rearing responsibilities, stage in the life cycle, health status, and so on. The questions that provide this information can be found in the illustrative schedule as follows:

Variable	Question No.
Sex	2
Work status	12 or 23
Child-rearing responsibility (determined by whether any child under 13 present)	3
Stage in the life cycle (determined from a combination of factors)	1, 3, and 4
Health status	22 or 29
Rearing environment	21 or 28

Other factors that we have considered for analysis in this category have to do with stability of the head's employment (Question 13) and the length of time he or she has worked (Question 14).

These variables can be used in various mixes. In the analyses in Chapters IV to VI, the following dichotomies of these factors are used throughout:

Working full time (breadwinning responsibilities)

   Female—children under 13 years in the household (more demanding with respect to child-care responsibilities)
   Female—no children under 13 years in the household (less demanding with respect to these responsibilities)
   Male   —children under 13 years in the household (more demanding with respect to child-care responsibilities)
   Male   —no children under 13 years in the household (less demanding with respect to these responsibilities)

Not working full time (no breadwinning responsibilities)
   [above subcategories repeated]

In the empirical work to follow, the decision-making role is taken into account in the original selection of respondents, and the life cycle factor is indirectly considered in the grouping of households according to child-rearing responsibilities.

Illustrative Briefing Sample

ACTIVITY SURVEY - BASIC SCHEDULE

Address of respondent: Interviewer's Name:

934- 7th Street NW   _Mary Duncan_

Hello, I'm _____, from Survey Research Associates. We
are conducting a survey about things that people do each day. We're trying to
learn from this survey how to plan better for the future.

This doesn't take but a few minutes. What I put down will be added in with
replies from others and therefore the answers won't be identified with names
of people in any way. All the answers you give will be strictly confidential.
Of course, you are not required to participate, but I hope very much that you
will, and I think you'll find it interesting. Can we begin the interview now?

First, I would like to ask you some questions about people living in this household.
Would you please give me a list of both adults and children who usually live in this
household. Let's start with the head of the household, then the oldest person, then
the next oldest, and so on. (RECORD BELOW)

WHOM TO INTERVIEW: YOU ARE TO INTERVIEW ONLY THE HEAD OF HOUSEHOLD OR SPOUSE

A. IF ONLY THE HEAD OF HOUSEHOLD   B. IF BOTH THE HEAD OF HOUSEHOLD AND
(WHETHER MALE OR FEMALE) LIVES   SPOUSE LIVE HERE, INTERVIEW THE MALE
HERE, INTERVIEW THAT PERSON.   IF A "1" APPEARS IN THE BOX AT RIGHT
                                          AND THE FEMALE IF A "2" APPEARS IN
                                          THE BOX.

		1. Relation-ship to head	2. Sex M	F	3. Age	4. Marital	Status:
PUT AN "X" BESIDE THE PERSON INTERVIEWED	X	1. HEAD	X		37	1	1 - Married
		2. Wife		X	35	1	2 - Widowed
	X	3. Daughter		X	12	5	3 - Divorced
		4. Son	X		7	5	4 - Separated
		5. mother-in-law		X	55	2	5 - Never Married
		6.					
		7.					
		8.					

2

OFFICE USE
ONLY:

8 _____

5. Now I'd like to ask you about the things you did and the places you went yesterday. I'm interested both in the things you do regularly and in the things that you happened to do yesterday, expecially things you did with other people, and things you did outside your home.

Let's begin with 4 a.m. in the morning. Were you up then? (IF AWAKE: About what time did you actually start doing that? THEN PROCEED WITH LISTING THROUGH ONE FULL SEQUENCE OF ACTIVITIES FROM "GETTING UP" TO "GOING TO BED") (IF ASLEEP: About when did you get up? (RECORD BELOW) Now, thinking back, what did you do next?

YESTERDAY WAS:

___ Monday
___ Tuesday
_X_ Wednesday
___ Thursday
___ Friday
___ Saturday
___ Sunday

ASK QUESTIONS A-D UNTIL THE ACTIVITIES FOR ONE FULL DAY'S EQUIVALENT (FROM "GOT UP" TO "WENT TO BED") HAVE BEEN COMPLETED. DO NOT ASK Q. C FOR SLEEP OR PERSONAL CARE ACTIVITIES. FOR Q. D (LOCATION) GET NEAREST CROSS STREETS OR EXACT ADDRESS. IF "AT HOME," CHECK BOX. IF "TRAVEL," CHECK BOX AND RECORD DESTINATION.

A. What did you do next? (Anything else at the same time?)	B. What time did you start?	C. Who did all that with you? (CHECK ALL THAT APPLY)	D. Where were you when you_____?	Q. 6 MORE	Q. 7 LESS	Q. 8 BEST
asleep	4:00 A.M.	[ ] Self only [X] Family in HH [ ] Rels. not in HH [ ] N'bors [ ] Friends [ ] Co-Workers [ ] Others	[X] Home Travel [Car] [Other] 934 - 7th St. NW	[ ]	[ ]	[ ]
Got up and dressed	6:30	[X] Self only [ ] Family in HH [ ] Rels. not in HH [ ] N'bors [ ] Friends [ ] Co-Workers [ ] Others	[X] Home Travel [Car] [Other]	[ ]	[ ]	[ ]
Fixed breakfast and lunches	6:40	[ ] Self only [X] Family in HH [ ] Rels. not in HH [ ] N'bors [ ] Friends [ ] Co-Workers [ ] Others	[X] Home Travel [Car] [Other]			
ate breakfast	6:50	[ ] Self only [X] Family in HH [ ] Rels. not in HH [ ] N'bors [ ] Friends [ ] Co-Workers [ ] Others	[X] Home Travel [Car] [Other]	[ ]	[ ]	[ ]

A. What did you do next? (Anything else at the same time?)	B. What time did you start?	C. Who did all that with you? (CHECK ALL THAT APPLY)	D. Where were you when you_____?	Q.6 M O R E	Q.7 L E S S	Q.8 B E S T
Cleaned up dishes	7:15	[X] Self only [ ] Family in HH [ ] Rels. not in HH [ ] N'bors [ ] Friends [ ] Co-Workers [ ] Others	[X] Home Travel [Car][Other]	[ ]	[ ]	[ ]
Got kids ready for school	7:20	[ ] Self only [X] Family in HH [ ] Rels. not in HH [ ] N'bors [ ] Friends [ ] Co-Workers [ ] Others	[X] Home Travel [Car][Other]	[ ]	[ ]	[ ]
Left for Work	7:30	[X] Self only [ ] Family in HH [ ] Rels. not in HH [ ] N'bors [ ] Friends [ ] Co-Workers [ ] Others	[ ] Home Travel [Car][X]Other Boarded bus at 7th St & new York ave NW	[ ]	[ ]	[ ]
Start work	8:00	[ ] Self only [ ] Family in HH [ ] Rels. not in HH [ ] N'bors [ ] Friends [X] Co-Workers [ ] Others	[ ] Home Travel [Car][Other] Ben Smith Hotel 18th & H St. NW	[ ]	[ ]	[ ]
Lunch	12:00	[ ] Self only [ ] Family in HH [ ] Rels. not in HH [ ] N'bors [ ] Friends [X] Co-Workers [ ] Others	[ ] Home Travel [Car][Other] Ben Smith Hotel	[ ]	[ ]	[ ]
Continue work	12:30	[ ] Self only [ ] Family in HH [ ] Rels. not in HH [ ] N'bors [ ] Friends [X] Co-Workers [ ] Others	[ ] Home Travel [Car][Other] Ben Smith Hotel	[ ]	[ ]	[ ]
Waited on street corner	5:05	[X] Self only [ ] Family in HH [ ] Rels. not in HH [ ] N'bors [ ] Friends [ ] Co-Workers [ ] Others	[ ] Home Travel [Car][Other] 18th & H St. NW	[ ]	[ ]	[ ]

A. What did you do next? (Anything else at the same time?)	B. What time did you start?	C. Who did all that with you? (CHECK ALL THAT APPLY)	D. Where were you when you _____?	Q.6 MORE	Q.7 LESS	Q.8 BEST
Husband drove me to mother's house	5:10	[ ] Self only [X] Family in HH [ ] Rels. not in HH [ ] N'bors [ ] Friends [ ] Co-Workers [ ] Others	[ ] Home Travel [X] Car [ ] Other	[ ]	[ ]	[ ]
Talked to mother and picked up kids	5:45	[ ] Self only [X] Family in HH [X] Rels. not in HH [ ] N'bors [ ] Friends [ ] Co-Workers [ ] Others	[ ] Home Travel [ ] Car [ ] Other 8th St & U, NW	[X]	[ ]	[X]
Drove home	6:15	[ ] Self only [X] Family in HH [ ] Rels. not in HH [ ] N'bors [ ] Friends [ ] Co-Workers [ ] Others	[ ] Home Travel [X] Car [ ] Other	[ ]	[ ]	[ ]
Changed clothes and dressed the children	6:25	[ ] Self only [X] Family in HH [ ] Rels. not in HH [ ] N'bors [ ] Friends [ ] Co-Workers [ ] Others	[X] Home Travel [ ] Car [ ] Other	[ ]	[ ]	[ ]
Left for church	7:00	[ ] Self only [X] Family in HH [ ] Rels. not in HH [ ] N'bors [ ] Friends [ ] Co-Workers [ ] Others	[ ] Home Travel [X] Car [ ] Other	[ ]	[ ]	[ ]
Church supper	7:30	[ ] Self only [X] Family in HH [ ] Rels. not in HH [ ] N'bors [ ] Friends [ ] Co-Workers [ ] Others	[ ] Home Travel [ ] Car [ ] Other 7th St & T NW	[X]	[ ]	[ ]
Visiting with friends at church	7:45	[ ] Self only [X] Family in HH [ ] Rels. not in HH [ ] N'bors [ ] Friends [ ] Co-Workers [ ] Others	[ ] Home Travel [ ] Car [ ] Other 7th St & T NW	[X]	[ ]	[ ]

A. What did you do next? (Anything else at the same time?)	B. What time did you start?	C. Who did all that with you? (CHECK ALL THAT APPLY)	D. Where were you when you_____?	Q.6 MORE	Q.7 LESS	Q.8 BEST
Drove home	8:00	[ ] Self only [X] Family in HH [ ] Rels. not in HH [ ] N'bors [ ] Friends [ ] Co-Workers [ ] Others	[ ] Home Travel [X]Car [ ]Other	[ ]	[ ]	[ ]
Telephoned friend on church business	8:15	[X] Self only [ ] Family in HH [ ] Rels. not in HH [ ] N'bors [ ] Friends [ ] Co-Workers [ ] Others	[X] Home Travel [ ]Car [ ]Other	[ ]	[ ]	[ ]
Gave kids bath and put them to bed	8:30	[ ] Self only [X] Family in HH [ ] Rels. not in HH [ ] N'bors [ ] Friends [ ] Co-Workers [ ] Others	[X] Home Travel [ ]Car [ ]Other	[ ]	[ ]	[ ]
Talked with husband	9:00	[ ] Self only [X] Family in HH [ ] Rels. not in HH [ ] N'bors [ ] Friends [ ] Co-Workers [ ] Others	[X] Home Travel [ ]Car [ ]Other	[X]	[ ]	[ ]
Watched TV		[ ] Self only [X] Family in HH [ ] Rels. not in HH [ ] N'bors [ ] Friends [ ] Co-Workers [ ] Others	[X] Home Travel [ ]Car [ ]Other	[ ]	[ ]	[ ]
Get ready for bed	10:15	[X] Self only [ ] Family in HH [ ] Rels. not in HH [ ] N'bors [ ] Friends [ ] Co-Workers [ ] Others	[X] Home Travel [ ]Car [ ]Other	[ ]	[ ]	[ ]
Retired	10:45	[ ] Self only [X] Family in HH [ ] Rels. not in HH [ ] N'bors [ ] Friends [ ] Co-Workers [ ] Others	[X] Home Travel [ ]Car [ ]Other	[ ]	[ ]	[ ]

6. Among the activities you mentioned doing <u>away from home</u> (other than work or transportation) were there any that you would like to do <u>more often</u>?

           [X] YES   [ ] NO   [ ] NONE AWAY FROM HOME

6a. Which ones? ("X" APPROPRIATE BOXES ABOVE)

7. And among those activities <u>away from home</u> (other than work or transportation), were there any that you would like to do <u>less often</u>?

           [ ] YES   [ ] NO   [X] NONE AWAY FROM HOME

7a. Which ones? ("X" IN APPROPRIATE BOXES ABOVE)

8. Now of <u>all</u> the things you did yesterday, which <u>one</u> did you enjoy doing most?

       IF <u>NO</u> ACTIVITY THAT ENJOYABLE, CHECK HERE: [ ]

       OTHERWISE CHECK ACTIVITY MENTIONED IN APPROPRIATE BOX ABOVE.

9. Are there things you didn't do yesterday which you usually do on (DAY OF WEEK)?

       [ ] NO

       [X] YES (SPECIFY: _Family usually goes out to supper and a movie_)

10. And are there things you did do yesterday which you don't usually do on (DAY OF WEEK)?

       [ ] NO

       [X] YES (SPECIFY: _Went to church supper with family_)

QUESTIONS (11-21) ARE TO BE ASKED ABOUT THE HEAD OF THE HOUSEHOLD. THIS IS ALWAYS THE MAN IF THERE IS BOTH A HUSBAND AND WIFE IN THE HOUSEHOLD. ONLY IF THERE IS NO HUSBAND LIVING IN THE HOUSEHOLD CAN A WOMAN RESPONDENT BE CONSIDERED THE HEAD OF THE HOUSEHOLD.

11. Now I'd like to ask you a few questions about (your/your husband's) work experience. (Have you/has he) ever worked on a full-time job (35 hours or more per week)?

    Ever worked [X]   Never worked [ ]
    full time   ASK Q.12   full time   GO TO Q.19.

12. (Are you/is he) now working full time, working part time, or (are you/is he) retired, not employed, or in school?

    Working full-time [X] } ASK   Retired   [ ] } GO TO
    Working part-time [ ] } Q.13   Not employed   [ ] } Q.16
                                      In school   [ ] }

13. In the last year (have you/has he) ever been unemployed for a week or more because (you/he) lost (your/his) job?

                    YES [ ]   NO [X] GO TO Q.14

    ┌───┐
    │ 13a. Why (were you/was he) out of work? CHECK ALL THAT APPLY   │
    │   │
    │   LAID OFF, FIRED   SICK OR   │
    │   OR LOST JOB   [ ]   QUIT [ ]   INJURED [ ]   OTHER [ ]   │
    │   │
    │ 13b. All in all, how many weeks (were you/was he) out of work (not counting │
    │   vacations)?   │
    │   │
    │   OVER A WEEK   OVER 2 MOS.   │
    │   UNDER 1 MO. [ ]   UNDER 6 MOS. [ ]   OVER 1 YR. [ ]   │
    │   │
    │   1-2 MOS.   [ ]   6 MOS-1 YR.   [ ]   │
    └───┘

14. When did (you/he) start working on (your/his) current job?

    Month December   NOT SURE [ ]
    Year   1964

15. What hours (do you/does he) usually work on the job?

    DAY SHIFT   [X]   NIGHT (GRAVE YARD) SHIFT [ ]
    SWING SHIFT [ ]   OTHER (SPECIFY)_____

16. What kind of business or industry (is/was) (your/his) (last) job in? (For example: TV and radio manufacturing, retail shoe store, State Labor Department, farm, etc.)? U. S. Department of Agriculture

17. What kind of work (do you/does he) do? (For example: skilled operative, supervisor, clerk, manager, laborer, etc.) mail clerk

18. (IF CURRENTLY WORKING) In addition to (your/his) (full-time/part-time) job, (are you/is he) now working full- or part-time at another job?

    YES, EXTRA FULL-TIME JOB [ ]   NOT WORKING [ ]
    YES, EXTRA PART-TIME JOB [X]   EXTRA JOB

19. How would you say (your/his) main job rates as to (your/his) chances for getting ahead? Would you say the chances are .... (READ CHOICES)

    [ ] VERY GOOD   [ ] GOOD   [ ] FAIR   [X] POOR

20. (ASK EVERYONE) How many years of school (have you/has he) completed? __*12*__ Years

21. When (you were/he was) in elementary school, where (were you/was he) living most of the time? READ LIST

On a farm [ ]   Suburbs of a sizable city [ ]
Country, but not [ ] Central city of a metro- [ ]
 on a farm   politan area
A town or small city [X] NOT SURE   [ ]

22. Look at this picture of a ladder. Suppose the top of the ladder represents the very best of health, and the bottom the very worst of health. Where would you say (your/his) health falls on this ladder?

--[X]
--[ ]
--[ ]
--[ ]
--[ ]

ASK ABOUT HEAD'S WIFE IF HEAD IS MALE AND WIFE IS LIVING IN HOUSEHOLD. IF INFORMATION HAS BEEN PROVIDED UNDER Q.11, THIS QUESTION IS NOT APPLICABLE SO MARK "X" HERE [ ] AND GO TO Q.28

23. (Are you/is your wife) now working full-time, part-time, or (are you/is your wife) retired, not employed, or what?

Working full-time [X] } ASK Retired [ ] }
Working part-time [ ] } Q.24 Not employed [ ] } GO TO
            Housewife [ ] } Q. 27
            Student [ ] }

24. What kind of business or industry is (your/her) job in? (For example: TV and radio manufacturing, supermarket, State Labor Department, someone's residence, etc.)____*Hotel*____

25. What kind of work (do you/does she) do? (For example: skilled operative, checker, secretary, maid, etc.)____*maid*____

26. How would you say (your/her) main job rates as to (your/her) chances for getting ahead? Would you say the chances are .... (READ CHOICES)

[ ] VERY GOOD [ ] GOOD [ ] FAIR [X] POOR

27. How many years of school (have you/has she) completed? _____*8*_____ years

28. When (you were/she was) in elementary school, where (were you/was she) living most of the time? READ LIST

On a farm   [X] Suburbs of a sizable city [ ]
Country, but not [ ] Central city of a metro- [ ]
 on a farm   politan area
A town or small [ ] NOT SURE   [ ]
 city

29. Look at this picture of a ladder. Suppose the top of the ladder represents the very best of health, and the bottom the very worst of health. Where would you say (your/her) health falls on this ladder?

--[ ]
--[X]
--[ ]
--[ ]
--[ ]

Now, I want to ask you some questions which will help us to see how you feel about life in this community and about your ideas in general.

30. Let's begin with some general questions. I am going to read you some sentences. Please tell me whether you agree or disagree with it and how much. [HAND CARD TO RESPONDENT] Here is a card with the four kinds of answers you might give: These are

> A – Agree strongly
> B – Agree somewhat
> C – Disagree somewhat
> D – Disagree strongly

I'll read each one if you prefer, or you can tell the letter that indicats your answer. Here they are:

	A AGREE STRONGLY	B AGREE SOMEWHAT	C DISAGREE SOMEWHAT	D DISAGREE STRONGLY
a. When I go outside and look around me at the street and the neighbors' homes, I like what I see		X		
b. As a rule you can tell quite a bit about a person by the way he dresses	X			
c. It's hardly fair to bring children into the world with the way things look for the future		X		
d. It is worth considerable effort to assure one's self of a good name with important people				X
e. The raising of one's social position is one of the most important goals in life		X		
f. These days a person doesn't really know whom he can count on	X			
g. There's little use in writing to public officials because often they aren't interested in the problems of the average person	X			
h. Nowadays a person has to live pretty much for today and let tomorrow take care of itself	X			
i. In spite of what some people say, the lot of the average man is getting worse, not better			X	

31. Here are some words or phrases (SHOW CARD) which we would like you to use
to describe this neighborhood as it seems to you. In this case, we mean
by neighborhood roughly the area near here which you can see from your front
door. Please tell me which you think applies by the letter. For example,
take the first one, "noisy-quiet," if you feel it is very noisy around here
A would be your answer; somewhat noisy, B would be your answer; if it is
average, C would be your answer; if it is rather quiet, D would be your
answer, and if it is very quiet, then E would be your answer. Let's begin
with the first one.

YOUR NEIGHBORHOOD

A   B   C   D   E

a   Noisy:___: X :___:___:___: Quiet   a
b   Attractive:___:___:___: X :___: Unattractive   b
c   Unfriendly people:___:___:___:___: X : Friendly people   c
d   Enough privacy:___:___: X :___:___: Not enough privacy   d
e   Poorly kept up buildings: X :___:___:___:___: Well kept up buildings   e
f   People who are like me: X :___:___:___:___: People who are not like me   f
g   Pleasant:___:___:___: X :___: Unpleasant   g
h   Convenient: X :___:___:___:___: Inconvenient   h
i   Very poor place to live:___: X :___:___:___: Very good place to live   i
j   Safe:___:___:___: X :___: Unsafe   j
k Well kept up lawns and yards:___:___: X :___:___: Poorly kept up lawns and yards   k
l   Bad reputation:___: X :___:___:___: Good reputation   l

32. Just for statistical purposes, would you mind telling me about how much money you
and your family received last month or last year from all sources, before taxes
were deducted? Would you please give me the letter. SHOW CARD.

	Monthly	Annual			Monthly	Annual	
M	Under $250	Under $3,000	M	Ⓖ	$667 - 749	$8,000 - 8,999	G
L	$250 - 333	$3,000 - 3,999	L	F	$750 - 833	$9,000 - 9,999	F
K	$334 - 416	$4,000 - 4,999	K	E	$834 - 1,249	10,000 - 14,999	E
J	$417 - 499	$5,000 - 5,999	J	D	$1,250 - 1,666	15,000 - 19,999	D
I	$500 - 583	$6,000 - 6,999	I	C	$1,667 - 2,083	20,000 - 24,999	C
H	$584 - 666	$7,000 - 7,999	H	B	$2,084 - 2,499	25,000 - 29,999	B
	NOT SURE OR REFUSED [ ]			A	$2,500 and over	30,000 and over	A

```
POST INTERVIEW ITEMS TO BE FILLED IN
     AFTER LEAVING HOUSEHOLD
```

33. RECORD GENERAL RACE - ETHNIC CHARACTERISTICS OF RESPONDENT

[X] BLACK   [ ] PUERTO RICAN OR SP.AMERICAN   [ ] AMERICAN INDIAN

[ ] ASIAN   [ ] ALL OTHER

34. TYPE OF DWELLING IN WHICH RESPONDENT LIVES

[ ] Single family, detached house   [ ] Elevator apartment building
[X] Duplex   [ ] Store with dwelling above or behind
[ ] Row house   [ ] House converted to rooms or apartments
[ ] Walkup apartment building with lawn space [ ] Other (SPECIFY):_____
[ ] Walk-up apartment building without lawn   _____

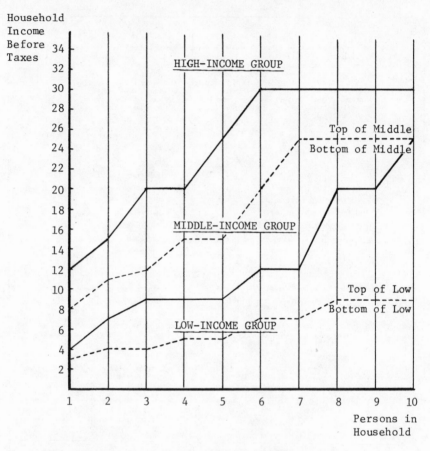

Figure III-3   Income strata on an income per-household-member basis.

Predisposing Variables. In Figure III-2, four categories of variables concerning the subject's attitudes were suggested: status concern, career opportunities, feelings about neighborhood safety, and an index of aliena-tion. The respondent's satisfaction with his neighborhood is a factor that might also be introduced here. Strictly construed in terms of the concep-tual framework outlined in Chapter II, this kind of factor belongs in the "opportunity" portion of the schema (see Figure II-1); it has a more direct bearing on the respondent's assessment of the quality of the environment and its facilities and services as these constrain activity choices. However, since this aspect of the framework is not dealt with in this volume, a proxy representing the respondent's general level of satisfaction with neighborhood surroundings may be informative to include with this list on an interim basis.

The questionnaire covers these variables as follows:

Variable	Question No.
Status concern	30 b, d, and e
Career opportunities	19 or 26
Feelings concerning neighborhood safety	31 j
Neighborhood satisfaction	30 a and 31 b, g, and i
Level of alienation	30 c, f, g, h, and i

As evident from the list of question numbers in the right-hand column, measures of status concern, neighborhood satisfaction, and alienation are based on indices made up from a combination of questions. These particular measures of predisposing variables are purely illustrative.[10]

Activity Listing. Questions 5 through 10 in the sample schedule illustrate a format for activity listing. This format calls for developing in chronological order the activities of the respondent for the previous day, starting with some beginning point in a 24-hour period. Practice varies on what the beginning point is. In the illustrative form, "4 a.m." is shown; this was selected as the low point in the activity cycle for the average respondent. For most, this would be a time when the respondent is "asleep"; for those working the graveyard shift, this would be an "at work" entry. The beginning times used in the coding of these schedules would begin with the "got up" time entry and run through to the "went to bed" entry. The Washington metropolitan area study used "midnight" instead of "4 a.m." in fixing the time for beginning the listing.

Implicit in this particular illustrative schedule is a continuous 7-day interviewing approach of the kind used in the national study. This is signified by the box in the upper right-hand corner on the first page of the listing form. In the format shown, the respondent is asked to give his itinerary for one day ("yesterday") only. The listing proceeds by rows; that is, A through D are completed on an activity before proceeding to the next. Questions 6, 7, and 8 are asked (see page 59 of the illustrative schedule) after the listing procedure is completed.

Participant Observation

The unique contribution of participant observation to the study of human behavior is in the qualitative assessment of activity which this field method affords. In the style of Goffman (1962, 1971), on-the-scene observation captures a wide range of nuances that go with an activity and permits the observer to identify more subtle differences between seemingly similar acts and to ascribe deeper meanings to otherwise surface interpretations of each observed act. In the style of the ethnographer, participant observation offers opportunities for exploring subcultural meanings to activity and interpreting the social significance of activities that are not readily understood from survey research. Participation has to do with an experiential approach to the study of activity and provides in effect the live matrix against which the activity being observed can be recorded and interpreted. The combination of participation and observation provides a means of assessing aspects of thoughtways and lifeways that slip through the net of survey research.

In the submetropolitan area community studies, participant observation was used as a complementary field study method to survey research. Under the most ideal circumstances, participant observers would be stationed in the study community from 6 months to 1 year before the survey research is scheduled to go into the field. This would enable the design of the survey to benefit from knowledge about an area and its people that grows out of the participant observer's residency in the community. This is extremely helpful in postulating the preconditioning and predisposing factors and in devising satisfactory measures of these factors. It is also useful in subsequent interpretation of survey results to have the participant observer resident in the area during the period in which the survey is in the field, in part, to monitor unusual events that occur over the period of the survey; in part, to provide feedback on how the survey is being received and the sincerity with which those in the sample appear to be responding to survey questions; and in part, to interpret the meaning of frequently reported activities. This third function is more nearly in the traditions of an ethnographic study. For an activity study, however, participant observation is especially helpful in defining patterns of over- or underreporting of some activities.

On the basis of our two submetropolitan community studies, we suggest that a residency of 1 year is the minimum span of time needed to provide for both a lead-in period and an overlap with the survey—roughly 9 months' lead-in and 3 months' overlap (assuming the survey is in and out of the field in 2 months). However, the length of residency beyond a year's time is dependent on other nonsurvey objectives in the study of community activity systems. These objectives can include a range of concerns. As suggested above, a full-fledged ethnographic study records in depth not only values, beliefs, and lifeways of the people whose subculture is being studied, but it also interprets demographic patterns in the area, economic conditions affecting the community, and social structure and political events as these are understood by the people.[11] However, there may be more focused interests of a policy-oriented nature, such as monitoring the use of service systems in the community (medical care, welfare, and other social services)—how they are used, not used, or misused, and with what consequences. A number of special studies focusing on the social functions of various institutions in the community provide other examples of the use of participant observation field methods, for example, studies of the pool hall, the bootlegger's establishment, the tavern, the card-playing group, or the racetrack.[12]

SOME METHODOLOGICAL ISSUES

In the course of carrying out the series of studies listed in Figure III-1, a variety of problems and issues have arisen from time to time which are worthy of comment, either because they need to be borne in mind in interpreting results summarized in subsequent chapters or because they provide a reference for others who undertake further work along the lines discussed. These comments appear under three topics: the classification of activities, time as a metric of activity, and measures of predisposing factors.

Activity Classification

In the last chapter it was brought out that classification of activity is essential if the behavior of relatively large numbers of persons is to be subjected to systematic study. To deal with sizable samples of subjects requires quantitative analysis, and to cope with large quantities of activities necessitates some kind of classification system compatible with uses to be made of the data. The necessity of classification is not an issue; rather, concern centers around at what stage in the study classification is undertaken and how much aggregation is introduced at the finest-grain level of the classification system.[13] The positions on this issue appear to form a continuum. At one end is essentially a basic research position which argues for a nonstructured form of field listing. At the other end is the applied research position, which argues that precategorization of activities is possible when applications of the data are known at the start of the study, and precategorization is an essential economy in mounting the study.

The basic research approach seeks the meaning of an activity to a subject and seeks to define a classification system that grows out of the subject's own characterization of the activity. The applied approach seeks a designation of an activity in terms of its meaning for suppliers of specific services or facilities, such as suppliers of medical care, adult education, and transportation. The former approach argues that the ordinary person has difficulty in objectively assessing the purpose of each particular activity with sufficient certainty to fit it into a set of precategorized classes of activity (Foote, 1961). In this connection the argument is made for recording full detail in the verbal form the respondent customarily uses in characterizing his activities. With this kind of detail, it is suggested that with the modern computer it is then possible to develop a "semantic dictionary" of key words, and once the exact words are coded and available on tapes, classification rules appropriate to particular uses of the data can be devised and programmed so as to group the data into desired classes (Kranz, 1970).

Under the pragmatic kind of approach, it is reasoned that since detailed forms of activity must be assigned sooner or later to summarizing classes if analysis is to be made for the specific uses planned for the data, who is better able to ascribe meaning to an activity than the subject himself, and when is there a better time to clarify the meaning than at the time of contact in the field? It is also argued that some taxonomy of activity must be cited in explaining the purpose of the survey, in specifying the kind of information desired, and in gaining the cooperation of the respondent. Furthermore, it is argued that not only are cues needed by the interviewer in getting the desired information, but these are needed to minimize variation among respondents in the information supplied owing to imperfect communications between them and the interviewer.

In short, the basic research interest is in coding activity information in the purest form possible, leaving the classification and aggregation of data into classes to the post-field stages of the study, when it is pursued according to the needs of each particular user. The applied research interest takes the position that some preestablished classification system must be introduced at the time of the interview in order to obtain meaningful results, and if this is necessary, the subject's own classification of an activity relative to an activity purpose is more appropriate than the researcher's. With each end of the continuum goes a preference for field listing technique. In the case of the former a premium is placed on diary techniques as providing the most accurate and complete record of the subject's characterization of an activity, and in the case of the latter, the technique identified earlier which calls for handing to the subject a listing of activities by general class and asking which of these he or she did "yesterday" or on a "typical weekday," Saturday, or Sunday.

Clearly each extreme has costs and benefits, each according to the reasons for which a study was made in the first place. In our studies the classification issue was handled in several ways according to the purposes of the study. In our pilot studies, we experimented with both unstructured listings (in the form of diaries) and highly structured listings ("Which of these activities did you do yesterday? . . . Any others, not shown on the list?"). In the five studies drawn upon in this volume, an intermediate position on this continuum came to be chosen.

For reasons somewhat unrelated to the classification issue, a "yesterday" listing of activities came to be the source of the activity data in these studies even though we used both retrospective and prospective techniques in the main Washington study. As brought out earlier, problems of diary keeping encountered among the illiterate, the elderly, and the poor affected our returns. Also among the poor, we were losing rapport with subjects in forcing on them a method of record keeping based on clock time.

A general level of classification was explicitly communicated to subjects by the cues that interviewers used. Cues used in the Washington metropolitan study were along these lines:

> Now, I would like to ask you the things you did and the places you went yesterday. . . . I am interested in everything you did . . . [such activities as work, housework and child care, shopping, travel, seeing or visiting people, medical care, classes attended, meetings, religious activities, going out (e.g., in the evening), recreation activities, and so on][14]. . . . I am particularly interested in things which you did with other people and free time activities. . . .

Subjects were informed that details of activities on the job could be omitted, and interviewers were instructed not to probe on personal care activities. Instructions to interviewers called for using the words of respondents and probing when an activity was not clearly attributable to one of the illustrative categories. The other studies had generally the same kind of lead-in to the activity listings, although, if anything, they were somewhat less specific in the cues used.

The activity classes used in cues had two kinds of applications in view. First, there was a specific interest in out-of-home activities, more particularly, an interest in community facilities used, utilization of medical care services, and the transportation dependence of subjects in these out-of-home activities. Second, there was a specific interest in discretionary forms of activity—detail in patterns of visiting, various forms of social interchange, participation, recreation, and the allocation of time to passive diversions such as watching television, reading, rest, and relaxation. Cues and probes sought to clear up any ambiguity in these kinds of activity.

The coding of activities was based on a "dictionary" of about 225 activity codes (see three-digit coding system, Appendix Table A-1). These are grouped into activity classes at two levels of aggregation according to the key shown in the Appendix, Table A-2, one forming 40 classes of activity, and the other forming 12 classes. Although summary data for the 40-class system are contained in the Appendix, analyses in later chapters are made on the basis of the 12-class system:

01	Main job	07	Participation (church and organizations)
02	Eating	08	Recreation and other diversions
03	Shopping	09	Watching TV
04	Homemaking	10	Rest and relaxation
05	Family activities	11	Miscellaneous
06	Socializing	12	Sleeping

For urban planning purposes, the 12-class system allows for summary analyses of broad categories of time allocation, whereas the 40-class system permits a more fine-grain study, including analyses of activity sets which are associated with particular kinds of land uses, community facilities, and public services.

The aggregation of activities from the 225 codes to the 12 classes can be carried a step further to an essentially two-class system consisting of obligatory activities and discretionary activities. In effect, what was described in the last chapter as a continuum, by this step is arbitrarily split up into two zones, one more or less obligatory and one more or less discretionary. To be more exacting in the assignment of activities to either category would involve interpretation of each activity on a whole set of contingencies—for example, the meaning ascribed to the activity by the culture and the social system in which the subject falls, the culturally defined household role being performed by the subject at the time of the activity, the subject's own tastes and preferences, and situational factors surrounding the occurrence of each such activity. Indeed, in the classical sense "leisure" has become so elusive in contemporary advanced societies (de Grazia, 1962), particularly among the more affluent (Linder, 1970), that there are real problems of interpretation at the level of generality involved in classifying activity as either "obligatory" or "discretionary." Although there are these empirical and conceptual problems, "discretionary activity" is introduced into this study as an internally consistent summarizing measure for scanning the results across the five data sets. (For the grouping of activities into discretionary-obligatory classes, see Appendix, Table A-2.)

Time Allocation as a Measure of Activity

The problems of activity analysis are not limited to classification alone. There are other issues; among these, the use of time as the basis for an accounting system in recording and measuring activities. Before looking at issues, it will be useful to review briefly the activity measures used in later chapters.

Activity Measures. Quite clearly the output of the analysis format shown in Figure III-2, like the classification system, is dictated by the uses to be made of the activity study. For the descriptive-explanatory concerns of this book where relatively general classes of activity are used in determining similarities and differences in living patterns among sub-societal segments in the metropolitan community, three summarizing measures are derived from the activity information appearing on the schedule (type of activity, its start time, and its location). Given information about each subject obtained in other parts of the schedule, these measures are as follows:

1. The count of persons from different ethnic and status groups and the characteristics of each such population segment which engaged in each class of activity on weekdays (or on Saturdays or Sundays)—usually called *participation rate*.
2. The mean hours of time allocated per participant or per capita by persons of these population segments and characteristics to each such activity class on weekdays (or on Saturdays or Sundays)—usually referred to as *mean duration*.
3. The mean sum of distances per participant from home to all out-of-home activity locations for persons of these population segments on weekdays (or on Saturdays or Sundays)—usually referred to as *mean locus*.

It might be noted that when descriptive and explanatory analyses are to provide the basis for simulation and evaluation, not only is a more fine-grain classification system required (for example, a shift in order of detail of the kind involved in going from our 12-class to our 40-class system), but also there are other requirements to be met for analyses at this more complex phase of study. With respect to data forms, simulation requires in addition to the first two measures above, data on "start times" of activities and travel data for each class of out-of-home activity at various time intervals of the day for weekdays, Saturdays, and Sundays.

To move into a simulation phase of course involves the design and development of models capable of generating in simplified form activity patterns of the kind recorded in the descriptive stage.[15] To do this, there is a need for repeat studies (usually smaller-scale panel-type studies). These enable the investigator to check out the stability of activity patterns and the trends of change in preconditioning and predisposing factors, so that adjustments can be introduced into activity measures and the parameters of simulation models. Finally, to move on to an evaluation format, an additional information system is obviously needed, one in which land uses, community facilities, and public services are recorded to standardized locations which are compatible with location data on activities. Thus in order to undertake evaluation studies, work must be activated on the lower as well as the upper branch in the framework diagrammed in Figure II-1—on the "opportunity" line of development as well as the "propensity."

Some Problems and Issues.   Most of the difficult technical problems arise in the later simulation phase of the research and development where modeling rather than standard statistical techniques is required. In the present descriptive-explanatory phase, the issues have more to do with measurement. One such issue relates to the bias that the use of clock-time measures may introduce into results. In this connection, there is the possibility that the use of time as a metric overemphasizes "the clock and calendar ethic" of middle-class Western society, and that survey methods designed around time measures may be misreading activity patterns of other subcultures. Even though the time aspect of the activity study is given a relatively mechanical metronome-like function, it is very easy to overlook the "content" of activities in the press of trying to carry out the time-based study, which under most circumstances is itself a formidable task. In our work, we believe we have kept the over- or understatement of time allocated to activities from this source to a minimum through special attention to this problem in interviewer training, through the design of instruments, and through the use of participant observation.[16]

A related issue centers around the qualitative meaning in the use of time. As will be noted in later chapters, we frequently find that people in two contrasting life styles actually spend on the average nearly identical amounts of their free time on the same class of activity. Experientially the use of time may be quite different. For example, during summer periods "rest and relaxation" in the low-income black community often includes "sitting on the front porch," an activity rich in social exchange with neighbors and passersby, whereas the same amount of time spent by a middle- or high-income person in his air-conditioned home or apartment might have been spent "taking a nap." It might be argued that these qualitative differences can be remedied with probing and improved survey techniques.

But even assuming more specification of activity content in the listing of activities, the qualitative differences involve another dimension, namely, the relative satisfaction-dissatisfaction levels of activities of essentially the same content. Referring back to the micro level models of human activity discussed in the last chapter, satisfaction levels have something to do with the frequency with which an activity is chosen and the probabilities that particular activity patterns will persist or be of less importance as time goes on. Here again survey research can record information that will tend to minimize this problem (for example, see Questions 6, 7, and 8 in the illustrative survey schedule), but it may be necessary to extend the purely quantitative measures of time use reported in this volume to include, at the very least, the proportion of the total participants in an activity who register high and low satisfaction levels.

Measures of Predisposing Factors

This leads directly into a third kind of problem, one of specification and technique in operationalizing the predisposing factors in the framework—the ones billed as "energizing" an activity as opposed to those that function as constraints. This third area of comment is a direct outgrowth of experience in the exploratory work in submetropolitan areas of Washington.

Some Questions of Specification. Earlier what we have been calling "motivations" were linked with a hierarchy of needs the individual experiences in the course of everyday life. In the above discussion of the content areas of the interview schedule, several questions were cited to illustrate how felt needs with respect to achievement, status, and security might be approached. These categories of need were selected because they encompass what are widely held to be the key areas of felt need that derive from the social context in which the individual pursues his everyday affairs. One problem that arises in this connection has to do with the selection of questions and the development of suitable indices that represent valid indicators of these categories of need. As brought out in Chapter VI, the exploratory work undertaken in the two submetropolitan communities, where trial measures of these categories of need were introduced, suggests the need for improved specification of these needs in future work.

The "motivation" component includes categories of need that extend beyond those defined by the social system, notably motivations to engage in activities that grow out of the individual himself and his own particular tastes and talents. Although these cannot be dissociated entirely from the social context, the satisfaction (or dissatisfaction) with the outcome of engaging in some activities may have more to do with enjoyment (or disappointment) evaluated against these tastes and talents than status, achievement, or security. The design of questions and the inclusion of measures of these sources of motivation should be a part of further exploratory work.[17]

The "thoughtway" portion of the predisposing component similarly requires specification and incorporation into survey instruments. This portion of the component also has a social as well as an individual aspect, and these too can overlap somewhat. Thus subcultures, especially those with a strong sense of identity and those that seek to maintain an ethnic consciousness, may develop common patterns of thought that predispose members of that ethnic group to act in distinctive ways, that is, pursue distinctive activity patterns. Although these do not escape pressures for social conformity, the biases and prejudices of individual thought processes also predispose a person to engage in certain activities, to break off or not to engage in them at all. These kinds of "energizing" factors involve the definition and development of suitable attitude questions and the development of appropriate indices as part of further exploratory work.

As brought out earlier, the ethnographic study used in conjunction with survey research offers opportunities to hypothesize the otherwise diffuse or unknown factors which may be important influences in predisposing people from different segments of society and different ethnic makeup to engage in particular kinds of activity. So, at least in submetropolitan community studies or in studies of particular ethnic groups, participant observation can serve to help define the scope of the predisposing element of the framework. For studies of larger areas, perhaps prior to survey research, the social structure of the metropolitan community can be established from screening surveys. Given some specification of the ethnic makeup of the larger community and its stratification, it would be possible to establish "sampling points," as it were, in which participant observers take up residency at one sampling point for a period sufficiently long to hypothesize key motivation and thoughtway factors of activity patterns and then move on to another sampling point. On a small-scale basis, this kind of short-term residency was used with some success in one of our submetropolitan area studies.

A Note on a Game Technique. One of the concerns in working with activity listings of the kind obtained from a survey schedule such as that reproduced earlier in the chapter is to determine the extent of variability in each individual's activity listings. As brought out earlier, studies of the stability of responses can be established through reinterviews with a subsample of the respondents interviewed in the original basic study. Though less exacting, some indication of the stability of activity choices can be established from questions of the kind appearing in the illustrative schedule (see Questions 9 and 10). So long as shifts in activity represent substitutions of one activity for another *within a class,* the contingencies for the choice can be assumed to remain constant. However, if the changes in activity involve shifts *between classes* of activity, this suggests some kind of change of the contingencies in the choice-making environment.[18] To explore this issue, a "game" on leisure-time activity choices was developed and tested in the context of the usual survey research interview. Noted earlier was our interest in discretionary activities for the more sharply focused perspective they give of differences in life styles. So in developing the choice contingencies of the game, except for opportunities to trade off free time for self-improvement, obligatory activities were not included.

Reproduced here is the game format in the last version tested.[19] Very briefly, as indicated on the face sheet of the game, a subject is asked to allocate a limited amount of time to selected "free-time" activities according to a few simple rules, considering his present family situation (responsibilities for children at their present ages) and other constraints (present place of residence and so on). Earlier we experimented with variable amounts of time allocation based on the actual amounts of time subjects spent on discretionary activities in their yesterday's activity listing. We also experimented with the notion of marginal utility in time use. After the subject finished making his time allocation on the basis of

A RESEARCH STUDY OF LEISURE-TIME ACTIVITIES OF URBAN RESIDENTS

(Third Modification)

A Project of the
Center for Urban and Regional Studies
University of North Carolina
at Chapel Hill

INSTRUCTIONS

In this game we are borrowing the trade stamp idea -- the green stamps that merchants give you when you are buying something. However, we will use black stamps. You will paste in your supply of stamps in the boxes shown according to the way you would like to spend your spare time. Assume that during the next 7-day week, after subtracting out the time taken up in sleep, work, meals, grocery shopping, doctors' visits and similar necessities, you have a total of _____ hours (to be filled in by interviewer) to use as you see fit for any of the activities you wish to choose on the other side of this sheet.

Your stamp supply corresponds to days of the week distributed, say, as follows:

M   T   W   Th   F

Sat. Sun. morning
afternoon
evening

There are a few rules we ask you to observe. You have to spend the full amount of time shown for any choice shown. Some choices call for four hours (four stamps), some three, some two, some single hours. We ask you to spend the full amount indicated for each choice you make. Thus, it is against the rules to put down one stamp in a place where a four-hour, three-hour, or a two-hour strip is called for.

The asterisk or star (*) by some choices indicates that these are things which you may want to do regularly, but not every week. In these cases, you may average the time you would spend on them, as long as you do not divide whole hours. For example, going to church is a two hour choice, but if you would only go to church every second or third week, you may put a single hour on this choice.

You will notice that the sheet has eight panels formed by the folds to the game sheet, each containing one or two major groups of activity. You may find it helpful to look these over before you start making choices. You should make your choices considering the present age levels of family members and your present income circumstances. Lay your stamps on the boxes in appropriate numbers, and after you are satisfied with your choices, paste them in.

INCREASING YOUR INCOME

(Choose as many single hours as you wish)

1. Bringing work home or working overtime on the job

(Choose by four-hour strips)

2. A second job (moonlighting)

   (Use as many strips of four hours as you wish, but you must fill an entire strip with stamps)

(Choose as many single hours as you wish)

3. Other activities to increase income such as

   ● taking care of rental property
   ● watching stock market prices
   ● earning income from some hobby
   ● military reserve, national guard, etc.

(Choose by two-hour strips)

4. Job-related activities (attending union or professional meetings, job training, night courses to learn new occupation, etc.

5. _____
   (specify other)

IMPROVING YOURSELF BY FURTHER EDUCATION OR
ADDING TO YOUR DEVELOPMENT IN OTHER WAYS

(Choose by three-hour strips)

1. Night classes not connected with job

    (Three hours set aside per evening
    includes study and time getting to
    and from class. Choose one or two
    evenings per week)

(Choose by two-hour strips)

*2. Attending evening or midweek
    church services, meetings,
    circles, choir practice or other
    church-sponsored activities

*3. Browsing in library, attending
    lecture, going to a museum,
    art gallery, symphony, etc.

(Choose by three-hour strips)

*4. Taking part in little theater,
    symphony orchestra, operetta,
    interpretative dance, etc.

(Use full two hours)

*5. Attending regular Sunday
    church services

(Choose by two-hour strips)

6. Acting, painting, writing,
    composing, playing an in-
    strument, singing, etc.

(Choose as many single hours as you wish)

7. Taking a correspondence
    course or following your
    own program of study

8. _____
        (specify other)

DOING THINGS WITH FAMILY

(Choose as many single hours as you wish)

1. Activities around home with children or grandchildren

   (playing games, helping with homework, teaching or helping with sewing, woodworking, etc.)

(Choose by three-hour strips)

2. Trip with children or grandchildren to library, movies, zoo, fair, circus, etc.

(Choose by four-hour strips)

*3. Family outing (picnic, etc.)

(Choose by two-hour strips)

*4. Taking a family drive in the car

(Choose as many single hours as you wish)

5. Telephoning or writing letters to RELATIVES

(Choose by two-hour strips)

6. Visiting with RELATIVES

7. _____
   (specify other)

79

SOCIAL ACTIVITIES

(Choose as many single hours as you wish)

1. Telephoning or
    writing letters
    to FRIENDS

    ☐ ☐ ☐ ☐ ☐

2. Visiting in the
    neighborhood

    ☐ ☐ ☐ ☐ ☐

(Choose by two-hour strips)

*3. Socializing in your house
    or friend's house. (Getting
    together for coffee, going
    to a tea, cocktail party, etc.)

    ☐☐ ☐☐

(Choose by four-hour strips)

*4. Evening at friends' house
    (dinner and visiting, possibly
    playing cards),
    OR entertaining friends at
    your house for evening

    ☐☐☐☐

    ☐☐☐☐

*5. Getting together with boys
    (poker, bull session, etc.)
    OR getting together with girls
    (bridge, hen party, etc.)

    ☐☐☐☐

*6. Square dancing or other com-
    munity dance, picnic, supper
    and similar socials

    ☐☐☐☐

(Choose as many single hours as you wish)

7. Spending an afternoon or
    evening at the club

    ☐ ☐ ☐ ☐

8. _____
    (specify other)

    ☐

80

RECREATION AND RELAXATION

A. Individual Activity   (Choose as many single hours as you wish)

1. Relaxing, nap-
    ping, looking
    through paper
    or magazine

2. Watching TV
    or listening
    to radio

3. Reading book,
    playing musical
    instrument, sing-
    ing, listening
    to records (for
    relaxation)

4. Hobbies such
    as gardening,
    sewing, crafts,
    woodworking,
    bird watching

B. Individual or Shared Activity

5. Walking, strolling or
    window shopping (just
    looking)

(Choose by three-hour strips)

*6. Movies

*7. Going to a
     play, band
     concert, etc.

*8. Evening out
(dinner, dance,
dropping in at
night spots)

(Choose as many single hours as you wish)

9. Driving around,
stopping at drive-in,
dropping in for a
beer, etc.

10. _____
(specify other)

RECREATION AND RELAXATION (CONT.)

C. Active Recreation & Sports

(Choose as many single hours as you wish)

1. Scrub ball, playing catch,
shooting baskets, passing
& kicking football, horse-
shoes

(Choose by two-hour strips)

*2. Individual sports such as
handball, squash, bowling

(Choose as many single hours as you wish)

3. Workout in gym, track,
judo, wrestling, boxing

(Choose by three-hour strips)

4. Seasonal sports--stamps can refer to
several sports according to season.

Check sports you are choosing

☐ Golf   ☐ Boating, incl.
water skiing

☐ Tennis   ☐ Skating

☐ Swimming   ☐ Skiing or
tobogganing

5. Playing on a team
(softball, bowling,
other)

82

D. Attending sports events

  *6. Going to baseball,
football, basket-
ball game, hockey
game, etc.

  *7. Going to fights,
races, tennis
matches, golf
tournaments

  8. _____
(specify other recreation or sports)

CLUB AND ORGANIZATIONAL ACTIVITIES

(Choose by two-hour strips)

*1. Clubs for hobbies & special
interests (garden club,
alumni clubs, crafts, etc.)

*2. Veterans organizations, their
auxiliaries, D.A.R., and other
patriotic groups)

*3. Groups interested in advance-
ment of human or social welfare
(peace, economic opportunity,
human rights, etc.)

*4. Attending meetings of civic club
(Rotary, Altrusa, etc.) or
fraternal group or its auxiliary
(Mason, Eastern Star, Elks, P.O.E.,
etc.)

5. _____
(specify other)

SERVICE AND CIVIC AFFAIRS ACTIVITIES

(Choose by two-hour strips)

*1. Helping out on occasional worthy
    projects (fund-raising, such as
    United Fund, Little League,
    fixing up toys, etc.)

2. Regular volunteer service (Scouts
   and similar young people's activities;
   hospital auxiliary; remedial reading
   for children of deprived families, etc.)

(Choose by three-hour strips)

*3. Civic interest activities (League of
    Women Voters, Good Government,
    Neighborhood Improvement Association,
    Taxpayers League, etc.)

*4. Political activities (campaigning,
    precinct work, volunteer time at
    party headquarters, etc.)

5. Running for office and serving
   term in elective positions (not
   as full-time job)

*6. Serving on appointive city, county,
    or state boards, commissions,
    advisory committees (not as a
    full-time job)

7. _____
   (specify other)

OTHER ACTIVITIES NOT ELSEWHERE COVERED

_____
(specify type)

_____
(specify type)

84

initial instructions, the interviewer then introduced a change in the contingencies: "now let's assume that you would have more free time during the week—a half day free on Tuesday and a half day on Thursday—but the same income you have now—please show how you would allocate these eight additional hours."

In the Washington metropolitan area study pretest, amounts of time were allowed to vary between two contingencies—30 hours a week and 50 hours a week—and between two income situations—continuing with the family's present income situation or an increase in the family income one-third more than the present level. Obviously, other contingencies can be explored with such a game, for example, a change in the life cycle, with the subject and his or her children being, say, 10 years older. Although samples were rather small in the pretest (94 usable returns from 100 possible respondent returns divided among the four contingencies), the results from an analysis of these returns suggest that when a subject is asked to project his activities under these contingencies, income changes do not appreciably affect choices but, not surprisingly, the number of hours available do appear to significantly affect the amount of time devoted to particular activities.[20]

Such a game functions somewhat in the manner of a primitive form of linear programming where the respondent seeks some optimal combination of activity choices in the allocation of free time, subject to a set of constraints. If the key constraints have been identified and introduced into the game, this device offers a means of eliciting reasoned indications of preference in the use of leisure time. Although it suffers from some of the same problems brought out above in connection with the use of diaries,[21] it is nevertheless a promising approach to preference studies within certain segments of the metropolitan community.

With this background on the five studies, the survey methods, and some of the problems associated with time allocation, we turn now to the results from these empirical studies.

NOTES

1. The Washington metropolitan area study in 1968 was supported by the National Center for Health Services Research and Development, U.S. Public Health Service (Grant No. HS 00094). The first national study in 1966 was made with support from the National Cooperative Highway Research Program sponsored by Highway Research Board of the National Academy of Sciences (NCHRP Project 8–6), and the 1969 recontact survey was funded by the National Science Foundation (Grant No. GS-2427). The inner-city black community study was carried out in 1969 under a grant from The Ford Foundation (Grant No. 68-719),

and the study of the transitional white community was supported by the Center for Studies of Metropolitan Problems, National Institute of Mental Health, U.S. Public Health Service (Grant No. MH 17858).

The Durham studies are summarized in Chapin and Hightower (1966); the national studies in Brail and Chapin (1973); the Washington metropolitan area study in Hammer and Chapin (1972) and in Chapin (1971); and the submetropolitan studies in Chapin, Butler, and Patten (to be published), Howell (1973), and Zehner and Chapin (1974).

2.   In the Washington areawide study, the investigation of activity patterns was proposed as a means of determining how medical-care episodes that occur during an average day in the lives of people included in our probability sample are handled in the context of all other activities happening in the course of the day. Although a history of medical-care episodes for the previous year was obtained for each of these subjects, the activity aspect was introduced to obtain some case studies on the way these episodes fitted into a day's routine for these people—what had to be done about getting time off from work or getting baby sitters for the children, what means of transportation was used, how long it took getting to the doctor or facility (including time spent hunting for a parking place if an automobile was used), and how much time was involved after arrival, waiting to be examined.

It turned out that the number of medical-care episodes occurring "yesterday" for our sampled subjects was too small for the sample size to warrant systematic analysis (61 week-day episodes for 1667 activity returns).

3.   For example, in the 1966 and 1969 national surveys, automobile, bus, or walking trips made during the day in connection with an activity were not reported as separate activities, as in the other three surveys, but the time involved in travel was merged with the time spent on activities generating that travel. In this connection, in order to maintain comparability in the form of results in all five studies reported in this volume, the travel time obtained in the other three studies is usually merged with the time of its appropriate activity category. Considerable interview time was also saved by eliminating the provision in the other three surveys that required the respondent to pinpoint locations of out-of-home activities to the nearest street corner; in the national studies, a check was made for each activity as to whether it occurred in or out of the home. The greatest saving of time was achieved by eliminating the double time required in the three Washington studies to obtain for each respondent not only "yesterday's" itinerary but another itinerary for a previous Saturday or Sunday (systematically alternated with each successive respondent). In the national studies, interviews were conducted so that respondents were interviewed on systematically assigned days of the week so that all seven days were covered approximately equally.

4.   Sample designs are discussed in the monographs on various individual studies (see note 1 for listing).

5.   The national studies involve some other departures. For example, the sampling design was based on a standard multistage probability sample to the level of small areas containing one or more city blocks, with quota sampling at the block level to obtain desired representation of heads and spouses, appropriate proportions of respondents by age and employment status, and equal representation of all days of the week in interviewing. The specifications also called for proportional representation of East, South, Middle West, and West, proportional representation within regions of SMSA-size class (less than 250,000 population in 1960; 250,000 to 1,000,000 population; and over 1,000,000 population), and equal numbers of interviews in central cities and suburban areas.

6. The definition of the household head follows the Bureau of the Census practice whereby in all situations where a husband-wife combination is found to "preside" over a household, the male partner is always designated as the head. A female head, therefore, can occur only when a female "presiding" member of the household has no partner present in the household. Households can have "family heads" or "primary individual" heads.

In our studies, respondents were selected on the following basis. Once the head of the household was identified from a list of every resident member of the household, the head or the spouse of the head was selected on a systematically alternating basis, except when a household had only one partner resident in the household, who then became the subject. This meant that heads would tend to be a somewhat higher proportion of the sample than spouses, and given the sex bias in the designation of heads (even taking into account higher male death rates), the effect is to produce a higher proportion of male heads in our sample of respondents than female heads. On the other hand, since interviews with sponses were systematically provided for (and by definition spouses would always be female), the sex distribution of respondents was brought more nearly into balance. Thus in the Washington metropolitan area, though the sex distribution of *heads of household* in the sample was 79.4 percent male and 20.6 percent female, the sex distribution of our *respondents* was 43.9 percent male and 56.1 percent were female.

7. Some experimental studies have been undertaken in which cooperating subjects using pocket-size transmitter-receiver radios are contacted at randomized time intervals during the sample day to obtain information on what is being done at the moment they are contacted, where the subject is, and with whom the activity is being done (Stone, 1970). This method of obtaining activity data would appear to be well suited to panel-type longitudinal studies; in many respects, it uses subjects as participant observers of their own activities.

8. Robert B. Zehner had much to do with the latest version of the basic interview format. Before him, Henry C. Hightower, Edgar W. Butler, Philip G. Hammer, Jr., Linda A. Fischer, and John C. Robson made contributions in the design of the activity schedule.

9. In the Duncan 100-point scale, these consist of scores 1–35, 36–85, and 86–100 (see Reiss, 1961, Appendix B, App. Table B-1, Column 3).

10. The questions shown in the illustrative schedule are based on those used in exploratory work in the submetropolitan transitional white community study. Much more testing is required before the questions shown could be recommended for general use.

11. See Valentine (1968) for a check list of topical guides, and see methodological appendices of Whyte (1943), Gans (1962, 1967), Liebow (1967), Lewis (1968), and Howell (1973). For a more systematic coverage of methodological approaches, see Bruyn (1966); and for a phenomenonological emphasis, see Goffman (1963, 1971).

12 For example, see Richards (1964), Cavan (1966), Polsky (1967), and Scott (1968).

13. In the urban planning field, there is a parallel in land use classification. During the fifties an extended debate developed around the need for a standard classification system, centering on what the makeup of the system should be. The publication of a standard coding system under sponsorship of the federal government defused the issue by shifting the emphasis from a classification system to a coding system (Urban Renewal Administration and Bureau of Public Roads, 1965).

14.   Based on the list used on the face sheet of the diary (with further detailed listing of illustrative classes of activity within each of these categories). Interviewers were instructed to use this kind of list in spelling out what was expected from respondents.

15.   Brail (1969) has proposed two approaches to the simulation of human activity. The first calls for the construction of two sets of Markov-like transitional matrices for each population segment (say, for each sex in each stage of the life cycle in each stratum of the metropolitan community). Briefly, the probabilities in the first set of matrices (one for each interval of time) determine how many people in the given population segment change their activities from what they are doing at time t to other activities in each and every activity class at time $t + 1$, and the probabilities in the second set of matrices determine how many of those changing activities who were in the ith grid cell go to the jth grid cell to do the next succeeding activity at time $t + 1$. The probability matrices would be constructed from participation rates per unit of time and accumulations of people at all grid coordinate locations per unit of time applicable in the descriptive phase of analysis.

The second approach uses a computer simulation model. On the basis of the descriptive stage of analysis, probability distributions are developed for (1) waking time, (2) activity choice, (3) mode of transportation (for activities requiring transportation), (4) the time spent in transportation, (5) the location selected within the appropriate radius, (6) the duration of the activity, and (7) the retiring time. The day begins for each person in each subsample category (for example, sex, stage in the life cycle, and socioeconomic segment) at a time determined by the computer from sampling the probability distribution for waking time. Then by sampling each successive probability distribution a person's first activity of the day is chosen, a mode of travel and duration of travel are determined (if appropriate), and the activity duration is established. The computer continues building that person's routine for the day until the sampling of the "retiring time" probability distribution results in his bedtime. In the course of this process, the computer maintains accounts on activity times and places for each person category. In contrast to taking *aggregates of people* through equal time intervals and establishing net balances of people engaging in each activity at each interval of time at each grid cell location involved in the transitional matrix approach, the computer simulation puts *individual persons* in the various population segments used in the analysis through a day's routine, with each such routine variable in its activity content, start times, locations, modes of travel, and durations. The matrix approach is deterministic; the computer simulation would be stochastic.

16.   In the inner-city black community study, we found that the use of time as a basis for recording activities was alien to the way people here thought about their activities. People in low-income circumstances, particularly low-income black persons, do not do things by clock time (Horton, 1967). A modified form of the activity listing format shown here was introduced. Although it was necessary to have time checkpoints, if results were to be summarized in ways used in the other studies, clock time was deemphasized. The approach followed in this study was to identify key break points in the subject's day (for example, getting up, noon meal, evening meal, and going to bed). Respondents were asked to furnish these times. Then, as the morning's itinerary, the afternoon's, and the evening's unfolded and were listed, the subject was asked to estimate the proportion of the morning, afternoon, or evening taken up in each activity. Wherever times were volunteered, these were used to refine estimates. Although the time emphasis was not eliminated, this procedure enabled us to obtain duration estimates roughly in keeping with time measures obtained in more direct fashion in the other studies. In this connection, it might

be noted that the same approach is well suited to interviews with illiterate subjects and elderly subjects who are sensitive about how much time they have to account for in these interviews.

17. At the present stage in the development of our model, the enjoyment of a discretionary activity relative to others is part of the residual of unexplained variation. An example of one approach to specifying degree of enjoyment is found in Questions 6, 7, and 8 of the illustrative schedule reproduced earlier in the chapter.

18. These within- and between-class distinctions assume that the classification of activities is highly developed and the substitutability of activities within classes has been fully explored. In this connection, it might be noted that in all likelihood subclassification systems for different subsocietal segments would need to be established in studying the substitutability of activities.

19. The original version (Chapin, 1965) and an assessment of its use appear elsewhere (Chapin and Hightower, 1965).

20. These findings are taken from an unpublished analysis by John R. Ottensmann in which the amounts of time allocated to the 10 generic classes of activity identified on the game sheet (with the recreation subcategories treated as separate activities) were dependent variables, and the total amount of free time and level of income in the four combinations were used as independent variables.

21. It is not easy to use with illiterate subjects; also, for subjects who are present-time oriented, the notion of making activity choices in terms of time is first of all somewhat alien to the way they go about choosing an activity, and second, the options of choosing between activities some of which have future payoffs and some have immediate payoffs tends to be a meaningless exercise. Similarly, for the elderly, such a game is an enigma. It asks them to accept a constraint (a limited amount of time) that is usually nonexistent in their lives; for them the filling of a day constitutes one of their most poignant day-to-day concerns.

REFERENCES

Brail, Richard K. (1969). *Activity System Investigations: Strategy for Model Design*, Ph.D. dissertation, University of North Carolina (Ann Arbor, Mich.: University Microfilms).

———— and F. Stuart Chapin, Jr. (1973). "Activity Patterns of Urban Residents," *Environment and Behavior*, **5**:2.

Bruyn, Severyn T. (1966). *The Human Perspective in Sociology* (Englewood Cliffs, N.J.: Prentice-Hall, Inc.).

Cavan, Serri (1966). *Liquor License: An Ethnography of Bar Behavior* (Chicago: Aldine Publishing Company).

Chapin, F. Stuart, Jr. (1965). *Urban Land Use Planning* (Urbana: University of Illinois Press), pp. 250–253.

———— (1971). "Free Time Activities and Quality of Urban Life," *Journal of the American Institute of Planners*, **37**:6.

————, Edgar W. Butler, and Frederick C. Patten (to be published). *Blackways in the Inner City* (Urbana: University of Illinois Press).

———— and Henry C. Hightower (1965). "Household Activity Patterns and Land Use," *Journal of the American Institute of Planners*, **31**:3.

———— and ———— (1966). *Household Activity Systems—A Pilot Investigation* (Chapel Hill: Center for Urban and Regional Studies, University of North Carolina).

Foote, Nelson N. (1961). "Methods for Study of Meaning in Use of Time," in Robert W. Kleemeier, *Aging and Leisure* (New York: Oxford University Press).

Gans, Herbert J. (1962). *The Urban Villagers* (New York: The Free Press of Glencoe, Division of The Macmillan Company).

———— (1967). *The Levittowners* (New York: Pantheon Books, Division of Random House, Inc.).

Goffman, Erving (1963). *Behavior in Public Places* (New York: The Free Press of Glencoe, Division of The Macmillan Company).

———— (1971). *Relations in Public* (New York: Basic Books, Inc.).

de Grazia, Sebastian (1962). *Of Time, Work and Leisure* (New York: The Twentieth Century Fund, Inc.).

Hammer, Philip G., Jr., and F. Stuart Chapin, Jr. (1972). *Human Time Allocation: A Case Study of Washington, D.C.*, Technical Monograph, (Chapel Hill: Center for Urban and Regional Studies, University of North Carolina).

Hollingshead, August B., and Fredrick C. Redlich (1958). *Social Class and Mental Illness: A Community Study* (New York: John Wiley & Sons).

Horton, John (1967). "Time and Cool People," *Trans-action*, **4**:5.

Howell, Joseph T. (1973). *Hard Living on Clay Street* (Garden City, N.Y.: Doubleday-Anchor Books).

Kranz, Peter (1970). "What Do People Do All Day?," *Behavioral Science*, **15**:3.

Lewis, Oscar (1968). *La Vida* (New York: Vintage Books, Division of Random House).

Liebow, Elliot (1967). *Tally's Corner* (Boston: Little, Brown and Company).

Linder, Staffan B. (1970). *The Harried Leisure Class* (New York: Columbia University Press).

Polsky, Ned (1967). *Hustlers, Beats and Others* (Chicago: Aldine Publishing Company).

Reiss, Albert J., Jr. (1961). *Occupations and Social Status* (New York: The Free Press of Glencoe, Division of the Macmillan Company).

Richards, Cara E. (1964). "City Taverns," *Human Organization*, **22**:4 (Winter 1963–64).

Scott, Marvin B. (1968). *The Racing Game* (Chicago: Aldine Publishing Company).

Stone, Philip J. (1970). "Technical Issues and Solutions Suggested by the International Time Budget Project," discussion of this paper presented at the World Congress of Sociology, Varna, Bulgaria.

Urban Renwal Administration, Housing and Home Finance Agency, and Bureau of Public Roads, Department of Commerce (1965). *Standard Land Use Coding Manual*, (Washington, D.C.: U.S. Government Printing Office).

Valentine, Charles A. (1968). *Culture and Poverty* (Chicago: The University of Chicago Press).

Whyte, William Foote (1943). *Street Corner Society* (Chicago: The University of Chicago Press).

Zehner, Robert B., and F. Stuart Chapin, Jr. (1974). *Across the City Line: A White Community in Transition* (Lexington, Mass.: Lexington Books, D. C. Heath and Company).

CHAPTER FOUR

METROPOLITAN AREA
ACTIVITY PATTERNS:
THE WASHINGTON STUDY

In some respects the activity patterns of a metropolitan community are a reflection of the ethos of that city. They are a blend of the cultural qualities that engender the values, beliefs, and life experiences of its different ethnic and status groups and give it an identity of its own among cities. Thus the base-line description of activity patterns in the Washington metropolitan area presented in this chapter might be used to indicate something of the character of this city in relation to that of others in some larger system of cities. Or it might be used in the framework of a cross-cultural comparative study of the kind Szalai (1972) and his colleagues made in their multinational time-budget project during the sixties.

However, for planning and policy applications of the kind contemplated from following the approach outlined in this work, such a baseline description of activity patterns has utility for examining the social fabric within a particular metropolitan community. For these purposes it provides a means of examining differences in life styles among ethnic groups and among various status levels within each such group in the community. If variations in activity patterns materialize from among these segments of the population (see Chapter V), these can be construed to indicate differences in life styles, perhaps warranting different em-

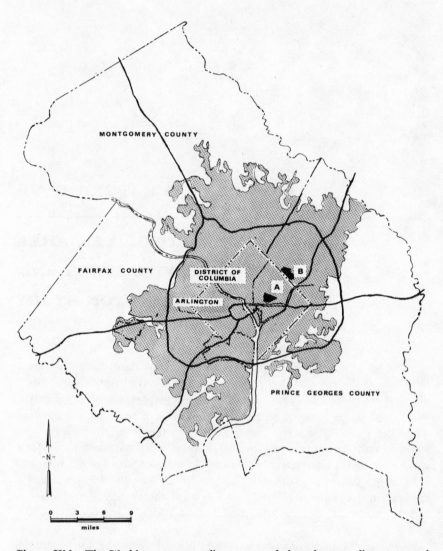

Figure IV-1   The Washington metropolitan area and the submetropolitan communities studied (inner-city study Area A and transitional study Area B).

phases in planning for community facilities and services. If no differences materialize and patterns are similar to those identified for the community (as defined in this chapter), then there is some basis for ascribing these patterns to the larger culture and following one common emphasis in planning for facilities and services. Here, where activities are aggregated into 12 classes, we concentrate on differences and similarities among these segments of society for *general* categories of activity, essentially defining the broad context for subsequent selective analyses of more specific forms of activity that go with particular facilities and services.

The chapter is organized into three sections. The first examines representativeness and general characteristics of the Washington area sample. In the next section, activity patterns are presented in three perspectives, by class of activity, by time of day, and by distance from home. The last section of this chapter examines variations in activity patterns for selected role and background characteristics of subjects.

THE WASHINGTON SMSA SAMPLE

For purposes of these analyses, the Washington area sample was drawn from the jurisdictions contained in the "old 1960 SMSA" consisting of the District of Columbia and four suburban counties (Arlington and Fairfax Counties in Virginia and Montgomery and Prince Georges Counties in Maryland, including the independent cities within these counties). The sample households were for the most part in the gray area in Figure IV-1, which shows roughly the solidly built-up areas in 1968. The area included in the old SMSA contained a 1970 population of 2,712,871, of which a quarter was black. More than three-quarters of the total black population of the old SMSA live in the District of Columbia, which in 1970 was 71.1 percent black.

Sample Compared to Census

To establish how closely our sample resembles the universe, rough comparisons are made on a few population characteristics between our 1968 survey results and the 1970 census. If the rules for selection of respondents followed in our survey in the spring of 1968 were followed in precisely the same manner at the time of the 1970 census, in 60.8 percent of the households the interview would have been with the head of the household, and in 39.2 percent it would have been with the spouse. This compares with results in 1968 of 64.4 percent and 35.6 percent, respectively. In 1970, this would have yielded 53.7 percent female respondents, whereas in the 1968 survey, we obtained 56.1 percent females.[1]

As to racial composition, from the 1970 census we learn that 23.6 percent of the households in the old SMSA were black; in our 1968 survey, 22.3 percent were black.[2] The following table compares the distribution of households among income classes:

Income Range Before Taxes for Families and Primary Individuals ($)	Percentage Distribution	
	1969 Incomes Recorded in 1970 Census (n = 994,924)	1967 Incomes Recorded in 1968 Survey (n = 1756*)
Under 5000	24.8	17.8
5000–9999	26.1	30.8
10,000–14,999	20.5	27.5
15,000 and over	28.6	23.9

* This figure represents the full sample of households; of these only 1667 respondents reported income and had weekday activity returns sufficiently complete to use in later analyses.

From these results it would appear that our sample somewhat overrepresents the middle two categories and underrepresents the bottom and top categories.

This may be explained to some degree in the lowest income group by the falloff in response rate in inner-city areas where civil disturbances broke out in the aftermath of Martin Luther King's assassination, an event that occurred when the survey was in progress.[3] For the top part of the upper-income category we were dealing with high-level government officials, capital representatives of corporations, and the like; for this group refusal rates ran high, not only because these persons are difficult to contact but also because they follow a practice in this politically sensitive community of refusing interviews. In this connection, we had hoped to check out some of the stereotype images of a capital city—the pageantry of entertaining in off-work hours—possibly getting some glimpses of influence peddling in the lives of high government officials, diplomats, and lobbyists. There may be some imprint of these activities in the collective patterns presented, but the underrepresentation of persons from these segments blurs results considerably in this relatively small sector of the community.

Characteristics of the Subjects

Since the characteristics of our subjects are of background interest in interpreting activity data, it will be informative to scan briefly some factors about our sample before examining their activity patterns. The rows of Table IV-1 show the variations in respondent characteristics by day of the week for which activity data were recorded, and in this respect it is evident that there are very small variations across rows between weekday and weekend day returns. This would be expected since Saturday and Sunday respondents taken together are the same persons who are listed for weekday respondents (minus 58 persons for whom a weekend day return was either incomplete or refused.)[4]

In the column listings, three characteristics are of special interest in later analyses—the respondents' work status, sex, and child-rearing responsibilities. Scanning the first column of the table for the weekday sample shows that 58.9 percent of our subjects work full time, 55.8 percent are women, and 43.8 percent have one or more children under 13 years of age in the household. Concerning the other characteristics shown in Table IV-1, the racial composition will be of interest in observing differences in activity patterns ascribed to ethnic groups in the SMSA's population in the next chapter. Similarly, the income group of subjects will be of interest in later analyses where we will be examining variations in time allocation for different socioeconomic groups.

THREE PERSPECTIVES OF HUMAN ACTIVITY

Each of the three perspectives taken up in subsections below provide a different dimension to the description of living patterns in the Washington metropolitan area. In the first, the emphasis is on *what kinds of activity* people engage in on weekdays, Saturdays, and Sundays: the proportion of the sample engaging in each activity and the mean time allocated to each. The second perspective emphasizes the temporal aspect of activities—*when people are doing these activities,* by different hours of day or night around the clock (for weekdays, Saturdays, and Sundays). The third perspective has a spatial emphasis—*where people are doing these*

Table IV-1 Selected Characteristics of Washington Metropolitan Area Sample Used in Activity Analysis by Day of Week, 1968.

Characteristics	Percent of Respondents by Activity Day		
	Weekdays (n=1,667)	Saturdays (n=807)	Sundays (n=802)
Work Status			
R works full time	58.9	60.3	58.1
R works part time	7.6	7.6	7.9
R does not work	33.5	32.1	34.0
Sex Distribution			
Male	44.1	43.7	44.3
Female	55.8	56.4	55.7
Life Cyclea/			
Young, no children	14.1	14.6	13.5
Child-rearing, some children under 13	43.8	46.0	42.8
Child-rearing, none under 13, some 13-18 yrs.	8.3	7.4	9.1
Middle years, no children under 19 present	24.2	24.0	24.2
Elderly, no children under 19 present	9.6	7.9	10.5
Race			
Black	21.4	19.9	22.5
Nonblack	78.5	80.2	77.5
Income Per Member of Householdb/			
Low Income--Bottom of Low	13.9	12.8	14.6
Low Income--Top of Low	21.6	21.7	21.7
Middle Income--Bottom of Middle	31.5	32.7	30.2
Middle Income--Top of Middle	20.3	20.7	20.0
High Income	12.7	12.1	13.6

a/ In later analyses, the samples are dichotomized such that the second category becomes "child < 13" and the other categories are combined to form "no child < 13."

b/ See Figure III-3 for the formation of categories.

activities and the mean "crow-flying" distances involved from home to the locations of out-of-home activities for persons who engage in these activities (weekdays only).

Patterns of Activity Choice

As brought out earlier, activity patterns presented here are at a level of aggregation best suited to analyzing the general content of daily pursuits of city life, that is, the 12-class system of grouping activities. We do not attempt here to examine activities at a more disaggregated level required for studying the use of specific community facilities and services, at the detail of a 40-class system.[5] Within the 12-class grouping of activities, special attention is given to activities of a discretionary character. Although some analyses are made of such "household maintenance functions" as work, homemaking and child care, shopping, and eating, primary attention is given to such categories as family activities; visiting and other forms of social interaction; participation in church and in the activities of various voluntary organizations; engaging in recreation and similar diversions; watching television; and resting and relaxing around home. Among these, the one nongeneric category is "watching television"; this activity was singled out as a separate category because it has been found to take up a larger proportion of discretionary time than any other category. It therefore not only merits attention as a special phenomenon in contemporary life, but if it were combined with another activity class it would overshadow all other activities in that category. Turning now to results from our studies, just what are the basic patterns of time allocation to these classes of human activity in the Washington metropolitan community, and how do they compare with SMSA patterns in the national scene?

Time Allocation Patterns in the Washington Metropolitan Area. Table IV-2 provides a summary view of time allocation during weekdays and weekend days for decision-making members of households in the Washington area during the spring of 1968. Using two measures—participation rates and mean durations of the time allocated to each of 12 activity categories and the travel associated with each—it provides a description of their activity patterns. The left-hand block of the table presents mean times devoted to various classes of activity figured on a per capita basis for all persons in the sample, and the right-hand block presents mean times calculated on a per participant basis for just those doing the

Table IV-2   Mean Duration of Time Heads of Households and Spouses Activities on Weekdays, Saturdays, and Sundays—Washington, 1968.

	Time Allocation Per Capita								
	Weekdays				Saturdays				
Activity Category[a]	% Engaging in Activity (n=1,667)	Mean Hours			% Engaging in Activity (n=807)	Mean Hours			% Engaging in Activity (n=802)
		Activity	Trav.	Tot.		Activity	Trav.	Tot.	
Main Job	57.9	4.49	.57	5.06	18.1	1.20	.13	1.33	11.7
Eating	96.2	1.56	.11	1.67	89.7	1.57	.11	1.68	89.5
Shopping	35.6	.36	.21	.57	48.0	.75	.34	1.09	14.8
Homemaking	75.8	2.70	.04	2.74	79.2	3.27	.05	3.32	73.6
Family Activities	30.5	.50	.02	.52	33.6	.95	.05	1.00	39.5
Socializing	36.4	.68	.06	.74	35.1	1.04	.12	1.16	36.8
Participation (Ch. & Orgs.)	6.5	.12	.02	.14	7.1	.15	.02	.17	33.2
Recreation, Other Diversions	32.0	.69	.06	.75	28.8	.76	.09	.85	30.9
Watching TV	66.9	1.65	.00	1.65	59.9	1.75	.00	1.75	66.8
Rest & Relaxation	57.4	.94	.00	.94	48.0	.99	.00	.99	67.0
Miscellaneous	89.6	2.53	.05	2.58	83.9	3.08	.06	3.14	85.7
Sleeping	99.5	7.46	.00	7.46	98.8	8.16	.00	8.16	99.0
Totals				24.82[b]				24.64[b]	

a/   Time allocated to concurrent activities is evenly split between these activities.

b/   Totals do not come to 24 hours due to rounding errors.

activity. Since the per capita durations in mean hours are computed on the same base for all activity categories, these can be summed to a 24-hour total. Most of the analyses from here on are made on a per capita basis, but the per participant data are of interest for the measure they give of "real time," that is, the mean duration of time actually spent on each class of activity by those who participated in it.

Earlier it was suggested that an "activity pattern" is determined by the extent of participation in an activity by a particular population. For the level of detail involved in the 12-class system of classification used in this volume, we have set a minimum participation rate of 25 percent as the cutoff point. Thus if at least 25 percent of the persons in a popu-

of Heads Spend on Daily Activities and Travel Associated with These

	Time Allocation Per Participant										
Sundays			Weekdays			Saturdays			Sundays		
Mean Hours			Mean Hours			Mean Hours			Mean Hours		
Activity	Trav.	Tot.	Activity	Trav.	Tot.	Activity	Trav.	Tot.	Activity	Trav.	Tot.
.73	.06	.79	7.77	.97	8.74	6.64	.73	7.37	6.23	.54	6.71
1.49	.12	1.61	1.63	.11	1.74	1.75	.12	1.87	1.66	.13	1.79
.07	.07	.14	1.02	.57	1.59	1.55	.72	2.27	.50	.44	.94
2.46	.05	2.51	3.56	.06	3.62	4.13	.07	4.20	3.35	.07	3.42
1.09	.07	1.16	1.62	.07	1.69	2.82	.16	2.98	2.75	.17	2.92
.87	.10	.97	1.87	.16	2.03	2.98	.33	3.31	2.38	.27	2.65
.62	.17	.79	1.82	.34	2.16	2.13	.25	2.38	1.89	.50	2.39
.80	.05	.85	2.15	.19	2.34	2.65	.30	2.95	2.59	.17	2.76
1.99	.00	1.99	2.46	.01	2.47	2.92	.00	2.92	2.98	.00	2.98
1.58	.00	1.58	1.64	.00	1.64	2.07	.00	2.07	2.35	.00	2.35
2.90	.05	2.95	1.47	.01	1.48	1.96	.00	1.96	1.90	.00	1.90
8.09	.00	8.09	7.50	.00	7.50	8.26	.00	8.26	8.17	.00	8.17

23.43[b/]

lation segment being studied engage in the activity during a day's period, this constitutes an activity pattern sufficiently widespread to warrant detailed study. By this criterion, for weekdays all 12 classes of activity except "participating in church and organizational activity" constitute distinct patterns in the Washington metropolitan community in the sense that at least a quarter of the population engage in them on weekdays. For Saturdays, all classes of activity but "participating in church and organizations" and "working at main job" constitute activity patterns; on Sundays only "working at main job" and "shopping" drop from the list of dominant activities.

If we examine the "mean hours" column of Table IV-2, the activities that dominate a day become quite evident. For example, if "main job" and "homemaking" are merged to eliminate the effect of sex role selection, we can see that 7.80, 4.65, and 3.30 mean hours of time on weekdays, Saturdays, and Sundays, respectively, are absorbed on a per capita basis in these prime "household maintenance functions." Except for sleep, which as a basic human physiological process remains fairly constant (showing the least variation of any activity around the mean), such prime maintenance functions take a major chunk out of the weekday, but as the week moves into Saturday and Sunday, the amount of time they preempt tapers off somewhat and discretionary forms of activity assume more importance. The residual category "miscellaneous activities" increases over the weekend (from a mean of 2.58 hours on weekdays to 3.14 on Saturdays and 2.95 on Sundays), the increase being attributable to "out-of-town" activities and other postponed or infrequent pursuits not covered elsewhere in the classification system.

Travel time associated with each activity is presented in Table IV-2 as a subtotal. Not surprisingly, on weekdays the largest amount of time spent in moving around in the community is work-related (one-half of all travel time); on Saturdays the largest proportion of travel time goes into shopping (one-third); and on Sundays the largest proportion can be ascribed to church attendance (about a quarter). The total amount of time devoted to travel, as might be expected, decreases on the weekend (with the column sum for weekdays showing a mean per capita time allocation of 1.14 hours; Saturdays, 0.97; and Sundays, 0.74).

Among the discretionary forms of activity (indicated by brackets in Table IV-2), "watching television" is clearly the most dominant one on all days of the week shown (a mean of 1.65 hours per subject in our sample for weekdays; 1.75 for Saturdays; and 1.99 for Sundays). Taken together, "watching television" and "rest and relaxation" account for a mean of 2.59 hours of passive activity on weekdays, 2.74 hours on Saturdays, and 3.57 hours on Sundays (or 44.2, 35.6, and 40.1 percent, respectively, of all discretionary time on these days). On weekdays, other forms of discretionary activity involve smaller amounts of time, with socializing and recreational activities being about equally important as secondary forms of "free-time" activity.

Table IV-2 indicates that weekend patterns popularly ascribed to American households are borne out. In addition to the heavier emphasis on television and "taking things easy around home" (rest and relaxation) on weekends, more time is allocated to socializing on Saturdays, and to family activities on Sundays, than is allocated to these pursuits on other days of the week.

Finally, it may be useful to examine two summarizing measures of time allocation, time spent on "out-of-home activities" and time devoted to "discretionary activities." The first is of interest primarily as a summarizing measure of the exposure people have to the "outside world," either moving around in the community (in transit) or engaging in activities away from home. The second is a summarizing measure of the amount of time devoted to "free time" kinds of activities.[6] By these measures time is allocated as follows:

	Weekdays		Saturdays		Sundays	
	Mean Hrs	% of 24 Hrs	Mean Hrs	% of 24 Hrs	Mean Hrs	% of 24 Hrs
All out-of-home activities	8.89	37.0	7.49	31.2	6.33	26.4
Discretionary activities	5.86	24.4	7.67	32.0	8.90	37.1

These figures indicate that the time devoted to out-of-home activities (including associated travel) falls off over the period of a week, going from weekdays to Saturday to Sunday.[7] This is not surprising since during the weekend the relative importance of work, usually the single largest use of out-of-home time, decreases, with "main job" (plus the travel associated with it) accounting for substantially less of the out-of-home activity (dropping from 56.9 percent on weekdays to 17.8 percent on Saturdays to 12.5 percent on Sundays). Discretionary activity shows a shift in the other direction. As would be expected, as a week progresses from the weekday to Saturday to Sunday, the proportion of time allocated to discretionary pursuits increases.

Comparisons with the National Scene. In examining time allocation patterns in Table IV-2 one begins to wonder how typical or atypical life in Washington is relative to life in urban America generally. Table IV-3 provides some insights in this respect for weekdays and, in addition, indicates how national patterns vary on selected dimensions. The first two columns in Table IV-3 are comparable to the per capita weekday data for Washington shown in Table IV-2.

Examining the extent of participation in discretionary forms of activity (those enclosed by brackets), it can be seen that Washington heads of households and spouses show higher rates for socializing, engaging in recreation and other diversions, and resting and relaxing than their counterparts in the national sample. In terms of the amount of time

Table IV-3 Mean Duration of Time Heads of Households and Spouses Spend on Various Classes of Activity on Weekdays, with Sample Grouped into Various Subsamples—National SMSA Survey, 1969.

Activity Category	Total Sample		Mean Hours Allocated to Activities for Various Subsamples[a]					
	% Engaging in Activity (n=902)	Mean Hours All[a]	Large SMSA[b] (n=139)	Medium SMSA[b] (n=295)	Small SMSA[b] (n=453)	Center City (n=307)	Inner Suburbs (n=292)	Fringe Areas[c] (n=164)
Main Job	40.6	3.55	3.70	3.61	3.03	4.28	4.19	4.57
Eating	94.5	1.51	1.50	1.47	1.60	1.67 *	1.86	1.84
Shopping	30.7	.44	.50 *	.35	.46	.36	.45	.38
Homemaking	85.5	4.08	4.16	4.00	3.90	3.51	3.71	3.36
Family Activities	33.0	.57	.57	.55	.61	.51	.59	.62
Socializing	29.2	.59	.59	.58	.58	.48	.58	.78
Participation (Ch. & Orgs.)	10.8	.26	.25	.26	.27	.07	.22	.17
Recreation, Other Diversions	30.9	.74	.70	.80	.71	.67	.59	.57
Watching TV	69.1	1.84	1.80	1.85	1.95	2.10	1.86	1.74
Rest & Relaxation	52.1	1.05	1.12	.99	.94	1.10	1.03	1.10
Miscellaneous	88.1	1.39	1.24 *	1.58	1.50	1.12	1.13	1.20

*Differences in durations to left and right significant $p \leq .05$ in difference of means test.

a/ All durations are on a per capita basis, i.e., mean time spent on an activity per person in the sample or subsample, as the case may be. In examining means across rows, it should be noted that the total n varies with each breakdown due to unreported data or excluded subjects (see Footnote c/).

b/ Large SMSA's are 1,000,000 and over at the time of the 1960 census; median SMSA's, 250,000–1,000,000; and small SMSA's, under 250,000.

c/ Includes outer incorporated suburbs, intensively developed unincorporated areas and scattered rural nonfarm. Subjects from small SMSA's excluded from this analysis.

allocated, however, only socializing takes up markedly more time in Washington than in the American scene generally, perhaps reflecting some of the capital city social pageantry noted earlier. Recreation and other diversions involve similar amounts of time in both samples. For the other activities, stating results the other way around, urban America appears to devote somewhat more time to family activities, participating in organizational activity, watching TV, and rest-relaxation than Washingtonians.

The remaining columns in Table IV-3 show variations within the national sample according to city size and the location of residence within the metropolitan area. When SMSA's are grouped by size (1,000,000 population and over in 1960; 250,000–1,000,000; and under 250,000), one can note only small gradations in mean times allocated to work, homemaking, watching TV, and rest-relaxation according to size, and very few with statistically significant differences. About all that can be said is that there are weak indications that during weekdays, the larger the metropolitan area, the more time spent at work (including commuting), the more time spent in homemaking, and the more time spent in rest and relaxation, but the less time spent watching TV.

When the sample is grouped by location of a subject's home in the metropolitan area, for our purposes there are no significant differences in time allocation. Here again, we can note only weak indications, especially in comparing center-city residential locations with fringe area locations, that the farther out from the center heads of households and spouses live, the more time allocated to prime household maintenance functions (work and homemaking) and to socializing, and the less time allocated to recreation and to watching television. Analyses in the next chapter suggest that variations in the discretionary activities may be in part attributable to factors other than spatial location, for example, income and education level.

The Temporal Patterns of Activity

With the foregoing overview on "what kinds of activity" our subjects engage in, we turn now to "when these activities take place," the temporal rhythm of activity during a weekday, Saturday, and Sunday in the metropolitan community. Figure IV-2 summarizes these temporal patterns. From the weekday chart it can be seen that the low point in the activity cycle occurs in the period from 2 to 5 a.m. For our population of heads of households and spouses, the proportions of people stirring, having breakfast, and subsequently at work, homemaking, and engaging in other

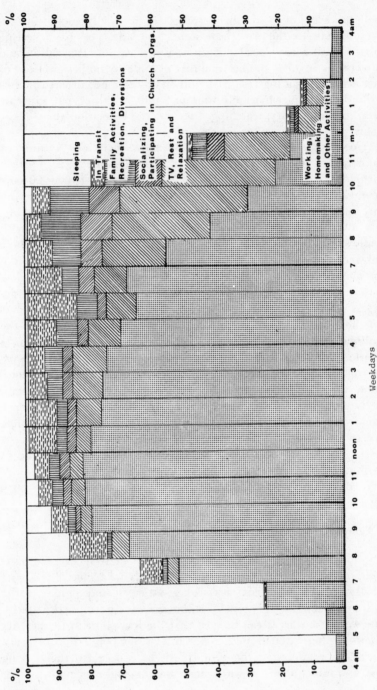

Figure IV-2 What heads of households and spouses are doing different hours of a 24-hour period on an average weekday, Saturday, and Sunday—Washington, spring 1968.

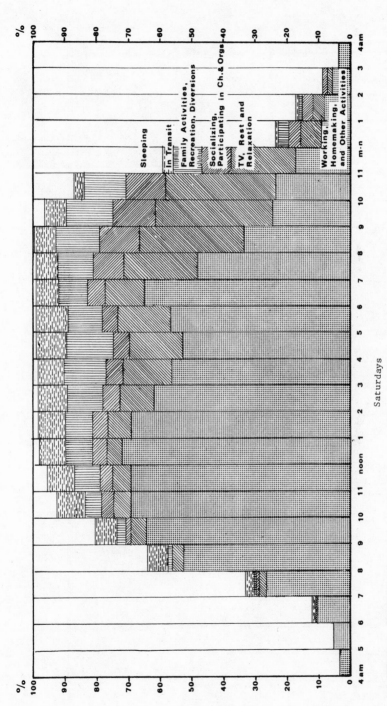

Figure IV-2 continued

105

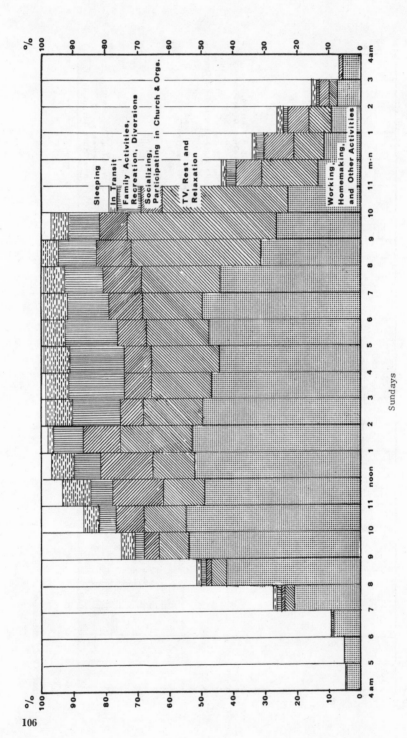

Figure IV-2 continued

household maintenance functions build up rapidly from 6 to 9 a.m. After 9 a.m. the proportion of the sample absorbed in these basic functions ascends more slowly to 11 a.m. and then gradually falls off until the dinner hour at 6 p.m.

People in motion begin with the journey to work starting about 7 a.m. and peaking in the morning at 8 a.m. As determined from detailed tabulations not shown here, shopping trips and other errands in mid-morning, lunch-hour travel at noon, and more shopping activity and errands in the afternoon account largely for the travel shown during late morning and early afternoon periods of the day. The proportion of the population in motion reaches an all-time peak at 5 p.m., when government offices are emptying. Some travel continues on into the evening, tapering off after 10 p.m.

The discretionary forms of activity are shown in Figure IV-2 by vertical and diagonal patterns of hatching. During weekdays, there is a steady but relatively small increase in these patterns of activity from 7 a.m. until the early evening. As would be expected, the more or less obligatory forms of activity involved in basic household maintenance functions give way to discretionary activities in the evening hours, finally dropping off in the period from 10 p.m. to about midnight. The white areas in the charts indicate the hours in which sleeping occurs.

Turning to the weekend day charts, as one glances from weekday to Saturday to Sunday, it can be seen that the base of the chart (consisting of work, homemaking, and other basic household maintenance activities) progressively flattens out, with discretionary activities increasing in importance. Saturday is an intermediate version between weekday highs and Sunday lows in time spent on these basic functions. On Sunday, except for church time, which peaks from 11 a.m. to 12 noon, and socializing around the 1 p.m. dinner hour, television and taking things easy around the house are the most prominent forms of discretionary activity. The proportion of a 24-hour period devoted to these passive forms of activity steadily increases from the dinner hour until evening, with these activities becoming the most dominant ones in the period from 8 to 11 p.m. On Sundays, however, family activities, recreation, and other forms of diversion are also prominent among discretionary activities.

Spatial Patterns of Activity

A third way of describing human activity in a metropolitan community has to do with its spatial patterns. Earlier the term "mean locus" was in-

troduced as a spatial measure of activity. Corresponding to "mean duration," which was used above for time allocation, mean locus provides a
summarizing measure of the extent of activity space. This measure is
constructed for each respondent by summing the "crow-flying" distances
from a person's home to every out-of-home activity location visited during a 24-hour period. The summation of these distances for each subject
is used as a crude indicator of the locus of his activity space. The mean
locus of an activity for the population as a whole or for a particular population segment is therefore defined as the mean sum of distances per
participant in that population or segment from the home to all out-of-
home places visited in a day's time—a weekday (as examined here) or a
Saturday or a Sunday.

The extent of activity space of persons in our Washington sample on
weekdays is summarized in Table IV-4, which gives the mean locus of
specific classes of activity as well as the mean locus of all out-of-home activities. A visual representation of crow-flying distances for four of these
activities on weekdays is given by the trace diagrams in Figure IV-3 for
the distance from home (identified by the dot at one end of the trace) to
main job, to shopping, to places of socializing, and to locations of recreation and other diversions.

The most clearly defined pattern in Table IV-4 is the extensive nature
of the "commutershed" involved in the journey from home to work as
compared to the mean sum of distances involved in other out-of-home
activities. The mean crow-flying distance between home and main job for
heads of households and spouses is 10.8 miles as compared to 7.8 miles
for eating and drinking out, and 6.0 miles for shopping, which are the
activities with the next largest mean sums of distances. In terms of travel
time, the main job absorbs 0.97 of an hour a day commuting for those
who work as compared to 0.57 of an hour a day for those shopping (see
right-hand panel of Table IV-2).[8]

The graphic displays for these two activities (the two upper diagrams
of Figure IV-3) not only bring out the marked dominance of "main job"
as an out-of-home activity (and also as a transportation phenomenon) as
compared to shopping, but they also bring out the contrasting spatial
patterns of these two classes of activity, the one in a concentrated pattern
around one dominant focal point and the other much more diffused and
multinucleated in pattern. Clearly these spatial patterns of activity are
shaped to an important degree by the land use and transportation configurations in the Washington area—what constitutes the "opportunity"
component of the model blocked out in Figure II-1. Despite the decentralization of government offices, which has been occurring slowly over

Table IV-4 Mean Locus of Various Out-of-Home Weekday Activities
on a per Participant Basis—Washington, 1968.

| Activity Class | Locus of Activity[a] | |
	Mean of Sums of Distances from Home to Activity (Miles)	n
Main Job	10.8	849
Eating and Drinking Out	7.8	636
Shopping	6.0	539
Socializing	2.4	668
Recreation	2.6	148
Other Out-of-Home	3.5	240
All Out-of-Home Activities	14.2	1,418

[a] The locus of activity is derived by computing first
for each respondent the sum of the distances as the crow
flies from the centroid of the grid cell in which the
home is located to each of the centroids of all cells in
which the indicated activity was carried on during the
weekday for which activities were recorded. The figure
shown is the mean of the sum of these activity distances
for all persons engaging in the indicated activity.

the past several decades (for example, the relocation of the Bureau of the
Census to Suitland to the east of the District and the establishment of
NASA in Gaithersburg to the northwest), the pattern of traces for the
main job in Figure IV-3 shows a high intensity convergence on the central complex of Federal office buildings. For the great majority of our
subjects, the main job is located in the area defined by the Capitol, the

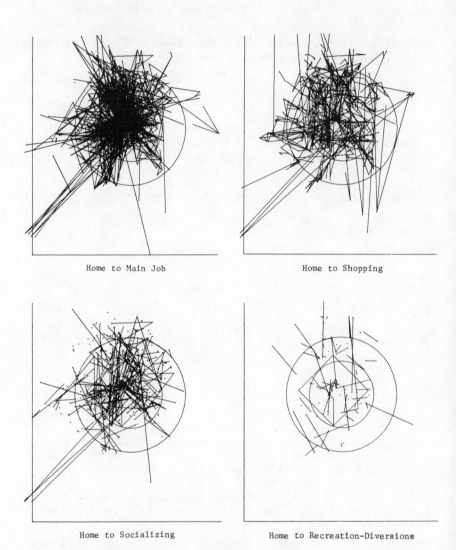

Home to Main Job

Home to Shopping

Home to Socializing

Home to Recreation-Diversions

Note: Dots signify home locations where activity is done at home; the radius of inner ring is seven miles from Washington Monument, and the outer ring, 12 miles.

Figure IV-3 Computer printouts of trace patterns from home to work, shopping, socializing, and recreation—Washington, 1968.

White House, the Pentagon, and the cluster of new buildings in south-west Washington fringing the south side of the great mall.

In contrast to this monolithic single-centered pattern, the shopping "traces" in Figure IV-3 bring out a multicentered pattern. Here again activity space is structured to an important degree by land use and transportation systems. The spatial patterns of activity are clearly a reflection of the decentralization of shopping functions to outlying shopping centers which have become so pronounced in the American scene in recent years, in conjunction with expressway building of the fifties and sixties. The crisscross patterns of shopping traces in Figure IV-3 indicate the characteristic suburban shopping configuration. If traces shown in the diagram were redrawn along routes actually traveled, many of the crisscrosses would follow Washington's beltway (located roughly where the inner circle is shown on the diagram).

Turning from obligatory to discretionary forms of activity, it can be seen from Table IV-4 that socializing and recreation outside the home involve lower-order mean distance values (2.4 and 2.6 miles, respectively). If "eating and drinking out," which involves a large number of instances where this activity is tied to the work trip (lunch-hour break or stop-offs after work), is ignored, these results suggest that for discretionary pursuits, activity space is more tightly drawn. People are less inclined to give up very much of their relatively limited free time getting to and from places where these activities take place. Although the lower left diagram in Figure IV-3 shows some long traces involved in socializing, these occur for the most part in conjunction with work trips, such as staying in town after work in order to socialize with friends. If these are eliminated the residual effect is that socializing involves short trips in random patterns, with an activity space somewhat less than the mean distance value indicated above. The larger number of dots in the socializing diagram of Figure IV-3 gives an indication of visiting and socializing in the home or in the immediate neighborhood.[9] Finally, with respect to recreation (the lower right-hand diagram in Figure IV-3), the relatively sparse pattern of traces indicates that less out-of-home emphasis is given to this activity during weekdays. Again the dots without traces indicate home- or neighborhood-centered recreation and other diversions. Had a larger sample been used, some evidence of multicentered activity somewhat similar in nature to shopping would undoubtedly have emerged in this diagram.

The information on activity space in Table IV-4 in conjunction with the spatial configurations in Figure IV-3 reflect the considerations that go into an individual's subjective notion of accessibility. When households move, the accessibility factor is commonly taken into account in the decision on the location of the new home place. Subconsciously the decision-making members of the household (the head of the household and the spouse) seek to minimize the time-distance in transportation as this consideration is traded off against others such as the cost of housing, the amount of space, its arrangement, the appointments of the new dwelling, and the attractiveness and character of the dwelling site and its neighborhood environment (see discussion in Chapter I). In many respects, the moving household is making subjective and imperfect assessments of information reflected in Table IV-4 and Figure IV-3.

Variations in Activity
by Role and Person Characteristics

We now consider several background variables about our subjects that affect activity patterns. The influence that such variables as work status, sex role, and stage in the life cycle have on the activities which a person is likely to engage in and the amount of time allocated are so pronounced and visible in everyday life as to be taken for granted. Certainly a person's breadwinning role in the household and whether or not he or she is working full time have very obvious effects on the makeup of a day's itinerary. Likewise, it takes no stretch of the imagination to conceive of the influence of sex role on a day's routine, especially in the seventies when the discriminatory aspects of culturally assigned roles have been under fire. Similarly, it seems fairly self-evident that whether a person is young and single or in the early young couple phase of family formation, in the child-rearing phase, in the middle years phase, or in the older retiree phase, the life cycle has something to do with the makeup of a person's activity routine. Although not taken up at this juncture, a person's health status obviously affects his activity choices. With respect to life cycle, since age is associated with stage in the life cycle, the two are merged in the analyses undertaken here.

Table IV-5 presents evidence concerning the influence each of these three factors has on the mean amount of time heads of households and spouses in the Washington SMSA sample allocate to the 12 categories of activity in a typical weekday. The influence of work status on activities during weekdays is quite pronounced; there are significant differences in the amount of time devoted to every class of activity between those working full time and those not working full time (see first panel of Table IV-5). In the case of sex (shown in the second panel), weekday variations are to be found more consistently in the obligatory than in the discretionary sector. For the two dominant obligatory activities, the patterns bring out the familiar emphases in role differentiation: the significantly greater amount of time devoted to "main job" by males than females would certainly seem to bring out the breadwinning role the culture assigns to men, and the significantly greater mean time devoted to homemaking by females provides evidence of the culture's assignment of this role to women.

With the male spending more time away from home and the female spending more time in the home, we might expect that the female would have more opportunity to become involved in family activities and socializing in the home and in the neighborhood. This appears to be the case (for weekdays); it can be seen in Table IV-5 that women spend significantly more time on family activities and socializing than men. For other discretionary activities such as recreation and related diversions, watching TV, and rest and relaxation—the kinds of activity which on weekdays customarily occur in the evening when man and wife are able to do things together—there are no significant differences in time allocation.

In the life cycle panel of Table IV-5, for weekdays clearly the most pronounced differences occur between the young single adult or young couple stage of the life cycle and the earliest child-rearing stages and between the "middle years" and the older "retirement years" stages. In total amount of time allocated to all forms of discretionary activity during weekdays (shown at the foot of the table), it appears, not surprisingly, that young single persons or young couples and senior citizens have significantly more relatively free time than those in the middle three stages in the life cycle. In the allocation of this discretionary time, both young couples and senior citizens devote significantly more time to socializing and to recreation and other diversions than do the three middle stages. Also, as might be expected, senior citizens allocate significantly more of their (larger amount of) free time to watching television and rest and relaxation than those in other stages of the life cycle.

In looking over Table IV-5 one is impressed by the consistent importance that work status has on the amount of time allocated in every class of activity, in this case all significant at the .01 level. To establish whether the differences in time allocation shown here might be an indirect reflection of the influence of the other two factors, we checked the effects on time allocation when work status, sex role, and child-rearing responsibility were cumulatively controlled, in that order. Because of the small numbers of subjects involved at the third control level, the life cycle factor was dichotomized into a child-responsibility factor (at least

Table IV-5   Mean Duration of Time Heads of Households
and Stage in Life Cycle—Washington, 1968.

Activity Category	Work Status Differences		Sex Role Differences	
	Working Full Time (n=982)	Not Working Full Time (n=685)	Male (n=736)	Female (n=911)
Main Job	8.02 *	0.82	7.35 *	3.26
Eating	1.60 *	1.76	1.74 *	1.61
Shopping	.39 *	0.81	.34 *	.73
Homemaking	1.23 *	4.89	.92 *	4.16
Family Activities	.43 *	.63	.41 *	.59
Socializing	.60 *	.92	.64 *	.80
Participation (Ch. & Orgs.)	.09 *	.20	.11	.16
Recreation, Other Diversions	.45 *	.68	.55	.55
Watching TV	1.30 *	2.14	1.57	1.71
Rest & Relaxation	.72 *	1.25	.93	.94
Miscellaneous	3.06 *	2.37	3.08 *	2.53
Sleeping	7.19 *	7.85	7.32 *	7.56
All Forms of Discretionary Activity	5.25 *	6.74	5.80	5.91

*Differences in durations to left and right significant p ≤ .05
in difference of means test.

one child under 13 years old living in the household, or no child under 13 living in the household).

Figure IV-4 shows the results of applying these controls to time allocated during weekdays to all forms of discretionary activity for the entire sample. The upper system of branches traces the effects of working full time on the amount of discretionary time available, with one subsidiary set of branches following these effects for women and another following them for men, and with both branches involving a final split according to child-care responsibilities. The lower system traces the same kinds of effects for those not working full time. As a general pattern, it can be and Spouses of Heads Spend on Weekday Activities, by Work Status, Sex,

Differences Among Various Stages in Life Cycle				
No children <19 present, Head < 35 (n=235)	Children < 19, Some < 13, Head Any Age (n=730)	Children < 19, None < 13, Head Any Age (n=138)	No children <19 present, Head 35-65 (n=404)	No children <19 present, Head 65 & over (n=160)
6.65 *	4.99	5.37	5.68 *	1.26
1.48 *	1.64	1.65	1.72	1.89
.45 *	.63	.51	.55	.49
1.02 *	3.41	2.87 *	2.18 *	3.42
.48	.65	.45	.35	.38
1.09 *	.68	.64	.56 *	.97
.13	.08	.27	.15	.27
.82 *	.41	.63	.51 *	.79
1.27	1.49	1.60	1.85 *	2.44
.71	.79	.85	.98 *	1.94
3.49 *	2.62	2.60	2.68 *	2.16
7.44	7.34	7.24	7.56 *	7.96
6.27 *	5.41	5.79	5.74 *	7.70

seen that for persons who are working full time (upper system of branches) the total amount of discretionary time is less than that for the persons of equivalent characteristics who are not working full time (lower system of branches).

By noting the significance levels in difference of means tests (designated by vertical broken lines in the diagram), it can be seen that work status continues to have a significant influence on time allocation even after sex role has been taken into account. Moreover, it continues to bring out significant differences in time allocation even after controlling for the effect of young children in the household. In this respect, however, it

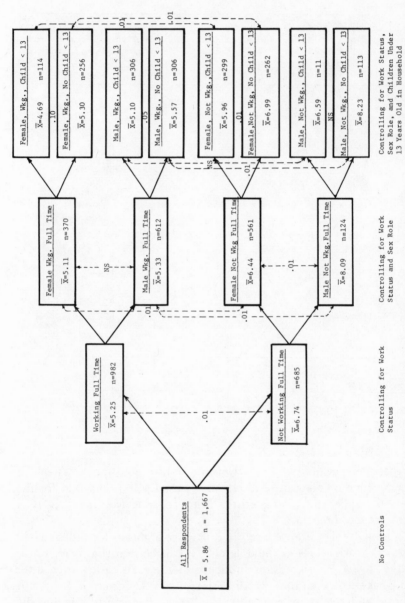

Figure IV-4 Effect on mean hours of weekday discretionary time by controlling cumulatively for work status, sex role, and children in the home under 13 years old—heads of households and spouses, Washington, 1968.

should be noted that the dwindling sample size in one category in the tier of boxes on the right-hand end of the diagram interferes with the significance level in one test.

In following the effects for sex alone and child responsibility alone in Figure IV-4, it can be seen that differences in time allocation between males and females show up with a higher level of significance for persons not working full time (following lower branch of the diagram). When results are examined at the third level of control (still following the lower branch), there are indications that child-care responsibilities have effects on the amount of discretionary time available at a somewhat higher significance level for those not working full time than for those working full time (upper branch). However, the small sample size noted above in one category prevents us from making an unqualified statement in this respect.

Although not reproduced here, tests similar to Figure IV-4 were made for individual classes of discretionary activity. The two classes of activity which consistently absorbed the largest amount of total discretionary time, watching television and rest-relaxation, follow the patterns shown in Figure IV-4 very closely. Though involving a somewhat lower proportion of total discretionary time, socializing similarly follows the Figure IV-4 patterns.

In the case of recreation and related diversions, the key importance of work status appears to be unchanged after controlling for sex, but when the presence or absence of young children in the household is taken into account, the situation is somewhat different. Here it would appear that regardless of whether a person is working full time or not, if there are young children in the household, subjects devote significantly less time to recreation and other diversions than those in households without young children.

In the case of family activities, although Table IV-5 indicates that work status significantly affects time spent on these activities, when sex and child-care responsibilities are successively controlled, work status loses significance in time allocation. This suggests that the significance level that work status brings out for this activity in Table IV-5 is more the result of differences in sex role and child-care responsibility that are implicit in the work status categorization.

In summary, then, work status appears to have an important influence on total time available for discretionary forms of activity, those working full time having significantly less time for these forms of activity than those not working full time, regardless of sex or child-care responsibilities. Among particular classes of discretionary activity, the same patterns persist for watching television, rest-relaxation, and socializing, with those working full time spending significantly less time on these activities than those not working full time, even after controlling for sex and child-care responsibilities. However, for recreation and related diversions, whether or not there are young children in the household seems to be a more crucial factor than work status affecting time allocation, and for family activities both sex role and child-care responsibilities appear to be a more important source of influence than work status.

SUMMARY

This overview chapter presents in quantified form a picture of how heads of households and spouses go about their everyday lives in the Washington scene. Results confirm a number of widely held subjective impressions about city life and in this connection bring out few surprises. For our purposes, the documentation on the extent of participation in various kinds of activities, the amount of time allocated, and the temporal and spatial patterns of these activities provide bench mark data for examining the activity patterns of selected subsocietal segments within the metropolitan community taken up in the next two chapters.

The following mean duration figures (in hours) indicate the broad swings in the use that our subjects make of their time in the course of an average week (with participation in these categories near the 100 percent level):

	Work and Homemaking	Activities for Residual Waking Hours		Sleep
		Other Obligatory	Discretionary	
Weekdays	7.80	2.88	5.86	7.46
Saturday	4.65	3.52	7.67	8.16
Sunday	3.30	3.71	8.90	8.09

The figures demonstrate the extent to which time preempted by prime household maintenance functions (i.e., work and homemaking) slacks off as the week progresses into the weekend, but they indicate that the released time does not go entirely into discretionary forms of activity. The figures show that some of it is absorbed in "other obligatory" activities (which include shopping and household errands on Saturdays and a host of miscellaneous postponed activities on Sundays), and some of it is spent catching up on sleep. Nevertheless, as might be expected, there is a notable increase in discretionary time during weekends.

Our Washington subjects taken as a whole divide up their total amount of discretionary time recorded above somewhat differently from one part of a week to another. For summarizing purposes, we collapse discretionary activities into three categories:

	Passive Forms of Activity		Activities Emphasizing Social Interaction		Other Diversions, Including Recreation	
	Mean Hrs	% of Discr.	Mean Hrs	% of Discr.	Mean Hrs	% of Discr.
Weekdays	2.59	44	1.40	24	1.87	32
Saturday	2.74	36	2.33	30	2.60	34
Sunday	3.57	40	2.92	23	2.41	27

Although *passive forms of activity* (watching television and resting and relaxing) are the dominant kinds of free-time activity on both weekdays and weekend days, there is a notable increase on Saturdays and Sundays in time devoted to *social interaction* (family activities, socializing, and participation in organizational activity) and an increased emphasis on *diversions* (recreation, hobbies, cultural pursuits, and others).

When subjects are grouped according to work status, sex, and child-care responsibilities, a number of variations in time allocation emerge. During weekdays, not only do those working full time spend significantly less time on all forms of discretionary activity than those not working full time, but also they spend a smaller proportion of their free time on passive and social interaction forms of activity than those not working full time. Working people appear to spend a larger proportion of their free time during weekdays on reading (mainly the newspaper and magazines), hobbies, and a variety of other diversions. On weekends, especially on Saturdays, however, those working full time spend a larger proportion of their discretionary time on social interaction, recreation, and other diversions than those who do not work full time. Although work status is the dominant source of variation, grouping subjects by sex brought out differences in time allocated to family activities and socializing, and grouping by child-care responsibilities brought out differences in out-of-home recreation activities.

NOTES

1.   Under our definitions of heads of households and spouses and under our rules of respondent selection, if we had no female heads of household and a 100 percent response rate, we would expect a 50-50 split. However, the higher representation of females in our sample (and the census) is not surprising since we do have some female heads of households (see Table III-1). But we expect a slightly higher representation of females in our sample than reflected in the census. This is because some attrition in male respondents can be anticipated simply because working heads, who are preponderantly male, are sometimes difficult to find at home, even on repeated callbacks. If by a third callback they are not interviewed, in our study they become a technical "refusal."

    This percentage figure (56.1 female) is based on the full 1756 households in our sample; it differs slightly from the percentages given in Table IV-1 where figures are based on respondents with completed activity returns.

2.   This percentage figure (22.3 black) is based on the full sample of 1756 households and differs slightly from Table IV-1 results, where figures are based on respondents with completed activity returns.

3.   In this connection, it was partly due to this underrepresentation that the inner-city submetropolitan community study (Area A in Figure IV–1) was undertaken to explore more fully the activity patterns of this important subsocietal segment in the metropolitan community. The work in Chapter VI uses results from this inner-city community for comparisons between low-income white and black segments of the population.

4.   By the rule followed in selecting the weekend day, we would expect that variation is due mainly to such personality factors as the patience levels of respondents and their willingness to take time to reconstruct a second day's set of activities.

5.   Since participation rates at the more detailed level of analysis are somewhat less than those involved in the more aggregated classification system, given the size of our sample there were distinct limitations in using the results of this particular study to make analyses at the 40-class level of aggregation.

6.   As brought out in Chapter III, few activities can be categorically assigned to the discretionary or the obligatory classification, since under some circumstances an activity can be one type, and under other circumstances the exact opposite. The characterization of an activity so as to take account of these kinds of situational factors has not been possible in our studies. Although we group activities in one or the other of these two classes (as defined in Table A–2), no particular significance should be read into what we call "total discretionary activity." It is simply an aggregation of activities that are commonly regarded as things people do when they are off work and are finished for the day with homemaking, shopping, eating, and other similar things they must do in order to subsist. (It should be noted that in the 12-class activity classification scheme, one class of activity called "miscellaneous" does not collapse into either the discretionary or the obligatory category, but includes activities in each category. This means that the figures used in the 12-class grouping of discretionary activity will not be identical with results shown in Tables A-3, A-4, and A-5 or other reports on the Washington study, for example, in Hammer and Chapin, 1972.)

7. Among the different weekdays, out-of-home activities on Thursdays (showing a low) and Fridays (showing a high) differ markedly from other days of the week:

Mean Durations in Hours

	n	Out-of-Home	Discretionary
Monday	292	8.48	5.54
Tuesday	290	8.17	5.92
Wednesday	252	8.80 *	5.87
Thursday	317	7.85 *	5.78
Friday	516	10.64	6.06
	1667		

*Differences in durations above and below asterisk significant $p = .01$.

However, the amount of discretionary time does not differ to any significant extent.

8. From the standpoint of transportation, since a considerable number of our respondents do their "eating and drinking out" at lunch time or before they go home at the end of the workday, their mean travel time for these purposes cannot be meaningfully compared with the mean distance recorded (which is the mean distance between the homes of those reporting this activity and the establishments they patronized).

9. Since locations are coded to grid cells 1000 by 1000 feet, some dots may represent socializing two or three blocks away. To the extent that the location of the activity and the home in relation to the grid system put some out-of-home socializing in the same grid cell, our measure of activity space may underestimate the mean sum of distances. This underestimation applies for corner-store shopping and for outdoor recreation in the near vicinity of the home. In the case of the main job, however, which tends to be more separated from the home environment, results are less likely to be affected.

REFERENCES

Hammer, Philip G., Jr., and F. Stuart Chapin, Jr. (1972). *Human Time Allocation: A Case Study of Washington, D.C.*, Technical Monograph (Chapel Hill: Center for Urban and Regional Studies, University of North Carolina).

Szalai, Alexander, ed. (1972). *The Use of Time* (The Hague: Mouton).

CHAPTER FIVE

VARIATIONS IN ACTIVITY
PATTERNS AMONG DIFFERENT
POPULATION SEGMENTS

In focusing on variations in activity patterns among different population segments in the metropolitan community, this chapter serves as a preparatory stage in the exploratory test of the activity model outlined in Chapter II. It examines the dependent variable of the model—the activities of people, especially the things they do in their relatively free time—for variations that emerge when people are grouped according to ethnic background and, within these ethnic categories, according to status measures.

This chapter is more descriptive than explanatory. It deals primarily with the systemic assumptions that go with the application of the model, although it also gives attention to role and personal characteristics which serve as one group of independent variables in the model. In effect, it tests the assumptions that activity patterns, particularly discretionary forms of activity, do differ with such environmental contingencies as the cultural milieu and the social structural context in which people live. Given these systemic influences, it then investigates the extent to which certain social roles and personal characteristics affect discretionary activity patterns.[1]

As brought out earlier, knowledge about variations in activity patterns among segments of the population of different socioeconomic composition provides important insights for planning and policy analyses relative to supplying public facilities and services. Although the level of detail used in activity classification in the analyses here and the descriptive emphasis involved in these analyses do not provide a sufficient basis for evaluating facilities and services in the detail envisioned in the four-stage R & D effort outlined earlier, it nevertheless provides a means for describing daily life in the metropolitan community and anticipating some of the stresses that investment decisions in land use, transportation, and community facilities are likely to produce in the social fabric of the community. To this extent, this description of activity patterns of different population segments enables those concerned with planning and policy to develop some sensitivity to the social implications of investment decisions.

The chapter consists of two parts. In the first, attention is devoted to exploring ethnic and status differences in discretionary activity patterns; the latter part examines the way in which role and person characteristics affect activity patterns.

VARIATIONS IN ACTIVITY BY RACE AND STATUS LEVEL

In setting up the cultural and social structural contingencies for analysis of activity patterns in the exploratory vein of the work undertaken here, the choices of subpopulation segments are fairly self-evident. The more complicated choices come later when more detailed bases for establishing contingencies are attempted. Certainly in the very large metropolitan areas, a case can be made to examine the black and nonblack segments of the population as an ethnic split since each possesses a very clear sense of group identity, and certainly since the sixties the black segment has become a more cohesive element in urban society as well. Moreover, since such status measures as income, occupation level, and education have been used widely in previous empirical work concerned with social stratification in metropolitan areas, it would seem appropriate to make use of these same kinds of measures in initial investigations of the influence of social structure on activity patterns.

From a planning and policy viewpoint, both bases of forming population segments are particularly appropriate in Washington. As brought out in the last chapter, this is a metropolitan area with a marked concentration of black population in the central city (71.1 percent of the District of Columbia population in 1970). Since this is the city from which the nation's policies and programs on employment, education, housing, and other opportunities for minority groups originate, there is a marked sense of black identity here and a high expectation that the elimination of prejudice and discrimination will be vigorously pursued. It is a community which is thus highly politicized along black-nonblack lines, but also within these groups it is a community in which status lines are prominent. Thus, though our sample is too small to disaggregate into other ethnic categories, certainly the racial split is highly appropriate here.[2] For planning and policy analyses, measures that group people by income, occupation, and education level have a similar pragmatic utility.

As in the previous chapter, activity patterns are examined in three perspectives. In the first, the extent of participation and the amount of time spent on each of the 12 classes of activity are examined. The other two perspectives are concerned with temporal and spatial patterns of activity.

Patterns of Activity Choice

Table V-1 presents data on weekday activity choices for the Washington metropolitan area sample disaggregated into black and nonblack segments. If the 25 percent minimum participation criterion used in the last chapter is introduced here as the threshold for the inclusion of an activity in the analysis of durations, by scanning the first two columns it can be seen that among the discretionary activities (identified by the brackets), only watching television and rest-relaxation meet this criterion. In order not to eliminate too many activities from consideration by this somewhat arbitrary cutoff point, particularly those that reflect something of the propensity for social interaction within each segment, analyses in this chapter include all activities for which at least one of the ethnic segments and one of the income groups reaches a 25 percent participation level.[3] This means that here, as in the last chapter, only participation in church and voluntary organizations is dropped from the analysis for having a relatively low frequency.

The remaining discretionary activities fall roughly into two groups: those with a generally high order of participation (watching TV and rest-relaxation), and those in which there is a distinctly lower order of participation (family activities, socializing, and recreation-diversions). It is of interest to note here that the first group is essentially passive in character and customarily home-oriented, whereas the second group involves activities which are not only more active in both a physical and a social sense, but may have a community orientation. In this last aspect, these activities directly involve the social fabric of the community, and some involve the availability of services and facilities and the opportunities open to sub-

Table V-1 Participation Rates and Mean Durations of Weekday Activities of Heads of Black and Nonblack Households and Spouses— Washington, 1968.

Activity Category	% Engaging in Activity		Mean Hrs. Devoted to Activity		
	Black (n=358)	Nonblack (n=1,309)	Black (n=358)		Nonblack (n=1,309)
Main Job	58.7	53.7	5.32		4.99
Eating	92.8	97.7	1.38	*	1.74
Shopping	19.3	40.3	.31	*	.63
Homemaking	70.9	77.9	2.63		2.76
Family Activities	12.9	35.3	.20	*	.60
Socializing	22.4	40.3	.48	*	.80
Participation (Ch. & Orgs.)	5.3	6.8	.11		.14
Recreation, Other Diversions	13.4	33.7	.36	*	.60
Watching TV	69.5	66.2	2.42	*	1.43
Rest & Relaxation	41.1	61.9	.98		.93
Miscellaneous	89.9	97.3	2.57		2.83
All Forms of Discretionary Activity	99.1	99.5	5.78		5.89

*Differences in duration to left and right significant $p \leq .05$ in difference of means test.

jects for making use of them—all of which affect the living qualities of the metropolitan area.

Variations in Participation by Race. We compare first the extent to which black and nonblack subjects engage in various classes of discretionary activity: the first two columns of Table V-1 show that in four out of five classes (omitting church and organizational activities) black subjects report substantially lower participation rates. Three of these four are in the second group of activities, in which the community environment is intimately involved. It is possible that the apparent lower frequency with which black subjects engage in these three activities (family activities, socializing, and recreation-diversions) as compared with nonblacks is a reflection of a genuine difference of preference in life style. But a more likely hypothesis in this respect is that a difference in economic opportunity serves as an intervening variable affecting the extent of participation, at least in some of these activities. Also, as discussed in greater detail in the next chapter, it could be that the differences in some activities are the result of underreporting by black subjects. On the basis of participant observation reports in the submetropolitan community studies, among black subjects in disadvantaged circumstances this is a real possibility in visiting forms of activity (socializing). In any event, on the basis of the data presented in the first two columns of Table V-1, because of economic necessity, underreporting, or free choice, black subjects appear to be less likely than nonblacks to engage in four out of five of the discretionary activities shown. Only in the case of watching television do black subjects have a higher participation rate.

Variations in Time Allocation by Race.   If we turn to the last two columns of Table V-1, it can be seen that, although there is no significant difference between racial groups in the total amount of time spent on all forms of discretionary activity, there are significant differences in the allocation of this total time to specific classes of activity. These differences show up in the same four out of five activities. In the case of watching television, not only are black subjects more likely to participate, but they also spend significantly more time watching television than nonblacks (41.8 percent of all their weekday free time as compared with 23.9 percent). Nonblacks appear to spend more time on the other four discretionary activities. For three of these—family activities, socializing, and recreation-diversions—nonblack subjects are shown to be spending *significantly* more time on these than blacks.

But these findings bear some closer examination. One suspects that the same two factors noted above may be affecting how much time is devoted to the more active forms of discretionary activity by black subjects, namely, economic opportunity and possibly underreporting. With respect to economic opportunity, one suspects that it involves such antecedent influences as prejudice and discrimination, though it is beyond the scope of this work to assess these sources of influence. It is, of course, not possible to establish how much underreporting there is in our data.

Variations in Time Allocation by Status Level.   Two tables are used to summarize how time is allocated when the black (Table V-2) and the nonblack (Table V-3) segments of the population are stratified for the three status measures, income, occupation, and education level. Before

Table V-2 Mean Duration of Weekday Activities of Heads of *Black Households* and Spouses by Income, Occupational Status, and Educational Status—Washington, 1968.

Activity Category	Income Per Household Member[a]		Occupation of Household Head[b]		Education Level of Subject		
	Low Income (n=249)	Above Low Income (n=109)	Unskilled or Semi-Skilled (n=219)	Skilled, Craftsmen, Clerical Occupations (n=113)	Less Than H.S. (n=217)	H.S.Grad.; Some College (n=109)	College Graduate; Some Grad. Work (n=32)
Main Job	4.51 *	7.17	4.77 *	6.81	4.65 *	6.48	5.90
Eating	1.40	1.34	1.40	1.29	1.41	1.26	1.53
Shopping	.31	.33	.37	.26	.28	.34	.43
Homemaking	2.98 *	1.85	2.85 *	1.98	2.95 *	2.16	2.14
Family Activities	.21	.17	.20	.13	.18	.20	.30
Socializing	.43	.59	.43	.51	.42	.56	.61
Participation (Ch. & Orgs.)	.13	.07	.12	.12	.11	.14	.02
Recreation, Other Diversions	.34	.37	.34	.31	.36	.35	.35
Watching TV	2.72 *	1.73	2.77 *	1.72	2.79 *	1.96	1.43
Rest & Relaxation	1.08 *	.76	.96	.94	1.11 *	.81	.69
Miscellaneous	2.28 *	3.25	2.18 *	3.46	1.99 *	3.21	4.36
All Forms of Discretionary Activity	5.92	5.45	5.86	5.47	5.90	5.68	5.28

*Differences in duration to left and right significant p ≤ .05 in difference of means test.

a/ For the formation of these income categories, see Figure III-3.

b/ Based on the Duncan socio-economic index (Appendix B-1 in Reiss, 1961). Developed on a 100-point scale, the first column is formed from households where the index score for the head's occupation is 1-35, and the second column is formed from those where the index score is 36-85. There were too few cases (n=7) to include the 86-100 category which covers top managerial and professional job classifications.

Table V-3 Mean Duration of Weekday Activities of Heads of *Nonblack Households* and Spouses by Income, Occupational Status, and Educational Status—Washington, 1968.

Activity Category	Income Per Household Member [a]			Occupation of Household Head [b]			Education Level of Respondent		
	Low Income (n=343)	Middle Income (n=759)	High Income (n=207)	Unskilled or Semi-Skilled (n=331)	Skilled, Craftsmen, Clerical Occupations (n=741)	Top Managerial, Professional (n=224)	Less Than H.S. (n=220)	H.S. Grad.; Some College (n=614)	College Graduate; Some Grad. Work (n=473)
Main Job	3.57 *	5.48 *	5.56	4.39 *	5.35	4.84	3.33 *	4.70 *	6.15
Eating	1.58 *	1.78 *	1.86	1.72	1.71	1.85	1.82	1.71	1.74
Shopping	.51 *	.64 *	.76	.63	.61	.70	.43 *	.77 *	.53
Homemaking	3.36 *	2.60 *	2.36	3.14 *	2.63	2.67	3.60 *	2.99 *	2.07
Family Activities	.73	.56	.50	.62	.58	.61	.59	.64	.55
Socializing	.95 *	.72	.86	.80	.78	.90	.72	.77	.88
Participation (Ch. & Orgs.)	.09	.17	.14	.09	.17	.12	.08	.12	.19
Recreation, Other Diversions	.58	.58	.69	.57	.60	.65	.57	.59	.63
Watching TV	1.86 *	1.35 *	1.03	1.78 *	1.34	1.26	2.28 *	1.44 *	1.03
Rest & Relaxation	.99	.88	1.00	.83	.96	.93	1.08	.87	.94
Miscellaneous	2.81	2.81	2.94	2.77	2.76	3.06	2.36 *	2.81	3.08
All Forms of Discretionary Activity	6.34 *	4.66 *	5.96	6.03	5.77	6.08	6.31 *	5.78 *	5.83

*Differences in duration to left and right significant p ≤ .05 in difference of means test.

a/ For the formation of these income categories, see Figure III-3.

b/ Based on the Duncan socio-economic index (Appendix Table B-1 in Reiss, 1961). Developed on a 100-point scale, the first column is formed from households where the index score for the head's occupation is 1-35; the second, 36-85; and the third, 86-100.

commenting on data shown in these tables, two general observations can be made about results. The first has to do with the consistency of differences in time spent on various discretionary activities by black and nonblack subjects (comparing the differences found in Table V-1 with those noted in Tables V-2 and V-3), and the second has to do with the consistency of results across status groups (comparing results horizontally for blacks in Table V-2 and nonblacks in Table V-3).

On the first point, by scanning all three tables it can be seen that, with one exception, the differences in the amount of time allocated to the various classes of discretionary activity by black and nonblack subjects, which were found in Columns 3 and 4 in Table V-1, carry over at the same general order of magnitude and direction to the figures for durations shown in Tables V-2 and V-3. This would seem to indicate that status factors do not alter appreciably the ethnic patterns brought out in Table V-1. The one exception is the rest and relaxation category. Table V-1 indicates that black subjects spend more time resting and relaxing than nonblacks (although not significantly more); Tables V-2 and V-3 show that this holds for low-status subjects, but the pattern of time allocation reverses for above-low-status persons. Blacks in above-low-status levels by these measures devote less time to rest and relaxation than nonblacks at corresponding status levels.[4]

On the second point, although stratification on each variable is obviously on a crude basis, it can be seen that for both blacks and nonblacks there are two obligatory activities and one discretionary activity which behave similarly for all three status variables. In the obligatory sector for all three, black and nonblack subjects alike, there are significant differences in time allocated to the main job and homemaking, particularly between the low- and middle-status levels. However, in the discretionary sector only viewing television shows this consistency across status categories—low-income subjects, those in low-index kinds of occupations, and those with a relatively low level of education devoting significantly more time to watching television than those in the next higher status group. Where three status levels are involved, the middle group, in turn, spends more time watching TV than the high group.[5] But since the amount of time black subjects devote to television as compared with nonblacks remains relatively higher in all status categories, this would seem to indicate that time spent on television is associated with both race and status level. Though no other discretionary activity behaves in the same consistent way from one status measure to the next, it must be borne in mind that had the frequencies of other activities been large enough to warrant treating them as separate activities, it may well be that a number of them (as discrete as "watching television") would also assume significance on both ethnic and status dimensions.

If we scan the bottom row in each of the two tables, it appears that there are no signficant variations in total amount of time black subjects devote to discretionary activity for the status measures used, but status level does make a difference in two out of the three measures for nonblack subjects. Thus for nonblacks, both income level and education level make a significant difference in how much time is available for discretionary activities, but only in comparisons between the lower and middle levels.[6] On both stratifying variables, low-status subjects have more time for discretionary activities than middle-status subjects.

Variations in Time Spent on Specific Classes of Activity. Turning to a discussion of the influence of status variables on individual classes of discretionary activity, we shall comment here only on income variations, not only because patterns of emphasis are quite similar for all three variables but also because in a sense income reflects the economic consequences of the other two. The first set of columns in Tables V-2 and V-3 demonstrates that not only does one activity, *watching television,* carry over the significant differences between black and nonblack subjects consistently in all strata as noted above, but that there are significant differences between all income groups. In this respect, results indicate that as income rises, the amount of time allocated to TV by both ethnic categories falls off. None of the other discretionary activities reflects at statistically significant levels the same regularity of pattern both with respect to race and income.

The tables indicate that, in the amount of discretionary time involved, *rest and relaxation* is second only to watching television, not only for both racial groups but also for all income groups within each racial category. Tables V-2 and V-3 indicate that low-income subjects from both black and nonblack households spend more time resting and relaxing than do middle-income subjects, although the differences are significant only for black subjects. Whether it was an unconscious interviewer bias or a respondent way of shortening the interview, "taking things easy around the house" or "relaxing" crept into activity listings of black subjects with a sufficient frequency that in retrospect this category appears to have been used to fill in times not otherwise accounted for in a person's itinerary. If this is the case, it is likely that many odds and ends of visiting from the front porch, over the telephone, or over the back fence were therefore blanketed into this class of activity rather than being reported as "visiting" (socializing).

Although dropping to a distinctly lower order in magnitude of time allocation, it can be seen that the third largest category of discretionary time is *socializing*.[7] If we take ethnic groups separately, we note first of all that among nonblacks, low-income subjects spend significantly more time on socializing than middle-income subjects. Indeed, for that matter, though not statistically significant, nonblack subjects from high-income circumstances also spend more time socializing than those in the middle-income category. There are plausible economic explanations for these results. It is not unreasonable to expect that low-income subjects, whose satisfactions from socializing are found at an informal visiting level of interaction, spend more time on this activity because they are underemployed, unemployed, or retired. On the other hand, it also seems reasonable to expect that high-income subjects, whose satisfactions are found in entertaining and social interchange in more formal ways, spend more time on socializing for business reasons and perhaps spend more time on socializing because of a deeper commitment to social mobility (getting ahead).

Curiously, the amount of time spent socializing by low-income black subjects as compared with above-low-income black subjects (for all purposes, the middle-income category) is the reverse of that of nonblack subjects. The results show that low-income black subjects spend less, rather than more time socializing, although the differences are not statistically significant. This seems surprising, since participant observation in the low-income black community (see Chapter VI) indicates a high level of social interaction. Indeed, on the basis of these clues from field observations and the above comments on rest and relaxation activities, it may be assumed that in the warmer periods of the year socializing is frequently a concurrent activity, not only with such discretionary forms of activity as rest-relaxation and recreation-diversions, but also with such obligatory forms of activity as shopping, homemaking, and even work. It might therefore be posited that, with full reporting on fragments of social interaction that occur in conjunction with other activities, the differences in socializing for black subjects between low- and middle-income groups would be eliminated (or possibly reversed). Further, results might even show that blacks in the lower-income category (if not the middle category as well) spend more time in social interaction than their nonblack counterparts. This is not to suggest that the form of socializing of blacks and nonblacks would be the same, or the content of social communications would be similar, but only that the amount of time devoted to socializing by blacks might be greater than reported here.[8]

When *family activities*[9] are examined by income level, the differences between low- and middle-income subjects, although in the same direction for both ethnic groups, are more marked for nonblack subjects. The more time that nonblack low-income subjects devote to family activities as compared to those from middle-income circumstances might plausibly be explained by the relatively higher unemployment or underemployment rates of those in the low-income categories. One might posit that because their weekdays may have substantial blocks of time free from work commitments, many low-income subjects spend more time on family activities.

Comparing the magnitudes of time allocated to family activities between low- and middle-income subjects of the black segments, however, one notes that for black subjects the amount of time thus spent does not vary appreciably between income groups. This is contrary to our expectations. If we can assume that underreporting is minor in the case of family activities, then for reasons of emphasis on upward mobility of their children, we would expect to find above-low-income blacks spending more time on family activities than the low-income subjects. The fact that both income groups spend about the same amount of time on family activities might plausibly be attributed to older children in the middle-income black family, assuming child-rearing responsibilities or relatives or friends functioning as substitutes in child rearing. According to participant observation, this occurs when economic pressures are such that both spouses feel compelled to work. The notable differences here, however, are between blacks and nonblacks; if underreporting is not a factor, the differences here may well reflect differences in the severity of deprivation between black and nonblack households in these two income strata. Greater deprivation in opportunities to earn income would mean that in black households heads and spouses experience greater inroads on time devoted to family activities than their nonblack counterparts.[10]

In the case of *recreation and other diversions*,[11] the notable fact here is that, although there is marked spread between black and nonblack subjects in the amount of time devoted to this activity, within both ethnic groups, there is little or no variation between income levels. This would seem to indicate that income per se is not a factor in how much time goes into recreation activity. The marked racial difference is probably either a case of black subjects having fewer opportunities of engaging in recreation-diversons because of the necessity of working longer hours than nonblacks to earn equivalent levels of income, or a case of their having different preference patterns (a difference attributable to genuinely different subcultural values).

In summary, by the measures used activity patterns appear to be affected by both cultural and social structural influences. In this respect, ethnic sources of variation, both for participation levels and the amount

of time spent on various discretionary activities, appear to be more pronounced than social structural sources, However, because the ethnic split
is on a black-nonblack basis, there is a strong possibility that economic
deprivation from prejudice and discrimination rather than genuine
choice is the underlying basis for the subcultural patterns of variation in
several activities, notably for family activities, socializing, and recreation-
diversions. This, however, is postulated from results presented here and
not a conclusion drawn from the analyses. The discretionary activity most
responsive to both ethnic and social structural sources of variation for all
measures used was "watching television."

Variations in Temporal and Spatial Patterns

In the preceding section, where the emphasis was on the amount of time
allocated to discretionary activities during the 24-hour period of a typical
weekday, we gave some attention to the proportions of black and nonblack and low- and middle-income segments engaging in these activities.
In this section, we first examine variations in these proportions by the
hour of the day for selected discretionary activities, comparing the temporal patterns in participation rates of racial and income groups for different periods of the day. We then examine variations in spatial patterns
of these discretionary activities for racial and income groups.[12] The
analysis concentrates on family activities, socializing, and recreation and
other diversions. These activities, as brought out above, have to do with
the social fabric of life in the community.

Participation Rates by Hour of the Day.   The import of temporal patterns can be illustrated readily in such activities as travel and meals (see
Tables A-7 and A-8). Low-income subjects in Washington reach a peak
in their weekday morning travel (mostly trips departing from home) in
the period between 8 and 9 a.m., and they reach an all-day peak of travel
in the afternoon (mostly trips returning home) between 5 and 6 p.m. By
comparison, middle-income subjects reach their morning peak between 7
and 8 a.m., and their afternoon peak between 4 and 5 p.m. One might
expect that mealtimes would reflect corresponding differences in scheduling, but this does not occur. For example, the proportion of low-income
subjects at supper reaches a peak at 6 p.m., immediately after the travel
peak, but for middle-income subjects, the supper hour peaks at the more
"sedate" hour of 7 p.m., two to three hours after the afternoon travel
peak. There are no marked differences in black and nonblack segments,

with travel for both segments peaking in the morning between 8 and 9 a.m., and in the afternoon between 5 and 6 p.m. Evening meals for both racial groups concentrate in the period between 6 and 7 p.m.

These homely examples illustrate the patterning of daily routines that this basis for summarizing the data brings out; they also indicate how the fixed times of obligatory activities structure the timing of discretionary activities in the period of a day. This can be seen readily in Figure V-1 where the temporal patterns of family activities, socializing, and recreation-diversions show their peaks in residual times of the day in the evening when time devoted to prime household maintenance functions (work and homemaking), associated travel, and meals no longer preempt time.

Focusing first on *family activities,* the upper diagram of Figure V-1 indicates that the markedly higher proportion of nonblack than black subjects involved in family affairs shown in Table V-1 applies at all hours of the day in which activities are recorded. The diagram also indicates that family activities for both races build up slowly during daylight periods of the day to a plateau in the evening hours, dropping off rapidly after 11 p.m. Although no similar diagrams are shown comparing income groups, the data indicate some variation in participation rates between low- and middle-income groups at different hours in the course of a day (see Table A-8). The proportion of low-income subjects engaging in family activities builds up gradually to a maximum at the supper hour and then falls off steadily into the evening. In comparison, the maximum proportion of the middle-income group occurs in mid-evening before falling off.

If the likelihood of underreporting of social exchange episodes by black subjects is disregarded, our data show that a larger proportion of nonblack subjects engage in *socializing* not only during the 24-hour period of a typical weekday but also for nearly all times of the day. This is reflected in the middle diagram of Figure V-1, which also indicates that although differences are less marked in daytime hours, they are quite pronounced in the evening hours. Even if underreporting of this activity has occurred among black subjects, it seems plausible to assume that underreporting will be fairly uniform over the hours of a day. If this is indeed the case, it can be concluded from Figure V-1 that social interchange among blacks begins in mid-morning and continues through the day and into the evening, with a near-constant proportion of black subjects involved at any hour. Comparing weekday participation rates by income categories we find that there are higher rates of participation by low-income subjects from mid-morning until the evening meal time, but in the evening,

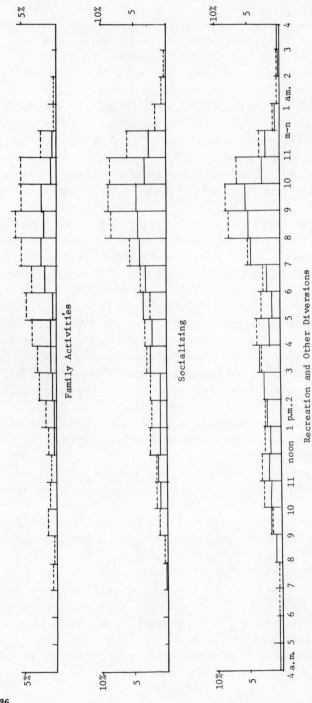

Family Activities

Socializing

Recreation and Other Diversions

Note: Solid lines designate proportion of black subjects engaging in the indicated activity; broken lines, the proportion of nonblack subjects.

Figure V-1 Proportions of black and nonblack sample engaged in selected discretionary activities at different hours of a weekday—Washington, Spring 1968.

middle-income subjects devote more time to socializing than low-income subjects (see Table A-8).

In the case of *recreation and other diversions,* not only does a larger proportion of nonblack than black subjects engage in these activities on weekdays in general (see Table V-1), but the lower diagram of Figure V-1 indicates that also for almost any hour of the day nonblack subjects are more likely to be participating in these activities than black subjects. The proportion of nonblacks engaging in recreation-diversions at different times of the day is nearly constant in daylight hours, rising moderately after evening meal times, falling off about 10 p.m., and tapering rapidly after 11 p.m. Levels of participation of black subjects during daylight hours are very similar to those of nonblacks, but during the evening their participation rates are a more restrained version of those by nonblacks. Turning to income differences, we have already seen that low-income subjects are less likely to engage in recreation-diversions than middle-income subjects. When participation is examined on an hourly basis (see Table A-8), we see that low-income subjects are more involved in recreation and other diversions during daytime hours (probably because a substantial proportion of them are underemployed, unemployed, or retired and are filling time on these activities), but in the off-work and off-housework hours of the evening, the middle-income people are more involved in this class of activity (these subjects more likely being employed during daylight hours and by this time of the day ready for recreation and diversions).

Spatial Patterns of Discretionary Activities.   As brought out in Chapter IV, the sum of "crow-flying" distances between the locations of out-of-home activity places and the home location provides a measure of the extent of activity space of a person. We refer to the mean of these sums of distances as the "mean locus" of activity space for a population. Table V-4 compares the mean locus of activity space of the black with the nonblack and the low-income with the above-low-income segments of the population.[13] As can be seen from the bottom row, nonblack and above-low-income subjects have a somewhat more extensive activity space than their counterparts, but not significantly more extensive. It can also be seen that when individual classes of activity are examined, the first three (main job, eating and drinking out, and shopping) involve a much more extensive activity space than socializing, recreation-diversions, and other out-of-home activities.

We examine the mean locus data first for black-nonblack differences. As would be expected, the journey to work for nonblacks (whose homes are concentrated in the suburban ring) involves a significantly greater

Table V-4 Mean Locus of Various Out-of-Home Weekday Activities on a per Participant Basis by Race and Income—Washington, 1968.

Activity Class	Racial Group				Income Group			
	Mean of Sums of Distances from Home to Activity (Miles)		n		Mean of Sums of Distances from Home to Activity (Miles)		n	
	Blacks	Nonblacks	Blacks	Nonblacks	Low	Above Low	Low	Above Low
Main Job	9.00	* 11.24	186	663	9.66	11.29	311	525
Eating and Drinking Out	6.48	8.08	115	521	7.39	8.03	216	409
Shopping	6.01	6.03	110	429	7.04	5.50	180	353
Socializing	3.05	2.26	130	538	2.71	2.20	220	441
Recreation-Diversions	2.32	2.64	27	121	3.02	2.45	43	107
Other Out-of-Home	3.01	3.61	38	202	3.16	3.77	71	161
All Out-of-Home Activities	12.11	14.82	303	1,115	13.96	14.26	490	911

*Differences in durations to left and right significant p $\leq$ .05 in difference of means test.

Note: The locus of activity is derived by computing first for each respondent the sum of the distances as the crow flies from the centroid of the grid cell in which the home is located to each of the centroids of all cells in which the indicated activity was carried on during the weekday for which activities were recorded. The figure shown is the mean of the sum of these activity distances for all persons engaging in the indicated activity.

distance than that of black subjects (even considering domestic employ-ment of black women in suburban white homes). Because of the concen-tration of eating and drinking establishments in the central area of Wash-ington and their heavier patronage at lunch, after work, or in the evening by whites, it is not surprising to see a marked difference in mean distances between homes and restaurants or bars patronized for nonblack as com-pared to black respondents. However, the somewhat greater distances that black subjects seem to travel for socializing, though not significantly greater than distances traveled by nonblacks, nevertheless is contrary to expectations: it would seem that residents of the white suburban ring would need to travel farther in order to visit with friends in other parts of the ring. The differences in mean locus of shopping places, centers for recreation-diversions, and locations of other out-of-home activities are roughly comparable for the two segments of the population.

Since a large proportion of the low-income segment of the population is black, the patterns of the differences by income are somewhat similar to those noted above. As might be expected, since both blacks and non-blacks are represented in these segments, low-income subjects have a somewhat more extensive activity space than black subjects. Also as might be expected, the greater extent of activity space of low-income sub-jects as compared to black subjects (last row of the table) reflects the greater distances nonblacks have to travel from their homes in the suburbs for the first three categories as compared with blacks who are concentrated in the central city. In comparisons of the mean locus of specific activities between low-income and black subjects, it can be seen that for the former the locus is somewhat more extensive for all activities except socializing. This one instance of a lower magnitude of activity space may well be the result of a higher representation of retirees from the low-income nonblack segment than in the low-income black segment, retirees being less likely to travel any great distance for socializing than other age groups.

Figures V-2 and V-3 present the trace patterns of socializing and recrea-tion-diversions. Apart from differences in relative busyness of pairs of diagrams (black vs. nonblack and low-income vs. above-low-income seg-ments), which is a reflection in part of differences in subsample sizes and in part of a lower participation rate of black and low-income subjects, these diagrams do not bring out any striking differences. However, a check of the extent to which subjects go beyond the immediate vicinity of their homes for these activities (i.e., the extent to which traces exceed dots in the diagrams) indicates some differences between racial and be-tween income groups.

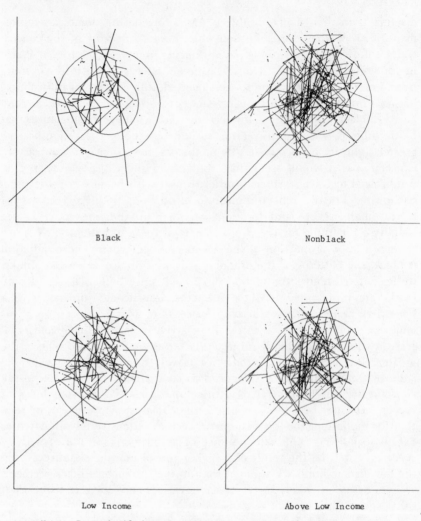

Black

Nonblack

Low Income

Above Low Income

Note: Dots signify home locations where activity is done at home; the radius of inner ring is seven miles from the Washington Monument, and the outer ring 12 miles.

Figure V-2 **Computer printouts of trace patterns from home to locations of** *socializing* **by race and by income level—Washington, 1968.**

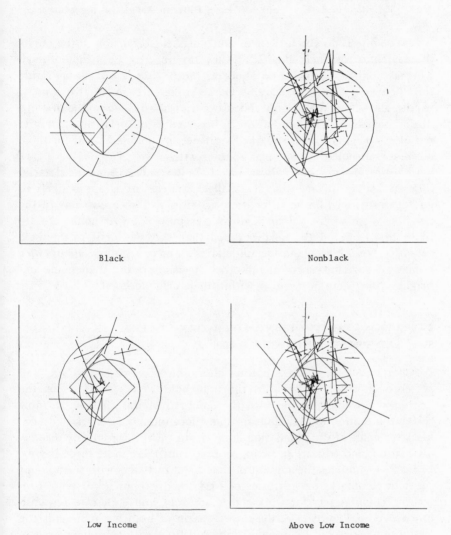

Black   Nonblack

Low Income   Above Low Income

Note: Dots signify home locations where activity is done at home; the radius of inner ring is seven miles from the Washington Monument, and the outer ring 12 miles.

Figure V-3 Computer printouts of trace patterns from home to locations of *recreation-diversions* by race and by income level—Washington, 1968.

Black subjects do about twice as much of their *socializing* in the immediate vicinity of their homes as they do outside the neighborhood, whereas nonblack subjects do about as much visiting outside as inside their home environs. There are no marked differences in socializing activities in and out of the neighborhood between low-income and above-low-income segments. The proportion of occurrences of socializing activities out of the neighborhood is markedly greater for nonblacks and for those above low income than for their counterparts.

In *recreation and other diversions,* there are more pronounced racial differences than income differences. Black subjects are about as likely to go out of the neighborhood for these activities as they are to stay in the neighborhood, whereas a markedly larger proportion of nonblacks are likely to go beyond the neighborhood than stay within it to do these activities. For both low-income and above-low-income groups, about twice as many engage in recreation and other diversions out of their home and neighborhood than at home or within their neighborhood.

VARIATIONS CONTROLLING FOR WORK STATUS, SEX, AND PRESENCE OF CHILDREN

In Chapter IV the effects on time allocation of work status, sex, and presence of young children in the household were examined for the sample as a whole. In line with the emphasis of this chapter, we now turn our attention to variations in time allocation among black and nonblack segments of the population and, within each, variations by income, occupation, and education, taking into account these same three factors. Figure V-4 compares the amount of time spent by blacks with the amount spent by nonblacks on all forms of weekday discretionary activity, controlling cumulatively for work status, sex role, and child-care responsibilities. As in Figure IV-4, the upper system of branches represents the amount of time spent by those working full time, with subsidiary branchings showing the time spent first by sex categories and then by whether or not there are young children present in the household. The lower system of branches shows similar time allocation information for those not working full time, controlling for the same categories.

Variations in Total Discretionary Time According to Race and Status

Subject to qualifications brought out earlier about the representativeness of these subsamples, Figure V-4 indicates that not only are there no sig-

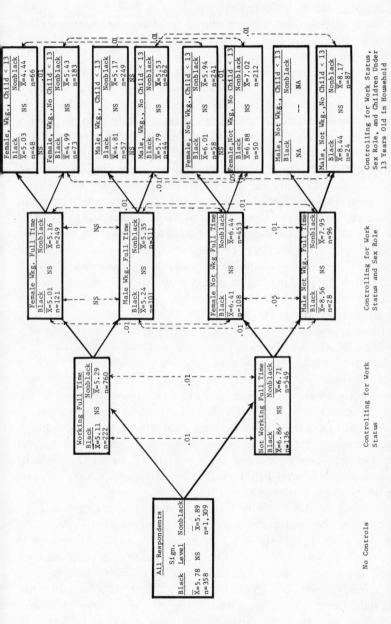

Figure V-4 Effect on mean hours of weekday discretionary time by controlling cumulatively for work status, sex role, and children in the home under 13 years old—black and nonblack heads of households and spouses, Washington, 1968.

nificant differences between blacks and nonblacks in the total amount of time spent on all forms of discretionary activity (as brought out in Table V-1), but it also brings out that no significant differences between races emerge even after controlling successively for work status, sex role, and child-care responsibilities.

However, for each branching in the diagram, the upper box, with one exception, consistently reflects the allocation of less time to all forms of discretionary activity than its paired-off lower box, indicating that working full time, being a female, and having young children in the household each put constraints on the amount of discretionary time available relative to the time shown for counterpart persons. The one exception is the lack of difference between black working females who have at least one child less than 13 years old in the household and those who do not have a child in the home under 13 (see pair of boxes in upper right-hand corner). These results may reflect a pattern noted earlier where in order to make ends meet both spouses in the household are working in support of the family, and older children, or members of the extended family or relatives are given the responsibility for looking after younger children. In this situation the working spouse with young children may extend this responsibility into the off-work period of the day, freeing her time for additional discretionary activities.

Since there appear to be no significant differences between blacks as a group and nonblacks as a group in the total amount of discretionary time at their disposal, it is not surprising to find that the significance levels of differences in time allocation along the vertical broken lines in the diagram based on work status, sex role, and child-care responsibilities follow fairly closely those in Figure IV-4 for the population as a whole. Thus for both ethnic groups, when these three controls are successively applied, work status has a pronounced influence throughout. Sex differences and differences in child-care responsibilities bring out significant variations in the amount of time allocated to discretionary activity primarily for those who are not working full time (lower branch).[14]

Having found no difference in results for blacks as a group as compared with those of nonblacks as a group, one wonders whether there are variations in weekday discretionary time when each racial segment is broken down into subsegments for the various stratifying variables used above—for income, occupation, and education level—and then controlling for work status, sex role, and child-care responsibilities as before. In other words, if these three role and background variables are controlled within these substrata, are the effects any different from those to be noted in Figure V-4?

In checking for income differences, we shall summarize without reproducing the charts and tables. We compare the total amount of weekday
discretionary time between low-income and above-low-income black subjects and between low-income and middle-income nonblack subjects,
these being essentially comparable income groupings for the two racial
categories. On the basis of initial analyses above in Tables V-2 and V-3,
income was found to be an important stratifying variable for the nonblack population but not for the black community. We now wish to see
what effect controlling for work status, sex, and child-care responsibilities
has.

The introduction of these controls when each racial group is stratified
on the basis of income produces some aberrations but no major changes
in income effects. Considering black subjects first, as we control success-
sively for work status, sex, and child-care responsibilities, for the most
part income stratification still does not bring out significant differences
in the total amount of time spent on all forms of discretionary activity.
In this respect there is one exception. It turns out that women from
above-low-income circumstances, not working full time, and without
young children under 13 years of age in the household, now are shown
to spend significantly more time on discretionary activities than their
low-income counterparts. Of the three control variables, work status
appears to be dominant and follows much the same pattern reflected in
Figure V-4, although for some categories the diminishing sample sizes
interfere with significance tests as controls are successively applied. Sex
differences are more pronounced among the low-income subjects not
working full time.

In the case of nonblack subjects, where a significant difference between
the amount of time spent on discretionary activity by those of low-income
and those of middle-income circumstances was found (see Table V-3),
these controls modify the influence of income in some respects. When
work status is controlled, results follow much the same pattern as shown
in Figure V-4 for both subjects working full time and subjects not working full time, but differences between income groups dissipate, indicating
that work status may be the underlying source of variation rather than
income. However, when sex role is taken into account, a significant difference between the two income groups reappears for those not working
full time, although at a weaker significance level. Even so, work status
continues to function in much the same dominant way as reflected in the
vertical broken lines in Figure V-4, after controlling for sex role. When
the third level of controls is introduced, work status continues to show a
strong basis of differentiation. At the same time, however, weak differ-

ences between income groups in time available for discretionary activities continue to appear in several boxes. Thus income affects the amount of discretionary time among nonblack women not working full time who have young children, with those from low-income circumstances spending significantly more time on discretionary activities than those from the middle-income group (a reverse emphasis in time allocation from that noted above for black women with young children and not working full time).

Shifting from income to occupation, the patterns of differentiation are somewhat different and in the black segment more pronounced. In Tables V-2 and 3 (bottom rows), it was brought out that for both black and nonblack subjects, there were no significant differences in the amount of time spent on all forms of discretionary activity on weekdays between those from households in which the head is in the lowest occupational group and those in which he is in the next higher occupation group (the lowest being a relatively unskilled occupation and the next higher being a skilled or clerical occupational category). When work status, sex role, and child-care responsibilities are taken into account, some differences between occupational groups show up for black respondents but none for nonblacks, the latter following closely the pattern in Figure V-4.

In the case of black subjects, where the occupation level of the head of the household does appear to affect the amount of time spent on discretionary activity on weekdays, these differences occur only after controlling for sex and child-care responsibilities. Results indicate that women from households where the head is in a lower occupational group, who have young children, and who are working full time spend less time on discretionary pursuits than their counterparts from households where the head's job is of a higher status. If these women are not working full time, however, then they spend more time on discretionary activities than their counterparts from households of the higher-status occupation group. Although the dwindling sample sizes in some categories undermine tests of significance, men from the lower occupational category appear to spend more time on discretionary activities than those from the higher occupational category, regardless of their work status. In this connection, results show that for households of the lower occupational category, men in both work status categories (those working full time and those not working full time) have significantly more discretionary time at their disposal than women in these categories, but in households of the higher occupational group, there are no significant sex differences.

When the subject's educational level is taken into account for each of the black and nonblack samples, time spent on all forms of discretionary activity on weekdays takes on somewhat different patterns for each racial group. As noted in Tables V-2 and V-3, education appears to make no difference in the total amount of time devoted to discretionary activities among black subjects but does appear to make a difference among non-blacks, at least in comparisons between the lower and middle levels. However, when work status, sex, and child-care factors are taken into account, in the black sample, among subjects not working full time, education level has a significant and different influence on the amount of time spent on discretionary activities according to sex. Women not working full time who did not complete a high school education, especially those with young children, have significantly less discretionary time than their women counterparts with a high school education or better; on the other hand, of men not working full time, those who did not complete a high school education spend significantly more time on discretionary pursuits than those who did complete high school or went on to a higher level of education (samples being too small at the third control level to determine effects of child-care responsibilities for men). In the nonblack sample, there are also sex differences, but instead of less time, women not working full time who did not complete a high school education, especially those with young children, spend more time on discretionary pursuits, whereas men of corresponding characteristics show reverse tendencies. It would thus appear that education brings out some significant black-nonblack differences in time allocation of an opposite order when work status and sex are successively controlled.

Up to this point, then, comparing blacks with nonblacks as aggregates, it has been established that there are no significant differences in the total amount of time spent on discretionary forms of activity. This holds even when controlling for work status, sex role, and child-care responsibilities. In investigating status variables within racial groups, we found earlier that significant differences develop between the lower- and middle-status levels of household income and respondent education level for nonblack subjects. For example, nonblacks from low-income circumstances and from the lower education level tend to spend more time on discretionary pursuits than their higher income and higher education counterparts. But in both racial groups, when work status, sex role, and child-care responsibilities are successively controlled, the patterns of difference in the total amount of discretionary time between income and education levels are modified somewhat, with different effects for blacks and nonblacks. With respect to occupation, which previously brought out no significant differences in total amount of discretionary time in either racial segment, the picture changes somewhat. After taking into account work status, sex, and child-care responsibility, occupation level assumes some importance among black subjects (though none among nonblack subjects), but these effects are weak.

Variations in Allocation of Discretionary Time According to Race and Income Level

Having considered the total time devoted to discretionary activities, we now turn to black-nonblack differences in the way this time is allocated to specific classes of activity. Because the complexity increases when discretionary time is disaggregated into component classes, these analyses are restricted to activities where significant black-nonblack differences were found in Table V-1 (notably for family activities, socializing, recreation and other diversions, and watching television) and to an analysis of status within racial groups using income as an indicator (notably comparisons between low- and middle-income levels). These analyses will seek to establish whether there are any differences in time allocation to these activities when work status, sex role, and child-care responsibilities are controlled.

Family Activities. As compared with results from the analysis of all forms of discretionary activity diagrammed in Figure V-4, time allocation to family activities brings out very distinctive black-nonblack differences, with black subjects reporting significantly less time devoted to family activities than nonblacks as each of the three control variables is successively applied. In short, the pronounced difference between blacks and nonblacks in time devoted to family activities noted in Table V-1 persists within work status, sex, and child-care categories. Within the black group, however, the time allocated to family activities is not significantly different between those working full time and those not working full time. In contrast, for nonblacks there is a significant difference according to work status.

If our reporting of activities has been equally effective with both blacks and nonblacks, it might be argued that these differences are attributable to disparities in income-earning opportunities, for instance, blacks of low-income circumstances being forced to take away more time from family activities than nonblacks in order to work on a second job or look for work. As suggested earlier, however, it may be that among blacks the assignment of child-care responsibilities to older children or the development of extended family systems of child care and child rearing do in fact result in less parental time allocated to family activities.

Unfortunately the dwindling sample of black subjects in the course of controlling for income and the three role and background factors does not permit us to deal conclusively with this problem in this study. However, among blacks working full time, men from low-income circumstances appear to spend significantly less time on family activities than men from above-low-income circumstances; this holds for men with young children in the family but not for those without young children (where income level makes no difference).

In the case of nonblacks, income seems to have a weak effect on men *not* working full time; here men from low-income circumstances spend less time on family activities than those from the middle-income category. If this segment has a marked representation in it of senior citizens who are retired and living on very low pensions, it would seem that the less time devoted to family activities is more related to stage in the life cycle than to income per se. Unfortunately, our sample sizes again interfere with drawing firm conclusions. We examine the question again with larger samples but in a somewhat more limited context in Chapter VI using the low-income subjects from the two submetropolitan studies. Within the limitations of the data in hand, at this point we note tentatively that there are indications of life style differences in time devoted to family activities, blacks reporting less time devoted to family activities than nonblacks, even when income is controlled.

Socializing Activities. When black-nonblack differences noted in Table V-1 for this activity are examined further, controlling successively for work status, sex role, and child-care responsibilities, it turns out that these differences are not affected appreciably when work status is controlled, but there are some new effects when sex role and child care are controlled. For men, regardless of work status, there appear to be no significant differences in the amount of time allocated to socializing between blacks and nonblacks even after controlling for presence of young children in the home, but for women significant black-nonblack differences do persist, with black women spending less time on socializing than nonblack women.

Within the black segment of the sample, as in the case of family activities, work status appears to have a relatively minor effect on time devoted to socializing, but within the nonblack segment, it appears to have a significant effect. When sex role is taken into account, although the work status difference for nonblacks persists, within both the black and the nonblack segments men and women do not differ appreciably in the amount of time devoted to socializing. This lack of sex difference holds even after controlling for child-care responsibilities. Again, if we disregard the possibilities of underreporting of socializing activities for our black sample, we are forced to conclude that there are life style differences in time allocated to socializing activities, blacks consistently reporting less time allocated to these pursuits than nonblacks. But if social interaction forms of activity are underreported by black subjects, then this conclusion would very likely be modified, either to finding blacks spending significantly more time in social exchange activities or to finding no difference.

When income is taken into account within each of the black and nonblack segments of the population, a few noteworthy differences in time allocated to socializing develop after controlling for work status and sex. Considering first the black segment, men working full time in the low-income category spend significantly less time socializing than those in above-low-income circumstances. Although within the low-income category, working men and women do not differ appreciably in time spent on socializing, there are significant sex differences within the above-low-income category, working women spending significantly less time socializing than working men. Since child-care responsibilities are not found to be a factor, it would appear that among those working full time, as income increases, sex role becomes more pronounced as a factor affecting time spent on socializing. Sample sizes are too small to check out these effects for persons who are not working full time.

Turning to the nonblack category, it appears that in this segment of the population, in contrast to the pattern noted above, it is among those not working full time where income exerts an influence on the amount of time spent socializing. Here it was found that low-income women not employed full time spend significantly more time socializing than women of similar employment status in middle-income circumstances. Within income categories, however, once work status has been controlled, sex role and child-care responsibilities do not appear to have a significant effect on time allocated to socializing.

Recreation and Other Diversions.   Table V-1 brought out that blacks spend significantly less time on these kinds of activities than nonblacks. When work status, sex role, and child-care responsibilities are introduced as controls, the importance of whether or not a person has a full-time job seems to be the key factor affecting these results. For those employed full time, blacks spend significantly less time on recreation and other diversions than nonblacks, regardless of sex or child-care responsibilities, but for those not working full time, with one exception, there are no significant differences between blacks and nonblacks in time devoted to these activities. In the last respect, the one exception is a weak difference between blacks and nonblacks for males with no child-care responsibility; here black subjects in this category spend somewhat less time on recreation than nonblack subjects in the same category.

Within the black and nonblack segments, whether or not a person is employed full time is the dominant factor affecting time devoted to recreational activities. Within the nonblack segment sex and child-care responsibilities seem to have some secondary importance, with men spending more time on these activities than women, especially men with no children under 13 years of age. Although similar tendencies are noted within the black segment, the differences are not significant. When income is introduced as a factor within each racial category, the patterns remain unchanged. In summary, the results show that differences between blacks and nonblacks in the extent of time devoted to recreation are tied to employment. Although our data will not permit us to explore such a notion satisfactorily, it may be that manual labor jobs of employed blacks leave them with less energy at the end of the day to engage in recreation than nonblacks in the same general economic level, who because of discrimination tend to have the somewhat higher-status jobs that involve less manual labor.

Watching Television. For this activity, differences between black and nonblack subjects brought out in Table V-1 are not appreciably affected by applying the three controls; black subjects consistently spend more time watching television than nonblacks at each level of control. At the same time, within both black and nonblack segments, work status is a key factor in how much time is spent at this activity, with those not working full time spending more time at it than those working full time. Only in the nonblack segment of the population are there pronounced sex differences, females spending significantly less time watching television than males.

SUMMARY

This chapter establishes that in the Washington metropolitan community there are differences in activity patterns along both ethnic and status lines. Although the grouping of subjects into black and nonblack segments brings out no significant differences between races in the total amount of time devoted to discretionary activities, or for that matter, to obligatory activities, it does bring out significant differences in the allocation of time within both the discretionary and obligatory sectors.

When each of the two racial segments are stratified on the three status variables (income, occupation, and education), significant differences between status levels in the total amount of discretionary time (and obligatory time) emerge in the nonblack but not in the black segment. Moreover, in the allocation of total discretionary and obligatory time, status variables appear to exert more influence in the obligatory than in the discretionary sector. In both racial segments there are significant differences along status lines in the obligatory sector in time devoted to prime household maintenance functions (main job and homemaking), but in the discretionary sector, only in viewing television. It is possible that the aggregation of specific activities into general classes obscures some differences, but our sample sizes limit opportunities to examine specific activities. The one exception is viewing television.

In the case of these three activities, the import of status may be more economic than social. Thus it is likely that time devoted to the main job, homemaking, and watching television bears a relationship more to economic differences in status than to differences in status ascribed to social processes. In any case, in the discretionary sector we find that in the case of television, status functions in the classical manner: for both racial groups, the higher the status, the smaller the proportion of subjects turning on their TV set in the first place, and the less time on the average spent viewing television. In this respect, there are relatively higher participation rates and durations found among black subjects. In an economic sense, this may be a result of having more limited alternatives for the use of free time, or it might be a reflection of genuine preference. We cannot tell from our data.

Once the population has been grouped successively on an ethnic and then a status basis, this chapter goes on to control for role and background characteristics of subjects (work status, sex, and child-care responsibilities) to determine how activity patterns are affected. In stratifying by income in each ethnic segment and controlling for role and background factors, there are differences in activity patterns between income groups similar for the most part to those shown in Tables V-2 and V-3. As reflected in Figure V-4, work status continues to bring out significant differences in amount and kind of activity in both racial groups. However, in the nonblack segment, differences between income groups in the total amount of discretionary time dissipate when work status is controlled, suggesting that work status is the primary influence; but when sex and child-care responsibilities are taken into account, significant differences between income groups reappear, suggesting that income is an intervening variable in the way sex and young children in the household affect activity patterns. In the black segment of the population, where discriminatory practices might plausibly have had a leveling effect, income stratification for the most part, even with the introduction of controls for work status, sex, and child-care responsibilities, does not bring out significant differences in total amount of discretionary time.

On the other hand, when we stratify on occupational status and apply these three control variables, in the black segment significant differences in the total amount of discretionary time emerge that did not show up before controls were applied. Occupational differences become important, however, only after controlling for sex and child-care responsibilities. Occupation level continues to have relatively minor influences on activity patterns of the nonblack segment of the population. When we stratify on education and apply the three controls, the significant differences that educational achievement brought out for nonblack subjects persist, and for black subjects education brings out some significant differences in activity patterns not previously in evidence.

From these analyses, we come to the general conclusion that once a population is subaggregated along ethnic and status lines, the influence that role and personal characteristics have on activity choices as examined in Chapter IV becomes much more focused. As in Chapter IV, work status usually has a primary effect on the total amount of discretionary time and how it is allocated, with sex and child-care responsibilities having additional but secondary effects.

NOTES

1. It can be argued that this analysis more properly belongs in the next chapter, where the joint influence of preconditioning *and* predisposing factors on activity patterns is examined. However, in the next chapter data from two submetropolitan surveys are used, since information on both sets of variables was not available from the areawide survey for such a joint analysis. Nevertheless because there is opportunity to examine one of the two groups of independent variables (the group containing the preconditioning factors) in the metropolitan area data sets, we do include in this chapter an analysis of these factors for the insights they add to our activity investigation.

2. In other SMSA's, splits that recognize Puerto Rican, Spanish-American, and even American Indian segments as well as European and Asian concentrations with ethnic identity may be similarly important.

3.   The participation rates of the black and nonblack segments and the comparable income groups in each racial segment are as follows:

			Black		Nonblack	
	All Black	All Non-Black	Low Income	Above-Low Income	Low Income	Middle Income
Family activities	13%	35%	13%	13%	35%	36%
Socializing	22	40	18	32	42	38
Recreation and other diversions	13	34	12	16	29	34
Watching TV	69	66	73	60	69	67

From this table, it can be seen that the only activity that unqualifiedly constitutes an activity pattern across all segments by our 25 percent criterion is still "watching television."

4.   It seems plausible to hypothesize here that the switches are a reflection of the relatively greater struggle that black subjects must make in order to hold or improve on their above-low status positions in society, not only spending less time resting and relaxing, but, it will be noted, allocating less time to all forms of discretionary activity than nonblacks.

5.   The tables indicate that not all these differences are statistically significant. However, significance levels here are probably curtailed by small sample sizes.

6.   With respect to the income measure, this is in contrast to "no difference" when black and nonblack are merged. Elsewhere in some analyses of our national samples we have taken some pains to show that how much total discretionary time heads of households and spouses have is not significantly affected by income, but how this total amount of discretionary time is allocated is significantly affected by income (Brail and Chapin, 1973). Though this same observation applies for the Washington data when black and nonblack subjects are treated as a total, the generalization does not hold for the nonblack subsample when comparing the low-income with the middle-income categories.

7.   This activity class includes visiting in or outside the neighborhood (primarily face-to-face and telephone forms of social interchange, but also correspondence with friends); it includes evening occasions (with drinks and/or meals) or simply drop-in visits in the subject's home or in a friend's home; and it includes informal get-togethers at clubs, restaurants, or taverns as well as formal receptions and the like.

8.   On the basis of these observations on underreporting of social interchange episodes and the possibilities that some social interaction may be included in time reported as rest and relaxation, it might seem plausible to combine socializing with rest and relaxation, treating them as a composite category. However, in such a combination not only would we miss social interchange concurrent with other activities, but we would be mixing quite different motivational and attitudinal factors and thus might seriously complicate our problem in the explanatory phase of the analysis.

9.   As a class, this category includes time spent in communication, with relatives as well as with members of the immediate family, time devoted to participating in the children's activities, and time devoted to activities planned primarily as a family occasion such as outings and drives. Subsistence-related activities, baby-sitting, and similar child-care-activities are not included, these being defined as part of homemaking. When activities

have a joint function such as a father and son expedition to a ball game, this is classed as a concurrent activity, and the time is split between "family activities" and "recreation and and other diversions."

10. Although child care (as distinct from child rearing) in our classification system is grouped with homemaking, nevertheless when older children, members of the extended family, or relatives outside the immediate family assume child-care responsibilities, it seems reasonable to expect subjects might come to depend on these sources for child rearing as well (which is classified under family activities), with the time that might otherwise go into family activities being absorbed in catching up on housekeeping, shopping, and even rest (especially if the subject is holding down two jobs).

11. This activity includes indoor and outdoor recreation whether as a spectator or a participant in sports, games, and other diversions; it includes engaging in hobbies and crafts, reading, going to musical events, museums, and attending evening classes (not related to vocation); and it includes walking, cycling, driving around town for pleasure, and going on out-of-town holidays.

12. It should be noted that for analyses of temporal and spatial patterns the sample is first split into racial categories and then pooled again before it is split into income categories. This is in contrast to other analyses in this chapter where income groups are examined as subsamples of each of the two racial categories.

13. As in Chapter IV spatial data are analyzed on a per-participant basis.

14. As in Figure IV-4, the same problem of sample size in one category in the lower right-hand set of boxes affects significance levels here.

REFERENCES

Brail, Richard K. and F. Stuart Chapin, Jr. (1973). "Activity Patterns of Urban Residents," *Environment and Behavior*, **5**:2.

Reiss, Albert J., Jr. (1961). *Occupations and Social Status* (New York: The Free Press of Glencoe, Division of the Macmillan Company).

CHAPTER SIX

DETERMINANTS OF
ACTIVITY PATTERNS

In this chapter, the empirical work focuses more directly on the model developed in Chapter II; in an exploratory way it applies an abbreviated version of the model to two submetropolitan areas of relatively low-economic status, one a predominantly black community and the other a predominantly white community. The analysis is based on special surveys undertaken in each community, the black community in the summer of 1969 and the white community in the summer of 1971. In these surveys, where sampling provided high-intensity coverage of the areas, interviews were designed to include test questions on several areas of investigation which held out promise in exploring explanatory factors in the analysis of activity patterns.

It will be recalled from the microconceptual view of human behavior sketched out in Chapter II that activities are seen to be regulated by physiological and learning processes. With respect to the latter, it will also be recalled that, in the theoretical traditions followed in the work here, in which satisfaction of felt needs of the individual is considered to be the underlying energizing force in the stimulus-response process characterizing learning behavior, the environmental contingencies are grouped into three categories: those derived from personality sources, those stemming from cultural influences, and those attributable to the social system.

In shifting to an aggregative model, the last two of these three sources of influence on learning behavior are given particular attention, with personality influences left as part of an undefined residual. According to the model, once people are grouped into population segments in which the systemic influences of cultural background and social stratification of the population can be controlled for, activity patterns can be explained in terms of what are called "preconditioning" and "predisposing" factors. In effect, these factors represent constraining and energizing forces operating in a collective and concurrent manner on the stimulus-response processes of people in each of the population segments. It will be recalled that the preconditioning element of the model consists of such role-related factors as work status and sex (in the sense that they mediate breadwinning and home-making roles) and such person-related characteristics as stage in the life cycle and health status. It will also be recalled that the predisposing element consists of motivations and related thought-ways concerning security, status, achievement, and other felt needs, including personal enjoyment.

In sum, the model says that within segments of the population with a similar cultural background and from a similar status level, people will be predisposed to choose free-time activities according to a particular combination of felt needs appropriate to that activity and previous experience in satisfying these needs, but subject to role and person constraints on engaging in these activities. In the present version of the model, satisfaction-dissatisfaction levels with particular activities are assumed to be recognized indirectly in the rates of participation in these activities by the people of the population segment. Given strong rates of participation in free-time activities (and thus assumed strong levels of satisfaction), significant differences in time allocation to these activities among population segments of different ethnic and status characteristics are seen to derive from differences in role and personal characteristics and in motivations and attitudes. In the previous chapter some analysis of the influence of role and personal characteristics on activity choices was made. In this chapter the joint influence of preconditioning *and* predisposing factors on the two submetropolitan area population segments is undertaken. Because weekend returns from the black community were relatively small (see Table III-1), the analysis is restricted to weekday discretionary activities.

The chapter is organized into three parts. In the first, the two submetropolitan communities are briefly described, first in terms of community characteristics and life styles as reported by participant observation and then in terms of population characteristics as determined from census sources and our own surveys. The second section examines the two communities in a comparative vein and, paralleling the analyses of Chapter V, is concerned with checking out the assumptions concerning ethnic and status differences. The final section examines each of the communities in terms of the abbreviated version of the model shown in Figure III-2.

THE TWO SUBMETROPOLITAN STUDY LOCALES

The locations of the two submetropolitan communities examined in this chapter are shown in Figure IV-1. Area A is the predominantly black community, located immediately northeast of the Capitol, and Area B is the predominantly white community, located in Prince Georges County beyond Area A, just over the District line. These areas were selected originally because the one contained a sizable concentration of low-income black households and the other possessed a large concentration of nonblack households of low-economic circumstances. In each instance the community was selected to provide a case study of the living conditions people in low-income circumstances encounter. In addition to the study of activity patterns, they were designed to provide information on the perception of community problems and the use made of community facilities and services, feelings of residential satisfaction, and patterns of social interaction and participation (reported elsewhere).[1]

Participant Observation Perspectives

By the initial selection of the two communities, the grouping of households by ethnic characteristics has been accomplished. Participant observation is introduced in order to define the general range of life situations in the two communities and identify general status distinctions. From these insights, we posit variations in activity patterns which go with status differences. The vignettes of the two communities below give only the briefest summary view of the environment, life situations, and activity patterns as distilled from field reports and analyses of participant observers.[2]

The Predominantly Black Community (Area A). The changes in housing occupancy in this community over the past 100 years provide an example of the classical process of residential succession. In its earlier years, after initial development in the mid-1800s, the area counted among its residents congressmen and high-level career government personnel, but by the late 1800s it had shifted into a community of predominantly middle-level government workers. In the period since the turn of the century, occupancy has shifted to lower-level white collar civil servants and blue collar residents employed both in and out of government. Since World War II, it has changed progressively from a predominantly white to a predominantly black occupancy.

Throughout this period of "trickle down" in housing occupancy, Area A has remained residential in character. Except for the business development along H Street, N.E., and a scattering of "mom and pop" markets, schools, and churches, it is an area of row housing in much the same mold in which it was originally built. In this kind of development, dwellings are built one attached to the next, forming in this community block-long brick facades. Some are set back to provide small front yards and adorned with bay windows and porches, and others appear more severe, with simple window openings and doorways facing directly onto the sidewalk. Except for an occasional block where painted trim, shrub beds, and unit air conditioners signify a different economic level, the overriding impression is one of neglect and deterioration. During the field period of the study, this effect was accentuated by occasional rubble heaps, boarded-up structures, and frequent gaps along the H Street frontage or in adjoining residential buildings burned out during the April, 1968 civil disturbances.

For residents of this area, the H Street business strip is not only the shopping district, but also a community center, a place to see people and keep up with what is happening. Along its length various forms of hustling are to be found. Depending on the time of day, the location, and the opportunities of the moment, these consist of such activities as panhandling, peddling hot goods, and drug pushing. Pool halls, snack shops, carry-out food stores, and taverns located here have their following and serve a function in the communication system.

But there are social communication centers also in a variety of random locations in residential sections: in homes where the card clubs meet or in the bootleggers' homes, in church basements where men's clubs or women's groups meet, at the places where street-corner men hang out, and on many front porches or steps throughout the community. For women, the chance element that goes with the card club offers both a hope and an occasional payoff for the solution of economic troubles, but these activities also serve a social communications function as well. For men, the counterpart is the pool hall. For both men and women, church groups serve an important social exchange function. Day or night, the bootlegger's is a gathering place for still others—a center of social interaction, a place to keep up with happenings in the community, and a refuge from the frustrations of "not making it." But perhaps the most active centers of communication and social interchange are the front porches and doorways, as is evident by the exchanges, banter, and laughter to be heard along almost any street in the heat of a summer's evening.

The patterns of interaction serve a broader function than just that of visiting. Many residents in the community come from rural backgrounds and are still in the process of adjusting to life in a highly urbanized setting. The communications aspect of interaction provides information for the adjustment process. Other factors of importance are the release from the feeling of powerlessness in coping with job discrimination (and prejudice generally), the sense of injustice from demeaning experiences in seeking public assistance, and the feeling of frustration at being "hooked" on the credit systems and the price gouging of retail establishments in areas of low income. For people living in such circumstances, social interchange provides outlets for commiseration and an antidote for frustration. These considerations lead us to expect a high rate of participation and a heavy commitment of time to the category of activity we call "socializing."

The foregoing discussion might imply a high degree of homogeneity in activity patterns among adults in this community. But on the basis of impressions gained from participant observation this does not appear to be the case: people from different life situations appear to emphasize somewhat different activities. In describing the fluctuating kind of life situaton that households in this community experience, Patten makes a basic distinction between households making ends meet and those not making ends meet (Chapin, Butler, and Patten, to be published, Chapter II). He then goes on to subdivide each of these categories into a typology of households consisting of what he calls "secure" and "equilibrium" households in the "making it" category, and the "fluctuating" and "survival-oriented" households in the "not making it" category.

If the relatively small number of households in the "secure" group are excluded, the remaining households in the community correspond roughly to the low-income sector used in our survey research analyses. The three remaining life situations fall along a continuum. At one end is Patten's "survival" group; at the other is his "equilibrium" group; and in between, his "fluctuating" group which he sees shifting back and forth across a "making it" and "not making it" dividing line. Thus at any point in time, the population of households in this stratum could be grouped into those "making it" (the equilibrium group plus that portion of the fluctuating group temporarily in an upswing) and those "not mak-ing it" (the permanent survival group plus the increment of the fluctuat-ing group temporarily in a downswing). Although Patten uses a variety of factors for characterizing these life situations, if a surrogate set of fac-tors were to be established as a basis for differentiating between those "making it" and those "not making it," this set would consist of at least two factors, one concerned with level of income, and the other with the employment stability of the head of the household.[3]

Unfortunately this definition did not emerge in time to include ques-tions in our survey that would establish the employment stability of the head. However, it is anticipated that for purposes approximating differ-ences in activity patterns, a crude differentiation between those "making it" and those "not making it" can be made on the basis of income levels alone, controlling for work status. Given a difference in the amount of free time between the "not making it" (low income) and the "making it" (above-low income) segments of the population, participant observation provides some clues on the use of the extra amount of free time involved. In particular, it would seem plausible to expect no significant difference in rate of participation in discretionary activities, but to expect differ-ences of some significance in the amounts of time devoted to family ac-tivities, socializing, watching TV, and resting and relaxing, with those not working spending more time at all of these activities. What the par-ticipant observation brings out, but what our 12-class activity classifica-tion obscures, are the qualitative differences in the kinds of socializing discussed above.[4]

So although we do not expect to have information that will either sup-port or negate expectations in this respect, we expect that for those not making ends meet, subjects will be involved in unreported activities that serve as work substitutes, such as checking in with the caseworker and in other ways maintaining eligibility for welfare assistance, engaging in one or more forms of gambling in the hopes of payoffs, hustling in one form or another, or some combination of these. Although these work substi-tutes can be expected to take up time in a weekday's itinerary for those "not making it," the time expended (on a per capita basis) could be ex-pected to run well below what those "making it" devote to a regular job. For men, a large part of the difference—the excess time that those "not making it" have because of not working—can be expected to go into dis-cretionary pursuits. These would consist of various forms of activity in-volving social exchange, such as hanging out on the street corner, at the bootlegger's, or at the pool room, but they would also include watching television and simply taking things easy around home.

For women, some of the excess time would go into housework, child care, and family activities. But a good portion of it could be expected to go into socializing (visiting in the neighborhood or, for some, social exchange with members of the card club or interchanges in conjunction with other activities). Also some of it could be expected to go into watching television and resting and relaxing at home. Thus for those "not making it," we expect more time going into these three particular classes of discretionary activity than for those "making it." However, we expect that underreporting of social interaction forms of activity will prevent us from drawing firm conclusions on socializing.

The Predominantly Nonblack Community (Area B).   In a variety of ways, Area B presents a marked contrast to Area A. In block after block, Area A shows a high-intensity building coverage, and it shows a high density of housing occupancy as well, through conversions of single-family dwellings into apartments and, in turn, the accommodation of large families in these units. In contrast, Area B reflects a lower intensity of land use and a considerably lower average number of persons per housing unit. Although Area A is almost wholly a community of brick-faced row houses, the dominant pattern in Area B is primarily one of single-family frame houses on small lots, with a few apartment buildings built in scattered locations and one sizable complex on the northern edge of the study area.

As its location would indicate, Area B comes from a later era in the development of the Washington metropolitan area. Initially brought into intensive use in the twenties and thirties as an end-of-the-trolley-line series of single-family developments for working-class families, Area B has remained unchanged over the intervening years. Only in the period of expansion in government employment during and after World War II, when the remaining undeveloped tracts were built up with two- and three-story apartment structures, has the character of the original development been altered. Nevertheless, in terms of community life, the apartment building era has had little effect. By virtue of differences in life styles and location, for all purposes these are separate communities. Also in contrast to the virtually unchanging occupancy in the original single-family home-owner developments, the apartment complexes are subject to more turnover. The single-family areas would appear to be more conducive to community life than the apartment areas.

The two kinds of housing and the differences in occupancy clearly suggest that residents of Area B presently come preponderantly from two stages in the life cycle. Those in apartments appear to come mainly from the earlier stages, young couples in the beginning period of married life and those beginning the family formation years. On the other hand, residents of the single-family sections are likely to be in the retirement period of life. This means that housing occupancy tends to consist of a sizable number of two- and one-person households. However, as this generation dies off, participant observation suggests that these dwellings are bought up as "investment housing" by real estate agencies and rented out to low-income families. Since these agencies have little concern for maintenance, wherever these units have been acquired, there are clear signs of deterioration setting in. Many of the new renter families are in the child-rearing stages of the life cycle, which indicates the likelihood of change in the composition of the population in the area.

In the years of social ferment in the inner-city sections of Washington, the older persons in this predominantly white community have become uneasy. With mounting anxiety, many old-timers have enclosed their yards in chain-link fencing, and some have acquired watchdogs. Despite the small lots, it is an area in which the victory gardening tradition continues, an area in which meticulous attention is given to yards, shrubs, and border planting. But here and there are yards with junked cars and rubbish accumulations, a sign of impending change in this hitherto stable community.

In contrast to Area A, whose territorial identity exists by virtue of a well-defined shopping district and the community focus that centers on H Street, Area B's physical identity is more associated with its edges—the open spaces of the Fort Lincoln Area on the District side, the Anacostia River, related drainage systems and their open space systems on the south and east, and the apartment complexes on the north. Area B residents go outside its boundaries to regional centers for much of their shopping. Though the original individual residential developments have been incorporated for some time, only one community has anything approaching a town center. Each of the four municipalities (Mt. Rainier, Brentwood, Cottage City, and Colmar Manor) has its municipal offices; some have their own elementary schools; and there is a scattering of churches. But none of these facilities serve the symbolic function of a community center.

Driving out Rhode Island Avenue or Bladensburg Pike, the main approaches from the District, one can pass through the area without realizing it. From the Rhode Island Avenue approach, Area B is more easily identified by the cluster of loan and finance company offices than by any of the usual shopping facilities associated with a town's center. Bladensburg Pike, the other main radial from the District, similarly gives no clue of the adjoining towns. It supports a string of taverns, supper clubs, auto repair places, and similar roadside establishments, but these are patronized more by outsiders than by residents of the four towns.

Almost as though it were a consequence of the absence of a center, Area B has no street life of any note. Indeed, at the end of the day, life appears to be almost wholly home-centered and family-related. Old-timers may be seen working in their gardens or in the yard, relaxing on the porch, or inside watching television. The occasional younger newcomer families can be identified by shouts from knots of children on a porch or in a yard here and there. Others can be identified by a man in T-shirt tinkering with a car, or a woman in curlers taking the wash off the line. Both partners may be relaxing on the porch or inside watching television. Old-timers may go off once a week to church meetings, and newcomers may go off to a bowling league game, but except for these, the once-a-week shopping expedition, or an occasional outing, most free-time activities occur around the home.

Although Area B has little of the sense of community that might be expected with the existence of separate little municipalities, these towns do manifest a political responsiveness. In contrast to Area A, which as part of the District depends on a distant government (at the time of this study one attuned to listening more to committees of the Congress than to wishes of the residents), in Area B the towns are governed by elected officials who "live up the street" or "on the next block." Though many such functions as education, health, social services, streets, parks, planning, and zoning have been assumed by the county or regional agencies, local elected officials frequently function as local advocates in appearances before these agencies, in addition to overseeing their own local services such as police and fire protection, and garbage disposal. Yet there is little of a town meeting kind of interest or activity. A threat of closing down a neighborhood elementary school and the accommodation of children in another existing school illustrates the occasional issue that brings out newcomers to community meetings. For the most part, however, the occasional flurry of community interest in municipal affairs tends to be more concerned with problems or services of interest to old-timers than to newcomers, much of it centering on issues of property protection (and implicit concerns about black families moving into the area).

Although the above sketch of Area B would seem to suggest life situations in this community drawn along tenure and life cycle lines, Howell brings out other factors about residents which are more difficult to pin down in quite such simplistic and objective terms (Howell, 1973, Chapter 12). Moreover, since there are parallels with Patten's typology of households in Area A and since it facilitates the comparative analyses being made in this chapter, we propose to group Area B households on the same basis. In Area B, however, the proportions of households falling in Patten's categories can be expected to be markedly skewed in the direction of "making ends meet," with the "secure" and "equilibrium" groups in this category being roughly equally represented. In this connection, those in the equilibrium group land there not because they "made it" after a period spent in a state of fluctuation as in Area A, but because they are on pensions, many on very modest pensions. In a very real sense, economically under the pinch of the dwindling purchasing power of fixed incomes, they face the possibility of dropping to the survival category. Among those not making ends meet, the "survival" group is very small and, though larger, the "fluctuating" group is not a sizable segment in Area B's population either.[5]

As was the case in comparing activity routines for the extreme differences in life situations in Area A, in Area B those in the "not making it" category can be expected to devote more time to discretionary pursuits than those "making it" simply because of the more time available to them (time not tied up in work). As in the black community, in Area B nonworking men tend to spend more time dropping in on friends, taking things easy around the house, and watching television; nonworking women can be expected to devote more time to housework and child care than working women, and more time to visiting, resting and relaxing, and watching television. Both men and women in "making it" households can be expected to devote more time to family activities and recreation and other diversions. Among both the "making it" and the "not making it" segments, especially among residents in the newcomer-renter element, there are examples of Howell's "hard living" life style (Howell, 1973, Chapter 12). According to Howell, this is a segment of the blue collar community consisting of residents who place a high value on toughness, enjoy their six-pack or pint every evening, take pride in their work skills, prize an independent life in which they are beholden to no one, are suspicious of politicians and government alike, and, though given to family altercations, place an emphasis on the home and male dominance in home life. This particular perspective has been used in survey research analyses of this community reported elsewhere (Zehner and Chapin, 1974).

In Area B, in examining activity emphases among households grouped into "not making it" and "making it" categories, the possibility of retirement households straddling the line should be borne in mind. For households in both groups, we may expect relatively low magnitudes of time preempted by obligatory forms of activity. The resulting relatively large amount of discretionary time can be expected to emphasize watching television, recreation and diversions (in this group, gardening, crafts, and the like), and rest and relaxation.

In summary, on the basis of the foregoing free-form interpretation of participant observation reports, we would expect to find subjects in the black community placing more emphasis on rest and relaxation and social-exchange kinds of activities than those in the white working-class community. Because of the likelihood of a problem in underreporting of the latter kinds of activity, we do not expect to be able to confirm this expectation. With respect to other discretionary forms of activity, we would expect to find Area B devoting somewhat more time to family activities and recreation and diversions than Area A, and with no marked difference in time spent on watching television.

Although our data from survey research do not demonstrate this, a comparison of the two communities on the basis of participant observation reports leads one to note certain parallels in these two communities when comparisons are made within each between the "not making it" and the "making it" categories. In both black and white communities the "not making it" segment (the lowest-income category and the one with the least stability in work history) is likely to reflect a higher incidence of alcoholism, more arrests, and a higher rate of family separation than the "making it" category. In terms of activity emphasis of concern in this chapter, in both communities we anticipate that those "not making it" (low income) are likely to spend more time resting and relaxing around home and watching television than those who are "making it." Those "making it" (above-low income) devote more time to family activities, socializing, and recreation and other diversions than those "not making it." When households are grouped on both a life situation and work status basis, we anticipate that the differences between communities will be very marked in the "not making it" situation, with those not working full time devoting more time to all classes of discretionary activity than those working full time, especially in passive forms of activity.

A Demographic Profile of the Two Areas

To round out the background on these two residential communities, selected comparative data from census sources and our own surveys are provided. As can be seen in Table VI-1, compiled from the 1970 census, each of the two communities contains small segments of the other racial category. In Area A, 6.4 percent of the population is nonblack, and in

Table VI-1 Comparison of Two Submetropolitan Communities for Selected 1970 Census Characteristics.[a]

Characteristics	Area A (Predominantly Black Community)	Area B (Predominantly White Community)
Total Population	20,359	10,468
Percent Black	93.6	4.3
Percent Nonblack	6.4	95.7
	100.0	100.0
Selected Age Categories (All Races, in Percents)		
Preschool Age (under 5 years)	7.9	8.7
School Age (5-17 years)	28.5	24.4
Early- & Middle-Year Adult (18-59 years)	49.8	51.0
Older Adult (60 years and over)	13.8	16.0
	100.0	100.0
Total Occupied Year-Round Housing Units	5,768	3,596
Percent Black	90.6	8.3
Percent Nonblack	9.4	91.7
	100.0	100.0
Owner-Renter Status by Race of Households (in Percents)		
Black Owners	34.1	62.8
Black Renters	65.9	37.2
	100.0	100.0
Nonblack Owners	32.1	58.5
Nonblack Renters	67.9	41.5
	100.0	100.0

a/ See Figure IV-1 for the general location of the two communities. Figures for Area A based on Census Tracts 0083.01, 0083.02, 0084 and 0085, and figures for Area B on Census Tracts 8044, 8046, and 8047. (A portion of 8048 which falls in the study area is omitted.)

Source: U.S. Bureau of the Census, Census Tracts -- Washington, D.C. SMSA, Report PHC(1)-226, May 1972.

Area B, 4.3 percent is black. Comparing the areas on age composition, the distribution patterns reflect no extreme differences. What differences there are follow the pattern expected from participant observation and relate to the proportions of young and old persons. The black community has a somewhat larger proportion of its population under 18 years old (36.4 percent as compared with 33.1 percent for the white community), and the white community has a somewhat larger proportion in the category of 60 years and over (16.0 percent as compared with 13.8 percent in the black community). The communities differ somewhat in the tenure of housing, the black community consisting of a large proportion of renters (65.9 percent of the black households) and the white community consisting of a substantial proportion of home owners (58.5 percent of the white households).

Table VI-2 presents a selection of characteristics about respondents from our own surveys. Comparison of the two columns indicates that our two population groups differ in several respects. The black sample contains a higher proportion of subjects not working full time and a higher percentage who are female than contained in the white sample. However, within sex categories the percentages of those working and not working full time are similar for the two areas; in both areas, two-thirds of the male subjects work full time and about one-third of the female subjects work full time. But more marked are the differences in the proportions reporting young children living in the household and proportions of households in low-income circumstances. Confirming expectations from participant observation, Table VI-2 indicates that subjects in Area A are much more likely to have young children and much more likely to fall in a low-income category than those from Area B.

There are some similarities between the study areas in residential mobility characteristics. Census sources indicate that 41 percent of Area A's black population lived in a different housing unit in 1965 from the one in which they were enumerated in 1970; the corresponding figure for the white population in Area B was 43 percent. In both areas, the great majority of those who moved came from another housing unit within the 1970 SMSA (84.2 percent in the black community and 84.6 percent in the white community). Of the roughly 15 percent of the subjects in both areas who moved into the Washington SMSA during the previous five-year period, two-thirds of those coming into Area A (the black community) and about three-fifths of those moving into Area B (the white community) were from the South. Though the numbers of arrivals from the South during the past five years have not been sizable, the proportion of nonnative adults with a Southern background in both

Table VI-2 Selected Characteristics of Washington Submetropolitan Area Samples—Predominantly Black Community, 1969, and Predominantly White Community, 1971.

	Percent of Respondents	
Characteristics	Area A[a] (Black Community) n=382[b]	Area B[a] (White Community) n=589[b]
Respondent Work Status		
Working Full Time	44.5	49.4
Not Working Full Time	55.5	50.6
	100.0	100.0
Respondent Sex (and Work Status)		
Male	32.2	43.3
Working Full Time	(65.8)	(66.9)
Not Working Full Time	(34.2)	(33.1)
	(100.0)	(100.0)
Female	67.8	56.7
Working Full Time	(34.4)	(35.6)
Not Working Full Time	(65.6)	(64.4)
	(100.0)	(100.0)
	100.0	100.0
Children in Household		
Child < 13 years	51.8	36.0
No Child < 13 years	48.2	64.0
	100.0	100.0
Income Per Member of Household[c]		
Low Income	58.4	40.9
Above Low Income	28.5	58.4
Income Unknown	13.1	0.7
	100.0	100.0

a/ For locations of Area A and Area B, see Figure IV-1.

b/ Only subjects with complete information on activities and all analysis variables are included.

c/ For the formation of these income categories, see Figure III-3. It should be noted that there are two factors affecting the comparability of results on income between the two communities. First, in the survey of the black community, subjects were asked to estimate total household income from all sources after taxes, whereas in the survey of the white community, this information was requested before taxes. Second, during the two-year period between the surveys, the purchasing power of the dollar decreased to a noteworthy degree. For purposes of analyses here, we assume that these two opposite effects cancel one another, making the two sets of data roughly comparable.

areas is sizable—71.1 percent of our adult subjects in the black study area and 43.8 percent of the subjects in the white study area migrated from nearby Southern states (Maryland, Virginia, West Virginia, North Carolina, and South Carolina).[6]

ACTIVITY PATTERNS OF THE TWO COMMUNITIES COMPARED

Before examining results from tests of the explanatory framework, we first identify discretionary activities with weekday participation rates high enough to constitute what was referred to earlier as an "activity pattern." We then go on to compare activity patterns in the two communities, using mean-time allocation during a typical weekday as a measure. Activities with fairly strong rates of participation and with significantly different mean durations are then used as dependent variables in the next section of the chapter in testing trial measures for preconditioning and predisposing factors, the independent variables.

Table VI-3 is the 12-code basic summary table for the two study areas (for the 40-code weekday summaries compared with the Washington area summary, see Table A-6 in the Appendix). In the first pair of columns Table VI-3 compares participation rates and in the second, mean durations of time allocated to various classes of activity on weekdays by subjects in the two communities. Following the same minimum participation rate for defining activity patterns noted in Chapter V (i.e., that at least one of the ethnic segments or one of the income segments, as the case may be, shows a 25 percent or greater level of participation in the activity), substantially the same results were obtained as emerged from that analysis. As shown in Table VI-3, in neither of the two study areas do the participation levels of subjects taking part in church or organizational activity on weekdays come anywhere near the 25-percent threshold.[7] When subjects are grouped into low- and above-low-income categories (or the "not making it" and "making it" households), a check of the percentages of people engaging in activities (not shown in the table) indicates that no activities dropped out of the analysis other than participation in church and voluntary organizational activities.

It can be seen from the second pair of columns in Table VI-3 that, though there is no significant difference in the total amount of free time that subjects have in these two study areas, there are significant differences in the way time is allocated for all but family activities. It would appear that subjects from the white community spend markedly more time in socializing and on recreation and diversions, and subjects from the inner-city black area spend markedly more time watching television,

Table VI-3 Participation Rates and Mean Durations by Income Category of Weekday Activities of Heads of Households and Spouses in Two Washington Study Areas—Inner-City Black Community, 1969, and Blue Collar White Community, 1971.

| Activity Category | % Engaging in Activity | | Mean Hours Per Capita Devoted to Activity | | | | | |
| | | | Totals | | "Not Making It" (Low Income)a/ | | "Making It" (Above Low Income)a/ | |
	Black Community (n=382)	White Community (n=589)	Black Community (n=382)	White Community (n=589)	Black Community (n=231)	White Community (n=241)	Black Community (n=109)	White Community (n=344)
Main Job	34.6	47.9	2.91 *	4.08	2.31	3.01	4.68	4.82
Eating	85.1	97.5	.95 *	1.39	.92 *	1.39	1.03 *	1.39
Shopping	25.1	39.7	.38 *	.60	.45	.60	.30 *	.61
Homemaking	76.9	78.9	2.96	2.66	3.38	3.26	2.00	2.23
Family Activities	13.9	31.9	.25 *	.38	.18 *	.42	.25	.36
Socializing	34.3	56.5	.73 *	1.36	.68 *	1.33	.84 *	1.39
Participation (Ch. & Orgs.)	5.8	8.0	.09 *	.18	.09	.21	.02 *	.17
Recreation, Other Diversions	35.9	63.7	.62 *	1.28	.40 *	1.27	.99	1.30
Watching TV	68.3	67.9	2.80 *	1.85	2.95 *	2.05	2.47	1.72
Rest & Relaxation	53.1	43.8	1.71 *	.89	1.80 *	1.08	1.44 *	.75
Miscellaneous	94.0	90.2	2.29 *	1.53	2.33 *	1.34	2.36 *	1.66
All Forms of Discretionary Activity	95.8	97.9	6.22	5.98	6.13	6.38	5.99	5.72

*Differences in duration to left and right significant p $\leq$ .05 in difference of means test.

a/ For definition of income categories see Figure VI-2.

resting, and relaxing. In all but the socializing activities, findings on community differences in emphasis bear out expectations from interpretations of participant observation reports. In the case of socializing, we suspected underreporting in the black community, and although we cannot confirm this from the data, the reverse emphasis in results (subjects in the white community spending more time socializing than subjects in the black community) would surely suggest that these findings need to be checked in further field studies.[8]

Using income as the basis for differentiating between the two status categories derived from participant observation, that is, differentiating on the basis of those "not making it" (low income) and those "making it" (above-low income), we see that differences between the black and white communities in the use of free time are more pronounced in the "not making it" or low-income pair of columns. The dominant patterns here are as follows: (1) In both communities, those "not making it" as compared with those "making it" record more free time spent on passive forms of activity (watching television, resting, and relaxing) and less time on recreation-diversions or social interaction (family activities, socializing, and participation in church and organizational activities); and (2) these differences in time allocation are more pronounced in the black than in the white community. These results confirm expectations from comparative interpretations of participant observation reports. Although other factors may be relevant here, one might at least pose as a hypothesis from these findings that the differences in activity emphasis between the two communities in the "not making it" life situation are associated with access to income-earning opportunities. Further, assuming prejudice and discrimination were eliminated as a constraint on blacks, such differences in activity patterns within this low-status situation would then tend to blur. This does not mean, of course, that blacks and whites in the "not making it," or for that matter, in the "making it" life situation, would necessarily choose the same detailed forms of activity within these broad classes of activity emphasis (i.e., choose the same life styles). This remains a matter of conjecture.

As brought out in Chapter V in the analysis of black-nonblack segments of the metropolitan area population as a whole, the time devoted to discretionary activities tends to vary with work status, sex, and child-care responsibilities. Since many of the same effects hold for comparisons of these two subcommunities, we do not reproduce a tree diagram similar to Figure V-4. Nevertheless, to give the reader some notion of the magnitudes of variation in time allocation according to work status, sex, and stage in the life cycle, Tables VI-4 and VI-5 examine these factors (one

Table VI-4 Mean Duration of Time Heads of Households and in Life Cycle—Inner-City *Black Community* in Washington Area, 1969.

Activity Category	Work Status Differences		Sex Role Differences	
	Working Full Time (n=170)	Not Working Full Time (n=212)	Male (n=123)	Female (n=259)
Main Job	5.69 *	0.68	4.07 *	2.35
Eating	1.03	.90	1.01	.93
Shopping	.39	.36	.20 *	.46
Homemaking	1.67 *	4.00	1.11 *	3.84
Family Activities	.11 *	.37	.23	.27
Socializing	.61	.83	.95	.63
Participation (Ch. & Orgs.)	.10	.08	.00 *	.13
Recreation, Other Diversions	.64	.60	.95 *	.46
Watching TV	2.39 *	3.13	2.93	2.74
Rest & Relaxation	1.20 *	2.11	2.13 *	1.50
Miscellaneous	2.45	2.16	2.77 *	2.06
All Forms of Discretionary Activity	5.07 *	7.14	7.22 *	5.75

*Differences in durations to left and right significant $p \leq .05$ in difference of means test.

at a time) in a format paralleling results summarized for the SMSA as a whole in Table IV-5.

Work Status Differences

Examining the first pair of columns in Tables VI-4 and VI-5, it can be seen that differences in time allocation attributable to work status are

Spouses Spend on Weekday Activities, by Work Status, Sex, and Stage

	Differences Among Various Stages in Life Cycle			
No children <19 present, Head < 35 (n=18)	Children < 19, Some < 13, Head Any Age (n=198)	Children < 19, None < 13, Head Any Age (n=37)	No children <19 present, Head 35–65 (n=88)	No children <19 present, Head 65 & over (n=41)
6.66 *	2.75	3.56	3.35 *	0.47
.84	.89	.84	1.01	1.29
.37	.50	.33	.14	.32
.75 *	3.70 *	2.55	2.29	2.17
0	.26 *	.01 *	.47	.09
.96	.82	.65	.49	.80
0	.06	.15	.11	.19
1.41 *	.38	.46	.67	1.42
2.87	2.76	2.39	2.79	3.35
.88	1.31 *	2.67	1.98	2.50
1.91	2.44	1.85	2.40	1.88
6.14	5.62	6.35	6.54 *	8.36

significant for almost all classes of activity in the white community, following closely the pattern shown in Table IV-5 for the metropolitan area as a whole. In the black community, there are fewer activities which reflect significant differences by work status.

As suggested earlier, one way to compare differences within the black and white communities is to determine how the excess of mean time released by those not working full time is absorbed in other activities. For

Table VI-5 Mean Duration of Time Heads of Households and Spouses Spend on Weekday Activities, by Work Status, Sex, and Stage

Activity Category	Work Status Differences		Sex Role Differences	
	Working Full Time (n=291)	Not Working Full Time (n=298)	Male (n=260)	Female (n=329)
Main Job	7.53 *	.70	5.87 *	2.66
Eating	1.36	1.42	1.38	1.41
Shopping	.41 *	.79	.44 *	.74
Homemaking	1.35 *	3.94	1.20 *	3.82
Family Activities	.31	.45	.26 *	.47
Socializing	1.04 *	1.67	1.09 *	1.57
Participation (Ch. & Orgs.)	.07 *	.29	.12	.23
Recreation, Other Diversions	1.11 *	1.45	1.47 *	1.14
Watching TV	1.27 *	2.41	1.71	1.95
Rest & Relaxation	.57 *	1.20	1.02	.79
Miscellaneous	1.56	1.51	1.66	1.43
All Forms of Discretionary Activity	4.41 *	7.51	5.71	6.19

*Differences in durations to left and right significant $p \leq .05$ in difference of means test.

the white community a substantial part of the per capita amount of time released when the subject does not work full time (a difference in the means of 6.83 hours) is absorbed in homemaking (a difference in the means of 2.59 hours). However, a major part is absorbed in free-time activities (a difference in the means for all discretionary activity of 3.10 hours), with the latter given over mainly to spending more time watching television, socializing, and resting and relaxing. For the black community, the difference in time between working and not working full in Life Cycle—Blue Collar *White Community* in Washington Area, 1971.

		Differences Among Various Stages in Life Cycle							
No children <19 present, Head < 35 (n=71)		Children < 19, Some < 13, Head Any Age (n=212)		Children < 19, None < 13, Head Any Age (n=39)		No children <19 present, Head 35-65 (n=158)		No children <19 present, Head 65 & over (n=109)	
5.44		4.33		4.40		5.26	*	.87	
1.44		1.31		1.44		1.47		1.42	
.63		.54		.89		.45	*	.83	
1.03	*	3.39		3.08		2.13	*	2.93	
.13	*	.49		.78		.33		.26	
2.42	*	1.25	*	.78	*	1.31		1.16	
.25		.08		.13		.22		.31	
1.71	*	.95		.80	*	1.28	*	1.85	
1.08	*	1.71		1.33		1.72	*	2.98	
.57		.80		1.03		.67	*	1.55	
2.08	*	1.43		1.47		1.53		1.42	
6.18		5.32		4.87		5.56	*	8.11	

time (a difference in the means of 5.01 hours) is similarly absorbed by homemaking (a difference in the means of 2.33 hours) and discretionary activity (a difference in the means of 2.07 hours), with most of the latter added in to television-viewing time and resting and relaxing. These results generally confirm expectations from participant observation.

In the last section it was suggested that work status must be taken into account in examining differences between those "not making it" (low income) and those "making it" (above-low income). The importance of work status has been brought out repeatedly in previous analyses, and so at this juncture it is introduced as a control in order to bring into sharp focus how these contrasting life situations affect activity choices free of these influences. To do this and determine the significance of differences in free-time activities recorded for the two communities, the following cross-tabulation was prepared:

| | "Not Making It" (Low Income) | | | | "Making It"(Above Low Income) | | | |
| | Working Full Time | | Not Working Full Time | | Working Full Time | | Not Working Full Time | |
Discretionary Activity Category	Black Com- munity n=77	White Com- munity n=81	Black Com- munity n=146	White Com- munity n=160	Black Com- munity n=82	White Com- munity n=207	Black Com- munity n=27	White Com- munity n=137
Family Activities	.05 *	.25	.25 *	.50	.16	.33	.37	.39
Socializing	.26 *	.94	.90 *	1.54	.96	1.09	.53 *	1.84
Recreation- Diversions	.36 *	1.17	.42 *	1.32	.89	1.09	1.28	1.61
Watching TV	2.61 *	1.33	3.12 *	2.41	2.29 *	1.26	2.99	2.41
Rest & Relaxation	1.09	.68	2.17 *	1.29	1.31 *	.54	1.82	1.07
All Forms of Discretionary Activity	4.53	4.44	6.97	7.37	5.66 *	4.43	7.00	7.67

* Differences in durations to left and right significant p ≤ .05 indifference of means test.

If the left-hand panel is compared with the right-hand panel, it can be seen that community differences are more significant in the "not making it" segment. The fact that these differences are significant in the group working full time as well as in the group not working full time suggests that the hypothesis posed above about "access to income-earning opportunities" might well be amended to read "access to income-earning opportunities *at adequate income levels.*"

It might be noted also that results from both panels indicate that in general the most time is spent on passive activities (last two rows) and the least time on activities involving social interaction (first three rows) in both these communities, confirming expectations from participant observation. Clearly the "not making it" group is spending less of their time on activities that bring them into contact with other people and giving more of their time to passive activities. These results would seem to be symptomatic of a state of alienation in both communities, but particularly in the black community.

Sex Differences

In the second pair of columns in Tables VI-4 and VI-5, except for similar patterns in recreation-diversions, the tables bring out different emphases between the sexes for the two communities. These comparative sex differences bear some further comment. As shown at the foot of the two tables there is a significant sex difference in the total amount of discretionary time in the black community but a smaller difference (at a weaker significance level) in the white community. When the two tables are compared, it can be seen that in the black community men have more free time than women, but in the white community women have more free time than men. When work status within sex groups is taken into account (not shown in the tables), in the white community it turns out that there is no sex difference for persons working full time, but for those not working full time, men have more free time than women. In contrast, in the black community the sex difference holds for both categories when work status is taken into account, but dissipates somewhat when child-care responsibilities are taken into account.

Generally confirming expectations from participant observation, in both communities, the "excess" of discretionary time for women not working full time is largely absorbed in homemaking and discretionary activities. For men, the "excess" is absorbed primarily in discretionary activities.[9] However, the sex differences for some individual classes of discretionary activity shown in the tables for the black and white communities present some contrasts that perhaps warrant further comment.

Among these, *socializing* provides the most notable contrast in the two communities. Although Table VI-3 indicates a higher level of socializing among subjects in the white community as compared to the black community (similar to results shown earlier in Table V-1 for the metropolitan area as a whole and both questioned on the basis of participant observation), sex differences in socializing take an opposite form in these two communities. Since the underreporting problem is not likely to be a factor for sex comparisons *within* communities, these opposite tendencies are notable. Table VI-4 indicates that in the black study area men devote more time to socializing than women (although the significance of these differences is at a relatively weak level); on the other hand, Table VI-5 indicates that in the white community women devote significantly more time to socializing than men. It is noteworthy that this community difference holds even after controlling for work status and child-care responsibilities (not shown in the tables). In contrast to these results, there was no sex difference in socializing in either the black or white segments of the population of the metropolitan area as a whole, even after controlling for work status and child-care responsibilities.

Although subjects in the black as compared to the white community appeared to spend significantly less time on *recreation and other diversions* (see Table VI-3), when sex is taken into account, it can be seen from Tables VI-4 and 5 that in both communities men spend significantly more time on these activities than women. Though not shown in these tables, these differences hold for the most part when work status and child-care responsibilities are taken into account, but working males with young children spend less time on these activities than females with young children. In short, recreation-diversions are much more of a male activity than female, though subjects in the white community spend more time at it than those in the black community; this differentiation by sex holds even when work is taken into account, and somewhat more selectively when child-care responsibilities are considered.

Going on to other free-time activities, it has already been noted that there is no significant difference between these two communities in time allocation to *family activities*. When these analyses are extended to take account of sex, there appear to be significant differences for the white community but none for the black community. Women devote more time to these activities in the white community than men, especially women who do not work full time. These results are in contrast to the no appreciable sex differences found among both blacks and whites in the metropolitan-wide analysis.

In the case of *rest-relaxation,* the findings in the two communities conform generally to results from the metropolitan area analysis: subjects in the black community devote significantly more time to these activities than in the white community. Within each community, there is a relatively weak sex difference, with men giving somewhat more time to these activities than women, even after controlling for work status. For *viewing television,* in the white community in the "not making it" group, women spend significantly more time watching television than men, but in the "making it" group, men spend somewhat more time than women. In the black community, the emphases are reversed: men spend more time viewing television in the "not making it" group, but in the "making it" group, women spend more time at it. These sex differences hold in both communities even after controlling for work status.

Life Cycle Differences

Turning to the life cycle variations shown in Tables VI-4 and VI-5, it can be noted that for various activity classes listed in the stubs of the tables significant differences between the life cycle categories occur more frequently for the white than for the black community. In the white community, the most pronounced differences are found between the pre-child-rearing and the initial child-rearing stages (first and second columns) and between the pre-65 year and the 65 and over stages (fourth and fifth columns). For the most part, the comparative community emphases in time allocation reflected here follow those noted earlier for the metropolitan community as a whole (Table IV-5). The life cycle categories at either end of the continuum, not surprisingly, record the largest amounts of free time, the younger age category putting much more of its free time into socializing and recreation-diversions and the older group putting more of it into recreation-diversions, watching television, and rest-relaxation. For the black community, the emphases in choice of free time are similar at these same two opposite ends of the life cycle, but in the "65 and over" category there is a heavier emphasis on passive forms of activity such as watching television and rest and relaxation than that shown for the white community.

In summary, then, data presented here do bring out differences in the free-time activity patterns of these two communities. Disregarding socializing differences, subjects in the white community put more emphasis on active pursuits (e.g., recreation-diversions), and subjects in the black community spend more time on passive pursuits (e.g., watching television and rest-relaxation). These differences in time allocation hold for "not making it" (low income) and "making it" (above-low income) segments of both communities but are more pronounced for the lower-status group.

Results also indicate that for the most part work status, sex, and life cycle considerations have similar effects on activity patterns in the two communities, with a few notable exceptions. In the black community, men have more free time than women, whereas in the white community the opposite prevails, women having more free time than men. For the most part these differences hold even after taking account of work status and child-care responsibilities. Also, in the distribution of their free time, men in the black community devote more time to socializing than women (underreporting presumably not being a factor here since it would be expected to apply similarly to both sexes). In the white community, women spend more time socializing than men, even after controlling for work status and child-care responsibilities. The sex differences in time spent watching television vary with the life situation of the household and follow reverse patterns in the two communities. In the black community in households "not making it," men spend more time viewing TV than women; in households "making it," women spend more time than men watching TV. In the white community exactly opposite patterns prevail. These reverse sex differences hold in both communities even after work status is controlled.

Finally, the life cycle differences are more pronounced in the white community than in the black community, especially in comparing either end of the life cycle continuum with its nearest intermediate stage. In the white community, distinctive patterns in the use of free time were expected for senior citizens, since this was an area identified earlier as containing a substantial number of retiree home owners; and distinctive patterns do emerge from the analysis, with socializing, recreation-diversions, watching television, and rest-relaxation being the most prominent activities. In the black community, senior citizen activities show similar emphases but the time allocations are not significantly different from those of the preceding stage in the life cycle.

EXPLORATORY APPLICATIONS OF THE MODEL

Having established in what respects these two low-income environments differ in their free-time activity patterns, we turn now to a trial use of the explanatory framework (summarized in Figure III-2). Focusing on the preconditioning and predisposing variables discussed in Chapters II and III, the analysis seeks to get some sense of the relative importance of these factors in explaining the weekday use of free time in each of the two communities for those activities where marked differences in time allocation were found. In the preceding section, some of the preconditioning elements of the framework (work status, sex, and life cycle) have been used as control variables for examining how the allocation of free time varies when these constraints are taken into account; in the analysis in this section the preconditioning variables are pooled with predisposing variables and the relative importance of both sets of factors is examined.

In keeping with the general exploratory stage in the development of this work where the range of variables and appropriate measures have still to be fully defined, no attempt is made to put the variables through rigorous statistical examination (e.g., through factor analysis). Rather, the analysis at this stage is more concerned with establishing rank order patterns and the general level of explanation these factors offer. For these purposes stepwise multiple regression analysis is used.

The Components of the Model

The activities examined (as dependent variables) are socializing, recreation-diversions, watching television, and rest-relaxation. These are the activities in which participation rates for both communities were at better than a 25-percent level and in which there were significant intercommunity differences in time allocation. In addition to these specific classes of activity, because of its summarizing nature, the category "all forms of discretionary activity" is included in the analyses as well, even though the mean duration figures for the two communities did not prove to be significantly different (a criterion used as the basis for the selection of the individual activities that are analyzed here).

Among the explanatory factors (or independent variables) used in these tests of the framework, the preconditioning factors are standard background variables, three of which have already been examined in this and earlier chapters and therefore need no further comment. In addition to work status, sex, and life cycle, the subject's evaluation of his or her state of health has been introduced. The specification of this factor is of a self-anchoring type and not based on a medical examination (see Questions 22 or 29 of the sample interview schedule in Chapter III).

The predisposing factors involve, of course, a different kind of variable, one where the phenomena being investigated are infinitely more difficult to measure. In this respect, well-honed measures would seem to be particularly important in exploring this aspect of the framework. Unfortunately, we cannot claim to have moved very far in this direction. At best, the measures used here are rough indicators of the factors discussed in Chapter II (status, achievement, security in the sense of personal safety, and security in the sense of mental health). It might be noted also that the questions used in the two communities differed somewhat, and so the specifications of the factors, though generally parallel, also differ somewhat (See table on the following page). It can readily be seen that these measures of predisposing factors were used in all regression analyses.[10] As can be noted in this list, the measures drawn from the black community study are less refined than those taken from the white community study. Because of the generally rough measures used for these predisposing factors and the limitations involved in tests that depend here on a truncated form of the framework, a fairly low level of explanation was anticipated.

Predisposing Factor	Black Community	White Community
Status concern	Direct question on importance of having neighbors who earn about the same income (graded from very important to not important)	An index based on attitudes about dress, social position, and knowing "important people"—see Questions 30 b, d, and e in sample schedule in Chapter III (graded from low to high status concern)
Head of household's chances of getting ahead	Direct question (graded from excellent to poor)	Direct question—see Question 19 (or 26) in sample schedule, Chapter III (graded very good to poor)
Neighborhood safety	Direct question on subject's feelings about crime and violence on neighborhood streets (graded from not a problem to a serious problem)	Direct question on feelings about safety in neighborhood—see Question 31 j in sample schedule, Chapter III (graded from safe to unsafe)
Alienation	Indirect question on extent of threat felt in relations with others (graded from often to never)	An index based on attitudes concerning trustworthiness of people generally, of public officials, and outlook about the future—see Questions 30 f, g, and h in sample schedule, Chapter III (graded most to least alienated)

Results from Trial Application

The summary of results from the tests of these various preconditioning and predisposing factors as explanatory variables is shown in Table VI-6. Interpretative comment focuses first on the explanatory factors, examined across activity categories (horizontally) and then on activity categories (vertically), examining the combination of factors which offers the most explanation. Since this chapter features comparisons between the two low-income communities, in both horizontal and vertical interpretations, intercommunity differences are noted as well. In this respect only the first

Table VI-6 Rank Order Importance of Preconditioning and Predisposing Factors in Explaining Various Weekday Discretionary Activity Choices of Heads of Households and Spouses in Submetropolitan Washington Study Areas—Inner-City Black Community, 1969, and Blue Collar White Community, 1971.

Factors Expected to be Associated With Subject's Activity Choice	Socializing		Recreation-Diversions		Watching Television		Rest and Relaxation		All Discretionary Activities	
	Black Community	White Community	Black Community	White Community	Black Community	White Community	Black Community	White Community	Black Community	White Community
Preconditioning Factors[a]										
S's Work Status	(3)	5	-8	5	(1)	-8	(1)	4	(1)	(2)
S's Stage in L. C.	-6	-8	(2)	(1)	8	5	(3)	(3)	(3)	(1)
S's Sex	-4	(1)	(1)	(2)	(3)	6	(2)	-5	(2)	6
S's Health	7	4	-4	-7	7	(2)	-4	(1)	-6	-4
Predisposing Factors[b]										
S's Status Concern	5	(2)	6	(3)	4	(1)	-6	-6	5	-7
S's Evaluation of Head's Chances of Getting Ahead	(1)	(3)	-7	6	(2)	(3)	5	8	-4	8
S's Concern About Neighborhood Safety	(2)	6	5	-4	-6	-7	7	7	7	-5
S's Degree of Alienation	-8	-7	(3)	8	-5	-4	-8	(2)	8	(3)
R²	.07	.05	.08	.04	.05	.11	.12	.04	.24	.07

Note: Rank order is established from step-wise multiple regression analysis; beyond the third rank, the remaining factors contribute very little additional explanation.

a/ Work status graded from working full time to not employed; life cycle, from young couple to elderly; sex, male to female; health, from bad to excellent.

b/ Views about social status graded from very important to unimportant; chances of head of household getting ahead, from good to poor; violence in the neighborhood, from no problem to serious problem; and degree of alienation, from most alienated to least alienated. It should be noted that because of different phrasings of questions and different measures used in original surveys, community comparisons of predisposing factors are approximate only.

three rankings are taken into account, since beyond these, little additional explanation of variance is contributed.

Relative Importance of Factors Across Activity Classes.   Using the frequencies with which the first three rankings occur across rows among the four specific classes of free-time activity, Table VI-6 indicates that by our measures preconditioning factors are more important than the predisposing factors as an influence on free-time activity in these two communities. If the rank order is used as a basis of weighting,[11] among the preconditioning factors sex is the most influential factor, followed by work status, life cycle, and health status. Also, it is apparent that the preconditioning factors are much more important in the black than in the white community. In the black community work status, sex, and stage in the life cycle are the key preconditioning variables, and in the white community sex and health status provide the greatest amount of explanation.

By the measures used predisposing factors do not occur in the first three ranks as frequently as preconditioning factors do, and fewer fall in the first rank. However, in the white community predisposing factors occur in the first three ranks with the same frequency as preconditioning factors; in the black community they show up with less frequency. In the predisposing category, the factor most frequently occurring in the top three rankings is "chances of the head of the household getting ahead," this factor being more important as an explanatory variable to the black than to the white community. Status concern shows up next most frequently in the rankings; but this factor is in the top three rankings only in the white community.

In sum, in the black community, such preconditioning factors as work status, sex, and stage in the life cycle have more to do with time allocation to most discretionary activities than predisposing factors. Among the latter, however, economic opportunity as determined by chances of the head of the household getting ahead on the job is a factor to be taken into account. In the white community, health status and sex are about equally important as preconditioning factors, with stage in the life cycle of somewhat less importance, and among the predisposing factors status considerations and evaluation of chances of getting ahead occur in the rankings with greatest frequency. The summary columns for all forms of discretionary activity (the last pair in Table VI-6) bring out the full effect of the way in which preconditioning factors (i.e., constraints on choice in the use of free time) in the black community appear to block out predisposing factors (opportunities to exercise felt need); these are work status, sex, and stage in the life cycle, their relative importance falling in that order. In the white community, stage in the life cycle, work status, and degree of alienation appear to be the most germane factors in the list affecting the amount of time allocated to discretionary activities, their importance falling in that order.

Factors Most Prominently Associated With Each Activity. Taking the activities in Table VI-6 one by one and examining the explanatory factors in the first three ranks by community, the following patterns can be noted:

Free-Time Activity	Black Community	White Community
Socializing	More time allocated if head of household has good chances of getting ahead, if there is no problem of safety on the streets, and if subject is not employed	More time allocated if subject is a female, if status considerations are of no particular consequence to subject, and if head of household's chances of getting ahead are poor
Recreation-diversions	More time allocated if subject is male, in later stages of life cycle, and not alienated	More time allocated if subject is in later stages of life cycle, is male, and if status considerations are of no particular consequence to subject
Watching television	More time allocated if subject is unemployed, if head of household's chances of getting ahead are good, and if subject is is male	More time allocated if status considerations are of some consequence to subject, if in poor health, and if head of household's chances of getting ahead are good
Rest and relaxation	More time allocated if subject is unemployed, a male, and in later stages of life cycle	More time allocated if subject is in poor health, alienated, and in the later stages of the life cycle
All forms of discretionary activity	More time allocated if subject is unemployed, male, and in later stages of the life cycle	More time allocated if subject in the later stages of the life cycle, unemployed and alienated

As can be seen from Table VI-6, the amount of variance explained is low, as anticipated. For the black community, the level of explanation is best for the summarizing category "all forms of discretionary activity" and for that portion of it spent on "rest and relaxation." For the white community, explanatory factors seem to show the most strength for time allocated to watching television.

Special Analyses of Low-Income Segments of Two Communities. Although Table VI-6 presents results for a sample representative of all households in each of the two communities, the subjects actually come from a gradation of life situations. To sharpen the focus of the analysis, we examined the free-time activities of subjects from the low-income segment alone, those roughly corresponding to the "not making it" life situation noted from participant observation in these two communities. As was seen above and in earlier analyses, work status and sex role are particularly prominent in the list of explanatory factors affecting the allocation of free time to various discretionary activities of subjects. Since there was therefore some likelihood that these two factors were suppressing the effects of the other six, the analyses were also modified to use these two factors as control variables. With these changes in the analysis format, we then reexamined the remaining six variables for their relative importance in explaining time allocated to socializing, recreation-diversions, watching television, and rest-relaxation.

As might be expected, in narrowing the focus to persons of one economic status and examining patterns in the choice of free-time activities for subjects of the same work status and sex, the framework turned out to be more sensitive to the performance of the residual group of factors. In effect, by focusing the analysis on subjects from "not making it" circumstances, a group that is likely to be somewhat more homogeneous than that studied above, there was greater likelihood of identifying strong and meaningful explanatory factors. Also, factors previously "robbed" of their influence by the presence in the mix of the more dominant work status and sex factors were now free to assert their influence "uninhibited," perhaps taking a different rank order with respect to the other residual factors.

As a result of these changes there were some marked increases, but also some decreases in the amount of variance explained. For example, the level of explanation turned out to be relatively high among men in the white community who were not working full time (R^2 varying upward of .50, depending upon the activity). In contrast, the amount of variance explained was at a relatively low level for men not working full time from the black community (R^2 falling to somewhere around the .05 level, depending upon the activity). Subjects who represent other combinations of sex and work status for the two communities were in between.

In examining rankings controlling for work status, we found several instances for both the black and the white communities in which predisposing factors had moved into the upper three ranks, in some cases edging out the remaining preconditioning factors. If the consistency with which explanatory variables recurred in the first three ranks for the four classes of free-time activity was used as an overall indicator of the importance of a variable, getting ahead and status concern (in the predisposing category) turned out to be the most prominent. However, stage in the life cycle and health status (the two remaining preconditioning factors) continued as high-ranking explanatory variables, especially in the white community. In both communities, among the six explanatory variables, getting ahead seemed to be a factor of particular importance in the amount of time allocated to socializing and watching television for both work status groups, particularly for those working full time. Stage in the life cycle seemed to be a factor of some importance in the allocation of time to recreation-diversions and rest-relaxation for both work status groups in the two communities.

When rankings were examined controlling for sex groups, the patterns were not so pronounced as they were by work status. Nevertheless, there was some indication in the rankings that among men the use of free time is influenced most markedly by considerations of getting ahead and by stage in the life cycle. For women, there appeared to be less pattern in the rankings, with both stage in the life cycle and health status prominent in the preconditioning category and with status concern and getting ahead showing up somewhat more frequently among the first three rankings from the list of predisposing factors. There were very few similarities in the ranking of factors in the two communities based on sex.

In summary, the results from the trial use of the explanatory framework appear promising as a basis for studying why people choose particular kinds of free-time activity. When applied to status segments of the population too broadly defined, its explanatory power was somewhat circumscribed, but when applied to fairly homogeneous status segments, particularly where sex role and work status were taken into account, the framework achieved an improved level of explanation.

When both work status and sex role were controlled for, the factors most consistently high ranking across all activity classes and all control categories were getting ahead, stage in the life cycle, status concern, and health considerations (in that order of importance). If work status alone was considered, the most important determinants in the choice of free-time activities *for those working full time* in the black community were stage in the life cycle, opportunity for getting ahead, and health status. In the white community, getting ahead, status considerations, and health turned out to be the most important ones (in that order). *For those not working full time,* in the black community, stage in the life cycle, status concern, and chances of getting ahead proved to be of first importance among the six factors; in the white community, getting ahead, health status, and stage in the life cycle were the three that averaged the highest among all six factors (in that order).

If sex alone was controlled for, similar factors were involved, but their ordering differed with sex in each community. *Among men* in the black community, stage in the life cycle, chances of getting ahead, and status considerations ranked of highest importance; in the white community, getting ahead, health status, and stage in the life cycle had the highest average rank among the six factors (in rank order). *Among women* in the black community, stage in the life cycle, chances of getting ahead, and health status were most important (in that order); in the white community, getting ahead, status considerations, and health were most important (in that order). These results generally correspond with expectations gained from participant observation reports on these areas.

SUMMARY

If free-time activity choices can be considered to be an indicator of life style, these analyses bring out several notable contrasts both within and between these two low-income environments. One of the pervasive findings about the weekday use of free time in all the studies is the relatively high proportion of discretionary time devoted to passive activities (here consisting of watching television, resting, and relaxing).[12] Although the allocation of some time to passive activities is usually considered to be an essential part of a person's weekday routine, the constrasts in these two communities are striking: in the black community, passive activities take up 72.5 percent of the average subject's free time, and in the white community, 45.8 percent, with the "not making it" segment in both communities accentuating the emphasis on passive pursuits still further (the "not making it" segments of the two communities being 77.4 and 49.1 percent, respectively). It is probable that the suspected underreporting of informal social exchanges in the black community would reduce the contrast somewhat, and a variety of miscellaneous activities that participant observation suggests go unreported (e.g., panhandling and hustling) would serve to reduce the difference still further, but it is unlikely that these would eliminate the contrast.

Consisting of a distinctly smaller proportion of reported free time, active pursuits (here consisting of socializing, recreation, and other diversions) are more heavily emphasized by subjects in "making it" circumstances in both communities. Though the underreporting of social exchanges casts some doubt on intercommunity comparisons, it would seem safe to accept the findings here of a generally heavy emphasis on passive forms of activity in situations of deprivation, with the strong likelihood that the emphasis would be much more accentuated in the black than in the white community under roughly equivalent economic circumstances.

Given the proclivity for subjects in low-status situations to spend a large proportion of their free time on passive activities, the question might then be asked: what factors best explain the emphasis given to these activities? Within the bounds represented by the list of factors that are incorporated into our explanatory framework, the results show that in the black community, the heavier emphasis on passive activities is most strongly associated with unemployment, the male sex, and being in an advanced stage in the life cycle. In the white community, those who spend large amounts of time on passive activities are likely to attach importance to status, be in poor health, reflect a marked degree of alienation, and be in the later stages of the life cycle.[13] It might be noted that the absence of opportunities in these two communities for choosing other alternatives (see the lower branch in the explanatory framework in Figure II-1) may have some bearing on the heavy emphasis on passive activities; but to determine how much such opportunities affect the configuration of explanatory factors must await another round in the R & D process.

NOTES

1. See Chapin, Butler, and Patten (to be published) and Zehner and Chapin (1974).

2. The impressions presented on Area A are drawn from the work of Frederick C. Patten, who headed the participant observation team, Thomas R. O'Neal, and Olivia J. Corgile; impressions on Area B are drawn from the work of Jospeh and Embry Howell.

3. Patten identifies other factors, including levels of living, occupation, the prestige of particular employers, and education.

4.   Even had our analysis been made on the 40-class level of detail, our techniques of activity listing do not yet pick up many of the kinds of activities reported by participant observers. As will become evident in the analysis of survey research results, with all the precautions of the kind brought out in Chapter III (see note 16) to improve on reporting, our techniques simply do not capture the random occurrences of social interchange of the kinds noted above in this chapter. Although the illegal nature of some forms of activity make it doubtful that they would be reported, it is also clear that activity listing is not getting at various less sensitive forms of social interchange that go with shopping, sitting on the front porch, and so on.

5.   Howell's Clay Street neighbors provide insights into these two segments in Area B. The Shackelfords are in the "survival" group, and June Moseby's children are clearly in the "fluctuating" group (Howell, 1973). In Area A, Patten sees the fluctuating house-holds as a group whose plight in part is a result of being black. The "survival" group is an outcome of a prolonged struggle in the "fluctuating" situation. A household drops to this situation after repeated tries at "making it," but because of prejudice and job discrimina-tion many do not make it and fall into a reactive syndrome of alcolohism, absenteeism, and family altercation. After a number of years of fluctuating up and down, the husband finally opts out of the value system of the larger society and turns to a floating life; the wife assumes the role of the family head and, depending on the mutual aid systems for taking care of the children, may work or turn to public assistance. In either case, the insufficiency of income puts the family in a survival category. Though the racial basis of discrimination is not involved, in Area B there are instances of a similar syndrome of alco-holism, absenteeism, and family altercation, with the eventual dissolution of the family. Indeed, participant observation brings out instances in which the wife rather than the husband becomes a societal "drop out"—for example, one wife left her husband and children for the nomad life of a motorcycle gang.

6.   These figures come from our own survey results. The place of origin for purposes here was the state in which subjects received the bulk of their elementary schooling.

7.   As reflected in the first two columns of Table VI-3, family activities was the only class of activity where a 25 percent participation level was not achieved by both samples, with the participation rate of black subjects in this instance falling below the criterion. Although not shown in the table, in both low-income and above-low-income categories the propor-tion of black subjects engaging in family activities also fell below the 25 percent level (for low-income black subjects, 14.1 percent as compared to 35.3 percent for low-income whites; and for above-low-income black subjects, 10.1 percent as compared to 29.4 percent for counterpart white subjects).

8.   Although we cannot establish from our data the extent of underreporting, on the chance that "rest and relaxation," as suggested in Chapter V, included a substantial proportion of the episodes of social interchange that did not get reported in activity listings, we checked on results combining socializing with rest and relaxation. This resulted in no significant difference between the two communities (a mean of 2.44 hours allocated to the combined category for subjects in the black community as compared with 2.25 hours for subjects in the white community). However, the cautions about mixing categories of a different functional nature cited in note 8 of Chapter V should not be taken lightly.

9. Sex comparisons of the "excess" and the use of this excess for the "not making it" and "making it" segments in the two communities are as follows:

	"Not Making It" (Low-Income Subjects)				"Making It" (Above-Low-Income Subjects)			
	Black Community		White Community		Black Community		White Community	
	Male n=58	Female n=165	Male n=91	Female n=150	Male n=56	Female n=53	Male n=165	Female n=179
Excess of Time[a]	5.34	4.52	6.11	6.12	5.86	4.29	7.57	6.16
Amount Going Into Discretionary Activity[b]	5.60	1.91	3.55	2.72	2.62	.58	4.19	2.80
Amount Going Into Homemaking[c]	- .30	2.26	1.17	2.54	1.81	2.73	1.27	2.42

[a] The net difference in the mean time recorded for "main job" by those not working full time and those working full time.

[b] A similar net difference for all forms of discretionary activity.

[c] A similar net difference for homemaking activities.

10. We pondered over using one set of all-purpose measures versus the use of differing measures designed around the special character of each activity class. In favor of the use of one set of general-purpose measures in analyses of all classes of discretionary activity was the advantage that a common base offers for establishing the consistency with which factors prove to be important or not important in their explanatory power across all classes of discretionary activity. Although the alternative of using a varying selection of measures especially suited to each activity would undoubtedly explain more variance, it was felt that it was more instructive at this stage to look into the relative importance of the several factors. As a technical footnote, it might also be noted that the linearity of several independent variables is ragged, with several showing curvilinear tendencies; consequently the results of tests do not have the sharpness that would be obtained in using transformations of measures for such variables.

11. For summarizing purposes, rank order of explanatory factors across activity classes is determined by ranking the average of ranks obtained from stepwise multiple regression analyses of the individual classes of free-time activity.

12. For the national SMSA sample in 1969, the proportion of per capita free time spent on passive activities (watching television, rest and relaxation) was 55.4 percent for those working full time, and 58.2 percent for those not working full time. For the Washington SMSA sample of 1968, these percentages were 38.5 and 50.3, respectively. For the inner-city black community in 1969, the corresponding figures were 70.8 and 73.4, respectively; and for the blue collar white community in 1971, they were 41.7 and 48.1, respectively.

13. These selections of explanatory factors are based on multiple regression results from the use of watching television, resting, and relaxing as one combined activity class called

"passive activities." Accordingly, the rankings of explanatory variables differ to some extent from those shown in Table VI-6. R^2 for results from the black community is .15, and from the white community, .12.

REFERENCES

Chapin, F. Stuart, Jr., Edgar W. Butler, and Frederick C. Patten (to be published). *Blackways in the Inner City* (Urbana: University of Illinois Press).

Howell, Joseph T. (1973). *Hard Living on Clay Street* (Garden City, N.Y.: Doubleday-Anchor Books).

Zehner, Robert B. and F. Stuart Chapin, Jr. (1974). *Across the City Line: A White Community in Transition* (Lexington, Mass.: Lexington Books, D. C. Heath & Company).

CHAPTER SEVEN

INTERPRETATION AND
A LOOK AHEAD

The work reported in the preceding chapters has sought to develop and test an approach to describing and explaining the patterned ways residents of a city go about their everyday life. Special attention has been given to an approach applicable to urban planning and policy studies, one that can eventually relate the spatial organization of the city and its services and facilities more closely to living patterns of residents. In this respect, at the exploratory stage of the work undertaken here, primary attention has been given to presenting the approach, conceptually and empirically.

The research focuses more on time allocation than on the spatial distribution of activities—more on the "what" and "why" of activity patterns than on the "where" and "why" of locational patterns. Certainly a more fine-grained level of definition for activity classes will be required when the spatial aspect is developed more fully and when activities are related more directly to services and facilities requisite to certain activities (which will necessitate somewhat larger samples than those available for these studies). Meanwhile the current stage of development offers a means of bringing into the public decision-making process more direct consideration of the social construction of the metropolitan community and the diversity of lifeways to be found there among different sociocultural segments of the community.

The findings emerging from this series of studies are of two kinds. One is concerned with applications to policy and planning and the other with refinement of the conceptual framework and research approach looking toward the next round in the transductive strategy of this R & D effort. Accordingly, in the first section below we review selected results from Chapters IV through VI and briefly examine their implications for planning and policy analysis. In both its conceptual and empirical aspects, these studies leave a number of problems and issues for further exploration; the final section indicates where work in extension of this effort will be particularly fruitful.

RESULTS AND PLANNING IMPLICATIONS

There are three aspects of the analyses in the foregoing chapters that are of particular interest for planning and policy studies. The first concerns a way of thinking about the people of the metropolitan community, and more particularly the basic "cuts" of the population that have significance in assaying the social construction of the community. The second has to do with activity patterns of segments of the population formed, especially the distinctive patterns that go with each "cut." The third has to do with the preconditioning and predisposing factors that appear to regulate activity patterns.

Population Segments of Planning and Policy Significance

According to the conceptual view of human activity systems set forth in Chapter II, some basis of disaggregating the household population of a metropolitan community which goes somewhat beyond the conventional demographic matrix of cohorts is required in activity analysis. The work here does not go deeply into the social construction of the community, but it is premised on the key importance of forming population segments along lines that enable the analyst to take account of systemic sources of social differentiation in the community. We argue that these "cuts" in the population are not only relevant for activity analysis, but are quite fundamental in assessing the social impact of public investments and policies in a wide range of other evaluation approaches.

At the beginning of Chapter II a caveat was set down for activity analysis that applies as well in a more general context of planning and policy studies. It was asserted that activity analysis should be approached not only with sensitivity to subaggregates of the population that constitute socially significant segments, but also with a sensitivity to "subpublics" of the "general public" which possess group identity and potential—if not a demonstrated capacity—for response as political constituencies.

On the basis of analyses undertaken in the preceding chapters, at least two dimensions in the social grouping of the population appear to warrant consideration in this respect. One seeks to identify cultural sources of influence on the lifeways and thoughtways of a metropolitan community, and the other seeks to make use of concepts of social stratification and status differentiation in planning and policy analysis. The first basis of subaggregating the population is usually evident on an ethnic basis, often as a spatial grouping in the metropolitan area, and frequently as a political constituency. The second basis of forming segments is less clear-cut since lines of differentiation are constantly being redrawn by society. Yet it has importance as a basis for interpreting group patterns of reactive behavior and in searching out equity differences in programming public actions.

In Chapter IV we presented a broad summarizing picture of activity patterns in the Washington metropolitan community. When the population was disaggregated into black and nonblack segments of the community in Chapter V, it was apparent that ethnicity was one key dimension by which to approach activity patterns. Although it was not possible to differentiate clearly between lifeways that were freely chosen as opposed to those that evolve in the form of "imposed" living patterns, this basis of grouping the population clearly brought out one important "cut" for getting at subcultural differences in activity patterns, and it also made considerable sense as a grouping to observe in a political action context. Other subcultures may well exist in other metropolitan communities which bear some analysis, for example, ethnicity based on waves of European, Asian, or Latin American immigration and their political identity and proclivity for group action.

The social-structural basis of disaggregation of a population into segments is dependent on the construction and application of valid indices for stratifying the metropolitan community. As brought out in Chapter V, our work utilized several status measures that might be incorporated into such an index, but we did not construct a composite index for grouping subjects by status.[1] Whether one measure is selected as the primary indicator of status differentiation in the stratification of the community (as we did in this exploratory effort, using income), or whether a composite measure is used, the designation of particular strata rarely has objective reality to residents of the community—at least to the extent that there is a clear consensus on the criterion and the division lines between status groups. The absence of clear division lines, in turn, works against the spontaneous formation of clear-cut political constituencies.

The most obvious exception to this observation is the establishment of a "poor people's lobby" or the banding together of "welfare mothers" in political reaction to congressional or city council inactions on programs from which there is high expectation of relief. But even in these instances, the "rest of society" is not disaggregated into other status gradations with any clear-cut political action base. It was for this reason that in Chapter V we used the ethnicity split as the primary subdivision of the population and, within each of the ethnic divisions, a somewhat arbitrary grouping of subjects by income status. (Occupational and educational status were also examined.)

In this connection, we note that in addition to the foregoing systemic ways of breaking down the population of the metropolitan community into population segments, there are the standard categories for grouping people used in conventional demographic analyses which provide still further ways of subaggregating the community into segments. Groupings based on stage in the life cycle and sex provide obvious examples. In recent years senior citizens, teenager groups, and women's liberation groups provide examples of political constituencies that have grown up around the special interests and activities of these segments of the population. For purposes here, life cycle and sex factors are explored as preconditioning factors in the choice of an activity rather than as basic divisions of the population into segments.

These ways of grouping the population indicate the diversity of "publics" which are so easily sublimated when the focus is on "the general public." Planning and policy analyses, whether for public investments or for regulatory actions, require a working knowledge of the segments of the population that are likely to be affected, for the possibility always exists of very considerable multiple social impacts and various side effects from public investment and related private development decisions. These may have much more far-reaching consequences than the purely cost-efficiency effects customarily taken into account.[2]

Activity Patterns with Planning and Policy Implications

Once population segments possessing some tangible sociocultural identity and political reality in the metropolitan community are defined, attention can be focused on household activity patterns within these segments. In this volume only the activities of heads of households and spouses of heads are investigated and only discretionary activities are examined in any detail. Although other research requirements dictated the selection of heads and spouses as subjects (see Chapter III), it can be argued that since they are usually the decision-making persons in the household and frequently provide the only means of household support, they are probably the most important sources to consult on the impact that regulatory measures and public investments have on living patterns of members of the family.

Though the emphasis here is on discretionary activities and their significance in bringing out differences in life styles among population segments, it should be noted that obligatory activities in many respects are of more direct importance in planning and policy studies. Because they relate in one degree or another to the necessities of life and, in terms of time commitment, form the most dominant part of the daily routine, there is strong justification for giving them priority attention. Indeed, they have been given priority attention as reflected in a large array of governmental programs on work opportunities, education, housing, transportation, medical care, and social services which have come into being in response to these concerns of households. Even though often given lower priority in the past, leisure-time activities of households are now assuming increasing importance in planning and policy studies. In a society moving toward a shorter work week, there is every reason to expect that discretionary areas of time allocation will receive much more attention in the future.

Previous chapters brought out that the total amount of free time adults have shows little variation from one segment of the population to another, once prime household maintenance functions such as work and housework are taken into account. But they brought out some marked variations in the way time is allocated within the discretionary sector. Table VII-1 recaps some of these variations. Horizontally, the table brings out variations by the day of the week in the mean hours spent by subjects for the three summarizing categories of activity shown along the top of the table, and vertically it indicates variations for different background variables—two used in previous chapters as basic controls for systemic sources of influence (ethnicity and income status) and three used as preconditioning factors for constraints on activity choice (work status, sex, and stage in the life cycle). The categories along the top provide a summarizing indication of what subsectors of free-time activity people of different background characteristics on the average emphasize on weekdays, Saturdays, and Sundays.[3]

In effect, Table VII-1 brings together the patterns of variation that were analyzed in Chapters IV and V, but presents them for all days of the week instead of weekdays alone. For purposes of illustrating the use

Table VII-1 Mean Duration of Time Heads of Households and Spouses Spend on General Classes of Discretionary Activity on Weekdays, Saturdays, and Sundays, for Selected Background Variables—Washington, 1968.

Background Variables	Social Interaction[a]			Recreation-Diversions[b]			Passive Forms of Activity[c]		
	Wkday.	Saturday	Sunday	Wkday.	Saturday	Sunday	Wkday.	Saturday	Sunday
All Persons	1.4	2.3	3.0	1.9	2.6	2.4	2.6	2.7	3.6
Ethnic Group									
Black	0.8	2.0	3.0	1.6	1.5	1.8	3.4	3.7	4.1
Nonblack	1.5	2.4	2.9	2.0	2.9	2.6	2.4	2.5	3.4
Income Group[d]									
Low	1.3	1.9	3.0	1.4	1.9	2.0	3.2	3.1	3.9
Above Low	1.4	2.6	2.9	2.0	2.9	2.6	2.2	2.6	3.4
Work Status									
Full Time	1.1	2.4	2.8	2.1	3.0	2.5	2.0	2.5	3.4
Not Full Time	1.8	2.3	3.1	1.6	2.0	2.3	3.4	3.0	3.8
Sex									
Male	1.1	2.3	2.6	2.2	3.2	2.5	2.5	2.9	4.0
Female	1.6	2.4	3.2	1.7	2.7	2.3	2.6	2.6	3.2
Life Cycle Stage[e]									
1	1.7	2.2	2.9	2.6	3.7	3.4	2.0	2.4	3.5
2	1.4	2.4	3.2	1.7	2.4	2.6	2.3	2.5	3.0
3	1.4	2.2	2.6	2.0	3.0	1.7	2.5	2.3	3.9
4	1.1	2.4	2.7	1.8	2.7	2.3	2.8	2.9	3.9
5	1.7	2.7	2.7	1.7	1.4	2.3	4.4	4.5	4.7

a/ Consists of family activities, socializing, and participation in church and organizational activities.

b/ Consists of recreation-diversions, and miscellaneous other discretionary activities.

c/ Consists of watching television, rest and relaxation.

d/ For the formation of income categories, see Figure III-3.

e/ Stages: 1 - under 35 years, no children present in household; 2 - have children under 13 years; 3 - have no children under 13 years, but some 13-18 years; 4 - age 35-64, no children present under 19 years; and 5 - age of activity analysis in the study of policy issues, three "cuts" of the population sample from this metropolitan area are particularly noteworthy: one relating to ethnicity, a second to income, and a third to stage in the life cycle. In regard to the first, vertical comparisons in Table VII-1 indicate that black and nonblack subjects (who on the average have equivalent amounts of total free time) emphasize distinctly different categories of activity: black subjects in Washington spend more of their free time on passive forms of activity than nonblack subjects, and nonblack subjects spend more time on recreation-diversions and social interaction than blacks, with the differences especially marked on weekend days. As brought out in Chapter V, the total amount of free time a person has, regardless of race, varies with work status, sex role, and child-rearing responsibilities. Even when these factors and income as well are taken into account, however, it is found that the patterns of emphasis in the use of free time by black and nonblack segments of the population remained essentially unchanged.

Although we cannot be certain from our data whether the differences can be ascribed to social choice or to discriminatory constraints on social choice, participant observation of life systems in one submetropolitan community gives some subjective insights in this respect. This work indicated that social interaction and passive forms of activity are dominant in the lives of black people in low-income circumstances,[4] but the presumption was fairly clear from this work that other options that would come with the availability of parks, recreation facilities, and adult education centers, for example, were not viable choices in the use of free time in this community. Either the facilities were missing or the program philosophy took no cognizance of the state of deprivation. The prevailing view was that the larger community and "the establishment" wanted it that way. The point to be made here is that time allocation measures can be used in defining the parameters in the use or nonuse of facilities and services. In conjunction with other lines of investigation, it should be possible to establish whether or not an emphasis on passive activity among black subjects as found here is a reciprocal effect of an absence of opportunities in recreation and diversions.[5]

With respect to income "cuts" for grouping the population, it was shown earlier that differentiation is most pronounced on a low- versus above-low-income grouping. On this basis, the most notable differences (vertically) occur in the "recreation-diversions" and "passive forms of activity" categories:[6] low-income subjects in Washington emphasize passive forms of activity, and above-low-income subjects emphasize recreation-diversions. In this respect, in Washington income and ethnicity would be expected to bring out similar emphases because so many of the black subjects are also the low-income subjects. The conclusions to be drawn are somewhat similar: either low-income people in this community in their preoccupation with problems of poverty have no inclination to engage in recreation-diversions, or the services and facilities suited to their needs are not available. As in the case of racial differentiation, supplemental lines of investigation concerning preferences in the use of free time could establish which situation prevails.

Turning to stage in the life cycle as a "cut" for grouping the population, the data in Table VII-1 indicate some distinct patterns of activity emphasis of policy significance. Examining patterns vertically, as might be expected, the first stage (young single heads of households or young couples without children) and the fifth stage (senior citizens) clearly show patterns that set them apart from those in the middle three stages of the life cycle: the younger stage tends to favor recreation and other diversions; senior citizens favor the passive forms of activity; and the three middle stages are strongest on social interaction kinds of activity.[7]

If we examine patterns horizontally, other notable variations can be seen. Results indicate that the amount of time devoted to *social interaction* forms of activity in Washington reaches a peak on Sundays for all stages in the life cycle.[8] But for those in the three middle stages, Saturday is also a day in the week when socializing is emphasized as well; for the youngest and the senior citizen stages, there is little difference in emphasis between weekdays and Saturdays. In the case of recreation and other diversions, Saturday is clearly the day of the week that the amount of time devoted to these activities reaches a peak; this is true for all but senior citizens, who allocate the highest proportion of their time to these actitvities on Sunday.[9] For passive forms of activity, those in the pre-child-rearing stage favor Sundays, as do those with older children; those with young children and those whose children are over 18 emphasize passive forms of activity on weekdays; and senior citizens devote more time to these activities on Saturdays than other days of the week.[10]

In applying activity data summarized by stage in the life cycle to planning analyses, the categories of greatest interest are likely to be "social interaction" and "recreation-diversions." With respect to social interacton, an analysis of friendship networks and intensities of social communications at different stages of the life cycle would provide a basis for assessing the relative vulnerability of these households to disruption and emotional stress when public investments are under study in the building of expressways, in urban renewal, or in other programs involving family relocation.[11]

With respect to *recreation and other diversions,* results from our activity analysis indicate that in Washington patterns of recreation vary from weekdays to weekend days in terms of absolute hours (see Table VII-1), proportion of all free time,[12] and participation rates. In this last respect, the percentages of persons in each stage of the life cycle engaging in recreation and diversions indicate that Stages 1 and 5 have differing patterns from those in the middle three stages:

Stage	Weekdays	Saturdays	Sundays
1	39.5%	33.1%	45.4%
2	25.5	26.7	26.6
3	27.5	31.7	32.9
4	27.2	27.9	25.8
5	38.8	23.4	29.8

On weekdays the frequencies of engaging in recreation and diversions are greater for the youngest and the oldest stages in the life cycle, whereas Saturdays or Sundays are favored by subjects in the intermediate stages.

As might be expected, a larger proportion of those in the younger first-stage group are participating in recreation activities and other diversions on any day of the week. Moreover, not only do they put into this subsector the largest number of hours on any day of the week (see Table VII-1), but they also spend higher proportions of their free time on these pursuits on any day as well.[13] Senior citizen participation rates indicate that subjects in this stage favor weekdays and Sundays (as do those in the youngest stage), but as would be expected, time allocation to these pursuits is at the lowest level. For the intermediate stages in the life cycle, participation rates show less variation horizontally by day of the week, but the amount of time given to these pursuits rises somewhat from weekdays to weekend days.

These data indicate the extent of participation and the amount of time Washington subjects allocate to recreation and other diversions. However, they do not reflect preferences, nor do they indicate what people would do, were there alternative ways available to spend their free time. Supplemental information is required on preferences in the context of the pragmatic contingencies faced when choices are made, and information is needed on the opportunities that existing services and facilities offer to residents in order to establish whether patterns in the use of free time at different stages in the life cycle are a reflection of genuine choice or simply a choice restricted by opportunities available.

Finally, it is clear that the subsector of leisure time given to *passive forms of activity* involves issues that are primarily in the realm of national policy. In some respects, the absence of local planning and policy in the other two subsectors may have an impact on passive forms of activity in the sense of "forcing" people to spend their time on more passive pursuits. Thus situations in which public actions have disrupted social communications, or where there is a failure to provide services and facilities consonant with the traditions and preferences of various subcultural groups in the population, may by default result in heavier emphasis on passive activities. However, the dominance of passive forms of activity at all stages in the life cycle is a national phenomenon.[14] In the Washington study, it is clear that not only are the proportions of subjects spending time on passive activities higher than in any of the other categories, but with few exceptions the results indicate that both in absolute figures and as a proportion of all an individual's free time, passive activities dominate the leisure time of adults on all days of the week and at every stage of the life cycle.[15] When it is considered that television takes up the major proportion of time in this category, it is evident that policies affecting programming of television time during leisure hours of a week are a very pervasive influence indeed.[16]

In the foregoing analyses, no attempt was made to examine more specific classes of activity, nor was any attention given to transportation associated with various activities. Table VII-2 gives the mean allocations of time to activities and associated travel disaggregated back to the 40-code level of detail (see Tables A-3, A-4, and A-5) and reconstituted in a somewhat different form. The 12-code classification utilizes activities that constitute the most common building blocks of time use in the average adult's weekday. For planning applications, there seems to be some advantage in reconstituting various discretionary activities from the 40-code system in groups that focus more precisely on social communications and on services and facilities of spatial significance, but still retaining the basic split used in Table VII-1. (Activity category labels are modified slightly to avoid confusion between the two tables.)

The functional significance of the first category in the daily life of the individual is conveyed in its name, "social communications." For purposes of planning analyses, the "visiting" and the "participation" subcategories provide a basis for flagging neighborhoods with a high degree of social interaction and where particular attention would have to be given to social impacts of proposed physical changes.[17] The "active diversions," "passive diversions," and "religious activities" represent functional categories of activity within which there is sufficient similarity as to pro-

Table VII-2 Mean Duration of Time Allocated by Heads of Households and Spouses to Activity Classes as Reconstituted for Planning and Policy Studies—Washington, 1968.

Generic & Specific Class of Activity	40-Code Category	Weekdays Total Duration	Weekdays (Travel Portion)	Saturdays Total Duration	Saturdays (Travel Portion)	Sundays Total Duration	Sundays (Travel Portion)
Social Communications		1.33	(.10)	2.21	(.19)	2.20	(.19)
Visiting with relatives, friends, and neighbors (socially or casually)	14, 18-21	.87	(.07)	1.45	(.15)	1.47	(.15)
Conversations, outings and other activities of immediate family	13, 15-17	.40	(.01)	.72	(.03)	.69	(.03)
Participation in activities of voluntary organizations	37-38	.06	(.02)	.04	(.01)	.04	(.01)
Active Diversions		.47	(.02)	1.21	(.04)	1.34	(.04)
Cultural activities (adult educ., concerts, museums)	25	.11	(.01)	.12	(.02)	.14	(.02)
Crafts and hobbies	29	.06	(.00)	.07	(.00)	.09	(.00)
Walking and cycling	30	.03	(-)	.04	(-)	.08	(-)
Participating in sports	32	.10	(.01)	.13	(.02)	.14	(.02)
Out-of-town recreation	34	.17	(-)	.85	(-)	.89	(-)
Passive Diversions		2.80	(.03)	3.09	(.03)	3.76	(.02)
Relaxing, loafing, napping	22	.38	(.00)	.51	(.00)	.52	(.00)
Reading, listening to radio	23-24, 28	.70	(.00)	.61	(.00)	1.18	(.00)
Watching TV	27	1.65	(.01)	1.75	(.00)	1.99	(.00)
Going to the movies	26	.05	(.01)	.13	(.02)	.04	(.01)
Attending sports events	33	.02	(.01)	.09	(.01)	.03	(.01)
Religious Activities	36	.08	(.01)	.13	(.01)	.76	(.16)
Miscellaneous Discretionary	31, 35	1.18	(.00)	1.03	(.00)	.84	(.00)
All Discretionary Activities		5.86	(.16)	7.67	(.27)	8.90	(.41)

vide options for substitution of one choice for another. In each such category, the out-of-home activities have distinct facility counterparts in land use.

A glance at time allocation figures in Table VII-2 indicates that in Washington facility-oriented activities have a use of relatively low intensity (measured in mean hours of time per capita devoted to them). Participant sports and cultural activities, especially on weekends, movies on Saturdays, and church on Sundays take up the highest per capita time expenditures. However, although it is not given in the table, it may be noted that the proportion of the sample engaging in these activities for all but "religious activities" is six percent or less. On Sundays, 32 percent of our sample are recorded as participating in attending church and engaging in other religious activities. Apart from watching television and on Sundays all forms of reading, Table VII-2 indicates that more free time is allocated to visiting (casually or socially) than to any other discretely defined activity. Also, except for television, the participation levels run higher (36 percent on weekdays, 35 percent on Saturdays, and 37 percent on Sundays).[18]

Travel data shown in Table VII-2 provide insights into leisure-time-oriented transportation habits. Glancing down the columns showing the per capita time involved in the various weekday free-time activities, it is evident that the level of time commitment for these purposes is minimal on weekdays. On weekends, however, time commitments to travel build up. On Saturdays and Sundays visiting takes the largest chunk of the time spent on travel for free-time activities, but church attendance also absorbs a major amount of Sunday's free-time travel.

In making adjustments in activity classification that give more direct recognition to social communications and to services and facilities, the modified system should also be suited to making analyses of the micro-environment of the residential community. For example, land use decisions embodied in zoning and subdivision ordinances have profound effects on human activity patterns. Michelson (1972), in his study on activity patterns in high-rise and single-family residential environments, provides insights into the social implications of housing design that should be given attention, not only in programming for community facilities but also in site planning.

Factors Preconditioning and Predisposing Activity Choices

Activity analysis is concerned not only with how people presently use their free time (i.e., description), but also with what factors prompt them to use their free time in these ways (i.e., explanation). As brought out in Chapter I, both are essential first steps in developing a capability to simulate activity patterns, which in turn is a step that paves the way to using time and spatial measures of human activity in the evaluation of public investment proposals and service delivery systems. The explanatory model thus serves as a diagnostic tool for pinpointing variables that then become parameters in the simulation of activity patterns.

In the work reported here, a truncated version of the model is used to examine what we call "preconditioning" and "predisposing" factors for their relative influence in explaining free-time activity choices. Both preconditioning and predisposing factors are seen to function in different combinations within segments of the metropolitan community differentiated according to ethnicity and socioeconomic status. As brought out in Chapters II and III, the preconditioning category consists of factors that are seen to put constraints on choices people have, for example, constraints represented by employment status, the roles society ascribes to the sexes, and the stage in the life cycle (including child-rearing responsibilities that go with some stages). On the other hand, the predisposing category consists of factors that are seen to energize choice (assuming opportunities to engage in these activities exist in the first place, that is, a set of facilities and services exist for engaging in such kinds of activity, or simply a congenial social environment exists for carrying on the activity). This last category has to do with felt needs for status, achievement, and security, and for individual preferences and tastes for particular activities. This truncated version of the model does not attempt to cover all sources of felt need, nor does it attempt to take into account in a direct way people's preferences and satisfactions as these temper the exercise of choice. Moreover, the opportunity aspect, that is, the choice options open to people and the accessibility and quality of these options, are not included in the trial version.

The framework was tested in an inner-city black community and a blue collar white community in the Washington area. By selection of these two areas, ethnic identity was taken into account, but by this choice of study areas, situated at one end of the socioeconomic continuum, we imposed some limitations on bringing status differences into the analysis. However, it was determined from participant observation that there were two kinds of life situations in these communities that seemed to result in different life styles: one situation where subjects come from households not making ends meet (referred to as "not making it"), and another in which subjects come from households that were managing to make ends meet (or "making it"). This basis of differentiation permitted us to parallel at a submetropolitan level the kinds of descriptive analyses done on a metropolitanwide basis and reported above. For purposes of these submetropolitan area tests, subjects from low-income circumstances as defined in Figure III-3 were considered to be "not making it," and those from households in categories above the low-income level were considered to be "making it."

When subjects were grouped on this basis, it became apparent that in both communities, there was a significant difference in the amount of weekday free time spent on passive forms of activity. As noted previously, passive uses of free time are prominent in the weekday routines of most people. But in these analyses the results brought out that those in the "not making it" situation devote substantially more of their free time to passive forms of activity than those "making it," even after taking account of employment status and sex role. These results also brought out that the proportion of discretionary time recorded in passive activities in the inner-city black community was considerably greater than what was recorded in the blue collar white community (roughly three-quarters as compared to half of all free time). The other side of the coin has to do with the free time taken up in more active pursuits, an emphasis which must obviously take up a somewhat smaller proportion of discretionary time. Here, not surprisingly, the "making it" segment devoted significantly more time to what has been relabeled above as "social communications" and "active diversions." This emphasis also holds, even after controlling for work status and sex.

Whether or not these differences between status groups can be construed as peculiarities of the two areas we happened to select for analysis (or with respect to intercommunity differences, whether or not they are attributable to the underreporting problem cited frequently throughout Chapter VI) cannot be resolved here. However, assuming these communities do typify the lower socioeconomic environment of the Washington area, the "not making it" versus "making it" activity comparisons within each community would seem to provide a valid indication of difference in life style.

Up to this point, these subcommunity analyses constitute an extension of our work on the metropolitan area as a whole. The explanatory phase of activity analysis comes into play when the "why" question is raised. With respect to these particular study areas, there is a strong inference from participant observation that the heavy emphasis on passive activities by those "not making it" is a consequence of "opting out of the social system," often reinforced by neglect of health and a further withdrawal from active pursuits. Applying the explanatory model to the passive class of activities and controlling for work status brought out very clearly that a marked degree of alienation and a poor state of health showed up most consistently as the top-ranking explanatory factors for those subjects in both communities who were not employed full time and who were in the "not making it" segment of the population. As might be expected, a person's stage in the life cycle was another high-ranking factor positively associated with passive activities. In short, these results say that people from "not making it" circumstances devote a much larger proportion of their free time to passive activities than those "making it." Among the explanatory factors used in our analyses, this heavy emphasis on passive forms of activity is most strongly associated with alienation, poor health, and an advanced stage in the life cycle in both communities by subjects not working full time.

In contrast, for those "making it" and working full time, there is less of a similarity between the communities in factors associated with time allocated to passive activities on weekdays. In the black community those in poor health and having the least concern for social status appeared to emphasize passive activities, and in the white community, those with a marked tendency toward alienation and those in the later stages of the life cycle appeared to emphasize these kinds of activities. Participant observation reports indicate that these are plausible results.

If we turn to the active weekday pursuits and take the polar extremes (those "not making it" who are not employed full time and those "making it" who are employed full time), again the explanatory factors appear to show more similarity in the two communities for those in less favorable than in more favorable circumstances. Thus in both communities those in the least favorable situation who are most predisposed to social exchange are persons who have a low sensitivity to social status and are the least alienated; those most apt to devote time to recreation-diversions are likely to be in the later stages of the life cycle and show a low sensitivity to status considerations. At the other extreme (the "making-it" and working-full-time situation), in both communities social communications activities are emphasized by those from households where there are positive expectations about getting ahead. Although congeniality of surroundings is a high-ranking factor in both communities for social interaction, in the black community a low sensitivity level to violence is the direction of emphasis. On the other hand, in the white community the emphasis is in the direction of a high anxiety about safety in the neighborhood. No patterns were found among the explanatory factors for recreation-diversions for those in more favorable circumstances.

Though field reports from participant observation give some support to these findings, with both investigative approaches attesting to the plausibility of the explanatory model, any claim to validity must await development and test of improved measures under carefully controlled conditions. Meanwhile, even in its present trial form, the model appears to have utility as a tool for exploring the kinds of factors that shape activity patterns. At the very least, this aspect of activity analysis can serve a purpose in scouting out the parameters of community problems.

A LOOK AHEAD

Experience from this trial use of the explanatory model brings out several elements requiring additional development and test and eventually other rounds in the strategy that has been followed in this research. At least three aspects of the conceptual framework would appear to benefit from additional work: (1) further refinement of the "propensity" element, (2) activation and test of the "opportunity" element of the model, and (3) exploration of the dynamics of the satisfaction-dissatisfaction feedback aspect of the schema. Although we do not go into the broader R & D agenda, it may be noted that, beyond these improvements in the descriptive-explanatory framework, there is work to be done in the area of simulation and evaluation.[19]

Further Work on Propensity Element of the Model

In the exploratory applications of the model, we found that, by the measures used, predisposing factors provided a lower level of explanation than preconditioning factors. Although there is no basis on which to conclude that one set of factors could be expected to yield a higher level of explanation than the other, there are some uncertainties connected with the measures used for the former which are not encountered in the latter. Thus work status, sex, and child-care responsibilities can be ascertained with little difficulty, but the individual's feelings of security, status, and achievement are less easily determined. Moreover, the full range of influences that prompt people to engage in an activity are likely to be less easily identified than those that constrain them from engaging in the activity.

Two lines of effort seem particularly important in improving on the performance of this aspect of the model. One would seek improvements in the specification and measurement of security, status, and achievement factors, and the other would seek to expand the scope of the predisposing element, bringing in other motivation factors and broadening this element of the framework to include enjoyment and thoughtway factors. In this last respect, the use of a more encompassing range of felt needs appropriate to each generic class of activity would seem to merit exploration (e.g., a wider selection from Maslow's hierarchy of needs). Also the specification of thoughtways, that is, the collective attitudes concerning particular activities (such as "in-things" to do, taboo activities, etc.), and the use of some measure of enjoyment would seem promising.

Improvements in specification and measurement could well involve offshoot investigations which would emphasize the development or adaptation of scales that provide acceptable surrogates of motivational factors relevant to social communications, recreation-diversions, passive diversions, religious, and other activity configurations to be used in activity analysis. For example, with respect to social communications activities, it may be feasible to merge indices of alienation, social prestige, and achievement, including measures of satisfaction and enjoyment of interpersonal exchanges, to obtain a composite measure that scales the felt need of subjects for social interaction. Used in a merged form or as a set of separate indices, these would certainly represent an improvement over the crude measures used in Chapter VI as predisposing factors. Somewhat different series of indices would probably be more appropriate for recreation and diversions, for passive forms of activity, and so on. Further work along these lines could be expected to bring some improvement in the performance of the model.

Although comments so far relate to the predisposing component of the model, this is not to suggest that the list of constraints included in the preconditioning component is necessarily complete. It may well be that other roles and other factors can be introduced usefully and improve on the performance of the model.

Extensions of the Model

As we proceeded with exploration of the truncated form of the model, there was a strong supposition that its performance could not be fully evaluated until the model included the opportunity component. Moreover, according to the conceptual framework, satisfaction-dissatisfaction levels from previous experience of the subject with an activity could be expected to affect levels of participation and commitment of time to that activity when subsequent opportunities arose to engage in it.

To indicate how these considerations are to be taken into account, Figure VII-1 modifies and enlarges on the beginning version shown in

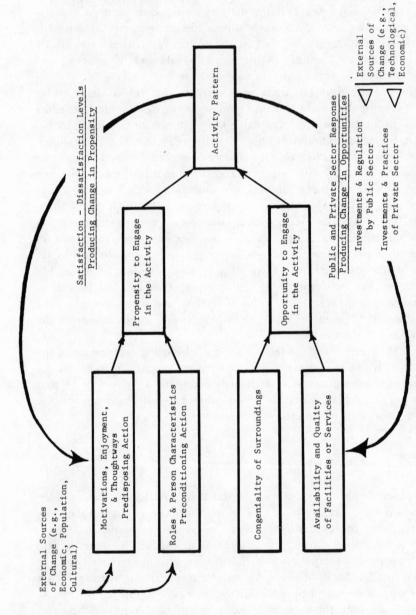

Figure VII-1 Extensions of General Model for Explaining Activity Patterns.

212

Figure II-1 in several respects. In the predisposing element of the upper branch of the model, the individual's enjoyment is made explicit as a factor to be examined in the next round of the research. It should be noted that the composite influence of all these predisposing factors produce what might be called "the preference function" for the activity.

There is a modification also in the opportunity element at the leftmost extremity of the lower branch. A box has been added labeled "congeniality of surroundings," and the original boxes for availability and quality of facility or service have been combined into one box. This modification retains the emphasis of the earlier version of the model on the availability of a service or facility of acceptable quality and accessibility. In this respect, to bring in the sensitivity of subjects to places offering acceptable opportunities, further experimentation in the use of Hightower's Index of Distance Sensitivity developed in the pilot phase of this work would seem important (Chapin and Hightower, 1966). The new box in Figure VII-1 concerning the general congeniality of surroundings has to do with the attractiveness of an opportunity for engaging in the activity, in addition to or in lieu of the availability of a service and facility. Thus in the case of social communications, the perceived congeniality of surroundings for interaction would be a factor affecting the individual's evaluation of the opportunity to engage in an activity. As an illustration, the use of an index of residential satisfaction with the individual's neighborhood, of the kind Zehner has used, would offer a means of evaluating the congeniality of the environment for localized social communications (see Lansing et al., 1970, Chapter 5; and Zehner, 1971).

Another change in the model is the addition of the feedback loop for channeling satisfaction-dissatisfaction back to the predisposing element of the framework. This loop provides the means of updating the preference function following the performance of an activity. The insertion of the feedback loop into the schema has particular relevance for longitudinal studies. It underscores the importance of recording levels of satisfaction or dissastisfaction with activities in an initial survey, so that changes in preference patterns can be assessed in connection with activities recorded in the next succeeding survey and their levels of satisfaction and dissatisfaction. An analysis of changes in satisfaction-dissatisfaction levels provides a basis for establishing the predictive use of preference indices and such devices as the leisure-time game reproduced in Chapter III.

In addition to these extensions of the schema, Figure VII-1 indicates something of the dynamic aspect of the opportunity element in the model. As suggested by the lower loop, activity patterns make an imprint on the public and private sectors whether they occur as planned or unplanned consequences. The point of conjunction between activity systems and land use, community facility, and service systems is indicated in the model by the interface between the propensity to pursue certain activities and the opportunities offered to pursue them through the public and private sectors. If planning and policy in the public sector give systematic attention to the functioning of human activity systems and to activities preferred by people, then appropriate regulatory measures and public investments can be introduced as reinforcement (following Skinnerian concepts) to ensure that opportunities in both the public and private sectors match up with preferences.[20] And if no systematic attention is given to these considerations, an equilibrium between the "demand" and "supply" parts of the model can be affected by the choices people make either in the market (via residential moves) or by social sanctions (for example, by organized consumer boycotts of the kind that have arisen in recent years when the public or private sectors have been unresponsive). Whatever the means, this model portrays how policy and public investment alternatives can be related more purposefully to needs and preferences of various segments of a population.

NOTES

1. Hollingshead and Redlich (1958) develop an approach for establishing an index of social position based on such factors as education and occupation (with a secondary level of differentiation on occupation according to broad income categories). Bogue (1969) proposes an income-education index for measuring social status.

2. In his goals-achievement matrix, Hill (1968) not only stresses the differential effects of favorable and unfavorable consequences accruing to different groups in the community but takes into account differential impacts that combinations of several goals may have on these groups.

3. See footnotes in Table VII-1 for assignment for 12-code activity classes to these three summarizing activity categories. It should be noted that because of proposals in Table VII-2 for regrouping activities, no special importance should be attached to these categories. Since they are based on groupings of activities analyzed in previous chapters, they provide a familiar basis for summarizing variations for background variables.

4. As brought out in previous chapters, participant observation leads us to suspect that the survey on which Table VII-1 is based probably underreports social interaction forms of activity of black subjects in low-income circumstances (who constitute at least a third of the black sample). However, with the relatively small increments of time that are involved in correcting for deficiencies here in interviewer-subject communications, the indications are that the basic emphases in time allocation are not likely to be appreciably affected by such adjustments in the results.

5.   Here a sharply focused investigation of preferences and subcultural attitude patterns with respect to existing alternatives in services and facilities for the use of free time, to perceived opportunities now available in this respect, and to the substitutability of choices at the margin for alternatives perceived by subjects (see the game described in Chapter III) would facilitate evaluation of the demand for recreation and other facilities and services for both black and nonblack subjects.

6.   There is little difference in total free time between low- and above-low-income segments of the population on weekdays and Sundays. Because totals differ for Saturdays (a mean of 6.9 hours for low-income as compared with 8.1 hours for above-low-income subjects), comparisons by day of the week should be on a percentage basis. Obviously the five-day government week is inflating the free time for above-low-income subjects in comparison to the longer work week that is likely to prevail in unskilled or semiskilled occupations where low-income persons are most likely to find employment, if employed at all.

7.   Since there are differences in the total amounts of free time persons at different stages in the life cycle in our sample have, these patterns can be examined more readily in terms of the proportion of total free time subjects within each stage of the life cycle devote to these three activity categories for each of weekdays, Saturdays, and Sundays:

Life Cycle Stage	Social Interaction			Recreation-Diversions			Passive Activities		
	Week-day	Sat.	Sun.	Week-day	Sat.	Sun.	Week-day	Sat.	Sun.
1	27.0	26.5	29.6	41.3	44.6	34.7	31.7	28.9	35.7
2	25.9	32.9	36.4	31.5	32.9	29.5	42.6	34.2	34.1
3	23.8	29.4	31.8	33.9	40.0	20.7	42.3	30.6	47.5
4	19.3	30.0	30.3	31.6	33.7	25.8	49.1	36.3	43.9
5	21.8	22.4	27.9	21.8	18.4	23.7	56.4	59.2	48.4

8.   However, if church attendance is lifted out of the social interaction category and made a separate class as in Table VII-2, Saturday becomes the key socializing day for all but the youngest stage in the life cycle.

9.   See note 7.

10.   See note 7.

11.   In this connection, the "location" and "with whom" information about activities obtained in interviews permits a screening analysis of the intensity of patterns of social interaction. By examining proportions of time spent on these activities within the home, within the immediate neighborhood, and outside the neighborhood, this information can be used as a basis of classifying neighborhoods into levels of internal interaction. When subjects are further grouped according to the extent that interactions are casual or sustained (as determined from the "with whom" information), it is possible to assess the resiliency of interaction patterns. This and attitudinal information concerning the emotional attachments people have to their neighborhood provide insights into the intensity of social disruption that is likely to be involved in programs of family removal.

   The lack of sensitivity to social communications needs of people and the emotional ties they have to their community have been brought out in urban renewal critiques (for example, see Fried and Gleicher, 1961; Rossi and Dentler, 1961; Anderson, 1964; and Bellush and Hausknecht, 1967) and in analyses of the impact of highway programs on residents in the path of expressways (for example see Lupo et al., 1971). The vacuum in planning and policy relating to leisure-time activity patterns and preferences is receiving increased attention (for example, see Gold, 1972).

12.   See note 7.

13.   See note 7.

14.   Referring to the 1969 national data in Table IV-3, compare, for example, the sum of time spent on weekdays on "watching television" and "rest and relaxation" (a mean of 2.89 hours) with the total time allocated on weekdays to discretionary pursuits (a mean of 5.02 hours).

15.   The percentage of subjects at each stage of the life cycle who are engaging in the three categories of free time for different days of the week are as follows:

Life Cycle Stage	Socializing*			Recreation-Diversions*			Watching Television*		
	Week-day	Sat.	Sun.	Week-day	Sat.	Sun.	Week-day	Sat.	Sun.
1	44.1%	47.5%	49.0%	39.5%	33.1%	45.4%	58.4%	52.5%	65.7%
2	35.7	31.3	37.1	25.5	26.7	26.6	65.2	58.0	63.3
3	31.9	33.3	30.2	27.5	31.7	32.9	68.1	60.0	65.8
4	31.7	37.1	34.0	27.2	27.9	25.8	71.5	62.9	71.7
5	45.0	29.7	32.0	38.8	23.4	29.8	75.5	75.0	72.6

* Highest subcategory participation rates are used here rather than generic category rates.

16.   The impact of television on the viewer has been the subject of a number of investigations (for example, see Bower, 1973; and the Surgeon General's Scientific Advisory Committee on Television and Social Behavior, 1972).

17.   See note 11.

18.   Breakdowns indicate that for the participation rate on weekdays spouses (many of whom do not work) are more heavily represented than heads, but that on weekend days there is more equal representation.

19.   Work is already in progress in simulation of human activity systems. For example, see Hemmens (1966, 1970), Brail (1969), and Tomlinson et al. (1973).

20.   It can be argued that an equilibrium can be achieved between the two systems through the creative use of an urban development guidance system (see Chapin, 1963, and Kaiser, 1971).

REFERENCES

Anderson, Martin (1964). *The Federal Bulldozer* (Cambridge, Mass.: The M.I.T. Press).

Bellush, Jewel, and Murray Hausknecht (1967). *Urban Renewal: People, Politics and Planning* (Garden City, N.Y.: Doubleday-Anchor Books).

Brail, Richard K. (1969). *Activity System Investigations: Strategy for Model Design*, Ph.D. dissertation, University of North Carolina (Ann Arbor, Mich.: University Microfilms, Inc.)

Bogue, Donald J. (1969). *Principles of Demography* (New York: John Wiley & Sons, Inc.), Chapter 14.

Bower, Robert T. (1973). *Television and the Public* (New York: Holt, Rinehart and Winston).

Chapin, F. Stuart, Jr. (1963). "Taking Stock of Techniques for Shaping Urban Growth," *Journal of the American Institute of Planners*, **29**:2.

———and Henry C. Hightower (1966). *Household Activity Systems—A Pilot Investigation* (Chapel Hill: Center for Urban and Regional Studies, University of North Carolina).

Fried, Marc, and Peggy Gleicher (1961). "Some Sources of Residential Satisfaction in an Urban Slum," *Journal of the American Institute of Planners*, **27**:4.

Gold, Seymour M. (1972)."Nonuse of Neighborhood Parks," *Journal of the American Institute of Planners*, **38**:6.

Hemmens, George C. (1966). *The Structure of Urban Activity Linkages*, (Chapel Hill: Center for Urban and Regional Studies, University of North Carolina).

——— (1970). "Analysis and Simulation of Urban Activity Patterns," *Socio-Economic Planning Sciences*, **4**:1.

Hill, Morris (1968). "A Goals-Achievement Matrix for Evaluating Alternative Plans," *Journal of the American Institute of Planners*, **34**:1.

Hollingshead, August B., and Frederick C. Redlich (1958). *Social Class and Mental Illness: A Community Study* (New York: John Wiley & Sons, Inc.).

Kaiser, Edward J. (1971). "Planning Urban Development Guidance Systems for Local Government," paper presented at the Annual Meeting of the American Institute of Planners.

Lansing, John B., Robert W. Marans, and Robert B. Zehner (1970). *Planned Residential Environments* (Ann Arbor, Mich.: Institute for Social Research, University of Michigan).

Lupo, Alan, Frank Colcord, and Edmund P. Fowler (1971). *Rites of Way: The Politics of Transportation in Boston and the U.S. City* (Boston: Little, Brown and Company).

Michelson, William (1972). "Environmental Choice: A Draft Report on the Social Basis of Family Decisions on Housing Type and Location in Greater Toronto" (Ottawa: Ministry of State for Urban Affairs).

Rossi, Peter H., and Robert A. Dentler (1961). *The Politics of Urban Renewal* (New York: The Free Press).

The Surgeon General's Scientific Advisory Committee on Television and Social Behavior (1972). *Television and Growing Up: The Impact of Televised Violence*, (Washington, D.C.: U.S. Government Printing Office). See also Reports and Papers, Vols. I–V, *Television and Social Behavior*.

Tomlinson, Janet, N. Bullock, P. Dickens, P. Steadman, and E. Taylor (1973). "A Model of Student's Daily Activity Patterns," *Environment and Planning*, **5**:2.

Zehner, Robert B. (1971). "Neighborhood and Community Satisfaction in New Towns and Less Planned Suburbs," *Journal of the American Institute of Planners*, **37**:6.

APPENDIX

Table A-1. Classification Code for Household Activities (Note: Index of Activities Follows the Coding System)

1. Homemaking

   10. Miscellaneous homemaking and repair activities

      100. Other homemaking, n.e.c.
         --farm work, when living on a farm
         --looking around one's new house or apartment
         --helping spouse or relative with work for school, job, etc.

      101. Trip preparation
         --packing for or unpacking from trips

      102. Preparations for moving
         --packing for or unpacking from a move

      103. Home maintenance and repair, location unspecified
         --other repairs and home maintenance, such as painting,
            carpentry, etc.
         --"work around the house"

      104. Home maintenance and repair, indoor
         --indoor painting, plastering, carpentry, wiring, fixing
            of household appliances, etc.
         --indoor plumbing, upkeep of heat and water supplies

      105. Home maintenance and repair, outdoor
         --painting, carpentry, roofing, etc.
         --snow and ice removal
         --outdoor cleaning (sidewalks, garbage)
         --yardwork and gardening (not hobby)
         --routine car maintenance, washing and cleaning (not hobby)
         --burn trash (outside)

      106. Pet care
         --feeding and care of pets, fowl, livestock, etc. (if not
            income-producing)
         --taking pets out (if this includes going for a walk, code
            concurrent with 640)
         --visiting the veterinarian (for driving a pet to the vet,
            code only travel followed by but not concurrent with 106)
         --pet-centered activities in general--playing with pets, etc.

220

11. Household Operation

110. Routine housework and child care
     --feeding, bathing, and putting (small) children to bed
     --darning and mending (not sewing or dressmaking as hobby--
       when in doubt, assume it isn't a hobby)
     --babysitting* (not for pay, not participating in children's
       activities--generally in home but not always)
     --babysitting* for someone else (not for pay--we can't always
       establish whether pay is involved)
     -- preparing and cooking food
     -- doing dishes, cleaning up after meals
     --laundry and ironing at home
     --waiting on the needs of other adults or teenagers, getting
       them up, bringing them things, helping in personal care
     --other indoor cleaning and housework
     --all baby care
     --cleaning silver

111. Other child-centered activities over and above their
     subsistence, n.e.c.
     --playing with children, indoor games and instruction
       (family "babysitting," nonpaying, with participation in
       their activities (could be 523 instead)
     --outdoor games with children (concurrent with 55_ or 57_)
     --taking children for a walk, for their enjoyment or benefit
       (concurrent with 640)--not for taking kids to school or
       busstop
     --talking, discussing children's activities and affairs
       with them
     --listening to child sing or play musical instruments
     --singing or playing musical instruments with children
       (concurrent with 551)
     --helping children with their hobbies
     --participating in family group projects and hobbies (con-
       current with 55_)

---

*Babysitting rule: If babysitting or childcare is explicitly mention-
ed and appears to be a concurrent activity, do not code it as a
concurrent activity unless

1) the other activity is not 110

2) babysitting or childcare appears to occupy a significant portion of the respondent's attention, and

3) simply recording the kids as participants is not
   adequate.

In all cases involving babysitting or childcare, the kids should be
listed as participants if that information is known.

111. Other child-centered activities (cont.)

-- taking children to lectures, talks, for their benefit
     or enjoyment (concurrent with 311)
-- taking children to visit other cultural places (concurrent
     with 313)
-- punishing children
-- sending children out to play or on errands
-- all other

112. Reading to children

113. Organizing, preparing for, and attending children's parties,
     (includes dances and parties), n.e.c.

114. Child supervision

-- helping with or overseeing children's homework, practice, etc.

115. Children's organized activities, n.e.c.: organizing, prepar-
     ing for, attending, or participating in such activities as

-- children's plays, recitals, sports (e.g., Little League)
-- Scouting, "Y," teen activities
-- various other organizational activities n.e.c. where the
     individual functions as a parent on matters specifically
     related to his own child (other than PTA meetings, con-
     ferences with teachers, etc.)
-- holiday activities and rituals, with the family or away
     from home, such as easter egg hunts, caroling at Christ-
     mas, Halloween trick or treating

116. Concern with children's education

-- PTA activities (if children take part, code 115)
-- conferences and visits with school teachers, officials,
     counselors, etc., about one's child

12. Shopping and household business

120. Shopping or household business, n.e.c. or unknown

-- window shopping (concurrent with 640)

121. Retail goods

-- convenience goods (food, drug, hardware, variety,
     optician, etc.)
-- shopper goods (clothing, shoes, fabrics, etc.)
-- consumer durables (home furnishings, sporting goods,
     automobiles, etc.)

122. Retail services

   -- caterers, etc.
   -- home cleaning services, domestic employment services
   -- laundry, dry cleaning, etc., laundromat
   -- tailoring, dressmakers for custom tailoring

123. Personal services

   -- barber, beauty, pedicure, sauna, masseur, etc.

124. Repair services

   -- repair of automobiles, appliances, and other consumer
       durables
   -- contractors, home repair services
   -- tailors, dressmakers for repair, mending

125. Nonmedical, non-real estate professional services

   -- special services of lawyers, accountants, tax consultants,
       financial institutions, and brokers (not routine banking, etc.)

126. Househunting on one's own; looking at houses, property for
     sale (when not owned by R)

127. Use of real estate services in househunting, seeing model homes

128. Other real estate services

   -- leasing out of rental properties
   -- handling the sale of properties, homes

129. Household business and related errands (not travel itself)

   -- routine use of governmental services and agencies (for non-
       routine, see 031)--e.g., post office, applying for and
       taking examinations for permits and licenses, welfare
       services, etc.
   -- routine use of private services (banks, ticket offices,
       telegraph offices, etc.)
   -- reading and writing letters for household business, writing
       checks, paying bills by mail, keeping records, etc.
   -- talking over household business matters with spouse
   -- telephoning for purposes of household business
   -- paying bills at company or agency offices
   -- seeing salesmen, peddlers who arrive unsolicited, agents,
       interviewers
   -- showing repair men, inspectors, etc., around
   -- writing invitations to parties
   -- paying hotel bills; checking into hotels, airports, etc.
   -- picking up or dropping off items, misc. errands
   -- picking up paychecks when not done on company time
   -- moving a car, finding a parking space, feeding the meter, etc.

2. Vocation-Oriented Activities

Work breaks will not be separated from work unless (1) R changes location or (2) specifically says what was done (e.g., played cards)

20. Miscellaneous vocation-oriented activities

200. Other vocation-oriented activities, n.e.c.

201. Military reserve duty (nights, weekends, summer camp)

202. Non-employment, non-job income-producing activities

-- managing or maintaining own property for rental
-- analysis of stock market
-- making a hobby pay
-- babysitting for pay (nonfamily) and related chores, such as bathing, feeding, etc.
-- contests
-- carrying groceries, running errands for pay
-- other income-producing activities

203. Job-hunting

-- reading want ads, use of employment services
-- medical examination for prospective employer, induction physical for military
-- interview, filing job application, etc.

204. Professional welfare

-- union activities: meetings and business, strikes and picketing
-- professional society or industry association activities, meetings, conventions, etc. and business and errands for these
-- other

21. Third job

210. Other job-required activities

-- worker-management relations
-- other

211. Job-required education and training

-- off-the-job civilian training, job sponsored or endorsed
-- off-the-job short courses for improving income-producing potential, including correspondence and TV courses, and related study time

212. Overtime work

    -- business phone calls during nonwork hours
    -- business transacted over meals (concurrent with 006)
    -- bringing work home from the office
    -- overtime work at the office, at a client's location,
        or at other locations

213. Work during regular working hours or shift

    -- all work-related tasks
    -- nonwork breaks, interruptions on the job, routine
        breaks, n.e.c.
    -- on-the-job training
    -- trips at work, waiting and delay time

22. Second job

220. Other job-required activities

    -- worker-management relations
    -- other

221. Job-required education and training

    -- off-the-job civilian training, job sponsored or endorsed
    -- off-the-job short courses for improving income-producing
        potential, including correspondence and TV courses,
        and related study time

222. Overtime work

    -- business phone calls during nonwork hours
    -- business transacted over meals (concurrent with 006)
    -- bringing work home from the office
    -- overtime work at the office, at a client's location,
        or at other locations

223. Work during regular working hours or shift

    -- all work-related tasks
    -- nonwork breaks, interruptions on the job, routine
        breaks, n.e.c.
    -- on-the-job training
    -- trips at work, waiting and delay time

23. Primary job

230. Other job-required activities

    -- worker-management relations
    -- other

231. Job-required education and training

    -- off-the-job civilian training, job-sponsored or endorsed
    -- off-the-job short courses for improving income-producing
        potential, including correspondence and TV courses,
        and related study time

232. Overtime work

    -- business phone calls during nonwork hours
    -- business transacted over meals (concurrent with 006)
    -- bringing work home from the office
    -- overtime work at the office, at a client's location,
        or at other locations

233. Work during regular working hours or shift

    -- all work-related tasks
    -- military service as principal job, either professional
        or normal tour of duty
    -- nonwork breaks, interruptions on the job, routine
        breaks, n.e.c.
    -- on-the-job training
    -- trips at work
    -- waiting and delay time
    -- preparation for work at place of employment, e.g., put-
        ting on uniform (unless it takes longer than one
        hour, in which case use code 230)

24. Education toward a degree, certificate, diploma, etc., including short courses and institutes, adult classes, and TV courses,
plus related study time; nonjob-required

    240. Other education, n.e.c., level unknown

    241. Pre-elementary education

    242. Elementary education*

    243. Junior high school*

    244. Senior high school*

    245. College or university

    246. Business or technical school

    247. Preparing for school, n.e.c.

    250. Education (study)-- O.K. if for a degree or if job-required

* No special rules as to what grades are included in each--accept the
respondent's classification, if given.

3. Religious and Cultural Activities

   30. Religious activities

      300. Other religious activities, n.e.c., unknown

      301. Family and private devotions

         -- reading the bible, praying, family religious instructions
         -- worship other than church services and Mass

      302. Retreats, revivals, religious conferences

      303. Non-social activities of church groups

         -- meetings and administrative activities of church
             auxiliaries, circles, etc.
         -- meetings of religious clubs or groups, such as the
             Knights of Columbus
         -- choir or organ practice

      304. Church services

         -- attending church services, singing in the choir at a
             church service
         -- teaching or attending Sunday School
         -- preparing Sunday School lessons (at home)

      305. Church organization and business (nonjob)

         -- meetings of elders, financial committees, etc.
         -- related administrative activities, whenever and
             wherever carried out (phone calls, etc.)

      306. Church beneficience

         -- church or church-sponsored group community service
             activities for the poor, sick, etc., requiring church
             membership for participation

      307. Attending funerals, visiting the cemetery, sympathy
         visits connected with death

      308. Weddings, christenings, confirmations, and ordinations,
         related receptions when in same place (receptions else-
         where, code 521)

      309. Other religious ceremonies

31. **Cultural activities**

    310. Other cultural activities, n.e.c.

    311. Lectures

        -- irregular symposia or seminars, not part of the activities of a member's organization, nonjob, non-educational curriculum
        -- occasional talks, speeches, n.e.c., but not political rallies, member's organization

    312. Theatre

        -- live shows, pagents, music festivals
        -- plays, concerts, operas
        -- burlesque, comedies

    313. Cultural facilities in the metropolitan area

        -- art galleries, museums, and special exhibits of professional, academic or civic societies and associations
        -- observatories and planetariums, etc.

    314. Visits to the zoo, botanical gardens, arboreta, etc.

    315. Visiting and touring interesting buildings and private or public agencies, such as the Capitol, the U.S. Mint, the Library of Congress (but not actual use of), etc. (but not historical sites and monuments per se)

    316. Visiting and using the library

    317. Listening to phonograph records, tapes*

    318. Listening to the radio*

    319. Watching television (news, nonlocal sports, etc.)*

32. **Reading**

    320. Miscellaneous reading, n.e.c., type unknown, including comic books*

    321. Reading books, encyclopedia, etc.*

    322. Reading magazines, pamphlets, etc.*

    323. Reading newspapers*

---

* Do not make these concurrent with relaxation

33. **Education for its own sake, not toward a degree, etc., nonjob related, including study time**

    330. Other, n.e.c., type unknown

        -- adult education, not toward a degree, not job-related
        -- speed reading courses, etc.
        -- driving lessons (if actually driving, concurrent with
            61_)
        -- other

    331. Academic instruction

        -- short courses and institutes, no degree, not job-related
        -- self-study, correspondence and TV courses

    332. Creative instruction

        -- music, singing lessons
        -- ballet, art, drama lessons

    333. Instruction in social activities

        -- ballroom dancing lessons, etc.
        -- instructions in etiquette, poise, charm schools, etc.

4. **Visiting**

    40. **Miscellaneous face-to-face visiting, talking, conversations**

        400. Other visiting, n.e.c., type not specified

            -- "husband got home" (when a duration specified)
            -- quarreling, fighting
            -- "drop in for a while"
            -- "spent some time there"

        401. Meeting and visiting by prior arrangement

            -- pre-arranged social calls, in person, wherever they
                occur, frequently concurrent with meals (006), as
                in the case of dinner with friends

        402. Visiting the sick, at home, in hospitals, etc.

        403. Helping others, n.e.c., not for pay (if for pay see
            202). Make sure codes 110, 129, 801 do not apply

41. Face-to-face visiting and conversations, not by prior arrangement (when in doubt, assume meetings are not by prior arrangement)

 410. Spontaneous conversations, location unknown

 411. Visiting in private clubs

 412. Visiting in public places, including street and yard area in front of house (must have participants, otherwise code 542)

  -- talking in streets, yards, parks, etc.
  -- conversations in stores, hotels, churches, etc.

 413. Visiting in catering establishments such as cafes, bars, restaurants, etc. (Code 519 unless R expressly mentions visiting, in which case code 413; not to be concurrent with 006--assumed to include 006)

 414. Dropping in and visiting in residences

  -- relatives, friends dropping in
  -- talking and gossiping with family members (not household business or helping in children's affairs)

42. Remote visiting and conversations

 420. Other, n.e.c., unknown, including phone calls of unknown nature

 421. Social telephone calls to friends, relatives

 422. Social correspondence by mail

  -- writing and reading letters to friends, relatives
  -- writing and reading Christmas, Easter, birthday, anniversary cards
  -- making and listening to recordings (e.g., as sent to servicemen)

5. Leisure and Recreation Activities

50. Miscellaneous leisure and recreation activities

 500. Other leisure and recreation, n.e.c., unknown

  -- "went outside" with no explanation of activities; taking pictures; "messing around," smoking, watching adult activities, e.g., card game (code watching of children as 110); watching misc. spontaneous events, e.g., fire, riots, gang fights, eclipses, etc. or just looking around.

230

501. Dating, n.e.c., activity unknown

507. Going for a walk for recreation*

508. Going for a bicycle ride for recreation*

509. Going for a drive around town for pleasure*

51. Amusements

510. Other amusements, n.e.c.

511. Spectator amusements (not movies)

    -- circuses, rodeos, horseshows

512. Participant amusements

    -- amusement parks; rides, shooting galleries, etc. at
       fairs and carnivals
    -- miniature golf, go-cart tracks
    -- pool hall, billiard parlor
    -- shooting pool anywhere

513. Shows and exhibitions (except when part of fairs or
     museums)

    -- dog, auto, boat shows
    -- fashion shows; dog field trials

514. Parades, holiday festivals, ceremonies

515. Boat and plane rides (not trips)

516. Excursions around town (not overnight)

    -- visits to memorials and monuments, historical sites,
       quaint parts of town, etc.

517. Movies

518. Gambling establishments

    -- slot machines, wherever located
    -- table gambling games in establishments

---

*Code 507, 508, 509 alone and not concurrent with a 600 code.

519. Nightclubs and bars

    -- nightclubs, including dinner and dancing (concurrent
         with 006 if eating is involved)
    -- taverns, bars, discoteques, music halls, etc.

52. Private or organizational parties and social life

520. Other social activities, n.e.c., unknown

521. Parties

    -- cocktail parties, receptions
    -- coffees, teas, brunches, luncheon parties (concurrent
         with 003) Note: dinner parties normally coded 401
         or 414 concurrent with 003
    -- showers, etc.
    -- attending adult birthday parties

522. Organized socials

    -- banquets and dinners (unless codable as the meetings
         of organizations, 72_) (Concurrent with 003 or 006)
    -- other organized socials
    -- church socials

523. Games

    -- table games: cards, bingo, monopoly, etc.
    -- parlor games: charades, twenty questions, etc.
    -- solitary games: crossword puzzles, solitaire, etc.
    if with children, indicate by participants--do not make
    concurrent with 111

524. Dances

    -- square or ballroom dancing at private clubs, organiza-
         tions, schools (except for nightclubs, children's
         activities)
    -- dancing at home

525. Picnics and outings

53. Vacation-site activities (Reserve these codes for activities
specifically related to the type of vacation site; use 110,
etc. for regular activities.)

530. Other vacation-site activities, nature unknown

531. Camp-making

532. Mountain-oriented, n.e.c.

533. Snow-oriented, n.e.c.

534. Water-oriented, n.e.c.

535. Farm-oriented, n.e.c., country home

536. Touring, not in Washington metro. area

537. Sightseeing, not in Washington metro. area

538. Honeymooning

54. Rest and relaxation

540. Napping, resting, lying down

541. Relaxing

-- sunbathing
-- sitting, rocking, daydreaming, thinking, planning
(not household business)
-- going outdoors to relax in the evening

542. Standing on the street corner (if talking, code 412).
No participants, if there are, code 412. Do not need to
code 542 and 412 concurrent.

543. Hanging out at a playground, recreation center, civic
building, or elsewhere, n.e.c.

-- hanging out at school when R did not have education
in mind

55. Hobbies and crafts

550. All other hobbies, crafts, collections and handiworks,
n.e.c. and nature unknown, including recording one's
voice when reason is unknown

551. Creative arts as hobbies

-- music, playing and practice (not in conjunction with
instruction)
-- painting, sculpture, creative writing (non-instructional,
non-income-producing)

552. Automobiles (other than normal maintenance)

553. Carpentry (other than normal house repairs)

554. Sewing and similar activities

-- dressmaking and non-housework sewing
-- crochet work, needlepoint, weaving, making hookrugs,
knitting, etc.

555. Gardening (other than normal yardwork)

    -- potting plants, etc., indoors or outdoors
    -- tending a garden, flowers, shrubbery, etc.

56-57. <u>Participant sports and sports lessons</u>

560. Other participant sports, n.e.c., unknown

    -- e.g., roller-skating
    -- playing in the streets n.e.c. , pitching pennies, craps

561. Field sports

    -- organized teams or neighborhood games of football,
        baseball, soccer, field hockey, lacross, rugby, etc.

562. Gym or hard surface: individual sports

    -- boxing, basketball practice

563. Gym or hard surface: team sports

    -- basketball, volleyball, etc.

564. Ice sports, individual

    -- skating

565. Ice sports, team

    -- ice hockey

566. Tennis

567. Golf

    -- regulation course
    -- par three courses, driving ranges

568. Bowling

569. Handball

570. Squash

571. Pool sports
    -- swimming, diving, water polo, etc.

572. Open water sports

    -- swimming, diving
    -- boating, sailing, waterskiing

573. Pick-up sports

    -- badminton, ping-pong, croquet, frisby, fly kites, etc.
    -- catch (football, baseball), shooting baskets
    -- workouts, gym or track, exercise, running, etc.

574. Park-oriented sports, sports not requiring special facilities

    -- walking (concurrent with 640)
    -- horseback riding
    -- cycling (concurrent with 642)
    -- automobile rallying (concurrent with 61_)

575. Sports in a natural environment

    -- hiking, climbing, spelunking (caving)
    -- hunting, fishing, shooting
    -- skiing, surfing, tobogganing

58. Spectator sports

580. Other spectator sports, n.e.c., unknown

    -- e.g., ski meets, winter sports events

581. Stadium (field) sports

    -- football, baseball, soccer, lacross, track, polo, etc.

582. Arena and gymnasium sports

    -- ice hockey, skating, etc.
    -- gymnastics, boxing, wrestling
    -- basketball, roller derby, etc.
    -- indoor tennis matches

583. Racetrack and speedway sports

    -- auto racing, horse racing, dog racing

584. Golf matches

585. Tennis matches (outdoor)

586. Pool sports

    -- swimming meets, diving exhibitions, etc.

587. Watching spectator sports on TV

6. Movement and Transportation

60. Other transportation

600. Other mode of transportation, n.e.c., unknown

61. Automobile transportation

    610. Automobile, individual status unknown

    611. Automobile, driver (not to serve passenger)*

    612. Automobile, drive to serve passenger (who must be in the car except for a round trip)*

    613. Automobile, ride as passenger

62. Public transportation

    620. Public transportation, n.e.c., mode unknown

    621. Taxicab

    622. Local mass transit (within whole metro area)
        -- bus
        -- subway, elevated, trolley
        -- tram
        -- boat, hydrafoil
        -- helicopter (e.g., downtown-to-airport service)

    623. Intercity travel (outside SMSA)
        -- bus
        -- train
        -- boat
        -- airplane

63. Terminal waiting time (excluding delays while in transit)

    630. Waiting at a particular location for a transportation vehicle (may be concurrent with other activities)
        -- waiting to be picked up by automobile
        -- waiting in an automobile to pick up a rider
        -- waiting for busses, trains, planes, boats, etc.
        -- picking up, dropping off passengers with duration

64. Self-locomotion and similar modes

    640. Walking

    641. Motorcycle and motor-scooter

    642. Bicycle

---

*If a trip was to serve a passenger (who need not be in the car for all trip segments) code 612 unless the trip was necessary for the respondent to participate in a non-passenger serving activity at the ultimate destination, in which case code 611.

7. <u>Public Affairs (Other than Church or Union Activities, and Other than Social Functions)</u>

70. <u>Miscellaneous membership organizations, n.e.c., unknown, when not an employee of such an organization</u>

700. Nature of activity unknown, n.e.c., all unknown "meeting" activities

701. Organization-sponsored community service activities (not church beneficience)

702. Attendance at regular meetings of organizations by members

703. Business and administrative duties for a member's organization

-- special committee meetings
-- elective office functions
-- errands, duties, business, etc., whenever and wherever carried out (including phone calls, writing letters, etc.), fund-raising, publicity, cleaning up, etc.

71. <u>Public-serving non-partisan organizations, such as the League of Women Voters, civic betterment groups, Jaycees and the Chamber of Commerce, etc., when not an employee of such an organization</u>

710. Nature of activity unknown, n.e.c.

711. Organization-sponsored community service activities

712. Attendance at meetings of organization by members

713. Business and administrative duties for a member's organization

-- special committee meetings
-- elective office functions
-- errands, duties, business, etc., whenever and wherever carried out (including phone calls, writing letters, etc.), fund-raising, publicity, cleaning up, etc.

72. <u>Fellowship and special interest organizations, such as lobbies and political influence groups (but not political parties, unions, or industry associations), alumni groups, patriotic and fraternal groups (e.g., D.A.R., V.F.W., Rotary, etc.), groups supporting the arts, etc., when not an employee of such an organization</u>

720. Nature of activity unknown, n.e.c.

721. Organization-sponsored community service activities

722. Attendance at regular meetings of organizations by members

723. Business and administrative duties for a member's organization

-- special committee meetings
-- elective office functions
-- errands, duties, business, etc., whenever and wherever carried out (including phone calls, writing letters, etc.), fund-raising, publicity, cleaning up, etc.

73. Hobby clubs, music appreciation groups, garden clubs, boys' clubs, church groups, etc. (for non-religious activities)

730. Nature of activity unknown, n.e.c., including hanging out

731. Organization-sponsored community service activities

732. Attendance at regular meetings of organizations by members (if hobby activity per se is performed, code concurrent with 55_)

733. Business and administrative duties for a member's organization

-- special committee meetings
-- elective office functions
-- errands, duties, business, etc., whenever and wherever carried out (including phone calls, writing letters, etc.), fund-raising, publicity, cleaning up, etc.

74. Volunteer community services where membership in an organization is not required

740. Volunteer community service, n.e.c., unknown

741. Fund-raising activities with community-wide appeal, such as those for the United Appeal or Community Chest, Heart Fund, etc.

742. Disaster relief (flood, fires, storms, etc.)

743. Hospital volunteer work (other than for an organization or church)

744. Working with civic agencies as a non-employee, non-member volunteer

-- volunteer work with Upward Bound, VISTA, Job Corps, etc., not as an employee or parent
-- other humanitarian and "cause" activities

745. Protests, rallies, demonstrations when not participating as a member of an organization (non-partisan, other than labor disputes)

746. Receipt of a community organization's services, n.e.c.; stopping by its offices or centers

75. Political party activities (when not a paid employee)

750. Nature of activity unknown, n.e.c.

751. Special committee meetings, strategy sessions, other policy decisions and administration

752. Routine office work, such as could be performed by volunteers

753. General meetings

754. Fund-raising activities, canvassing and campaign activities, in person or by telephone, special voter services such as driving voters to polls, etc.

76. Civic duties and responsibilities, non-organizational

760. Other duties, n.e.c., unknown

761. Registering to vote, voting

762. Attending public hearings, presenting opinions before public boards and committees

763. Jury duty, subpoenaed testimony

764. Serving as an ex-officio member of public agency boards, citizen review committees, etc., by appointment or election but without remuneration

8. Health and Medical Services

80. Health and medical services

800. Other health and medical activities, n.e.c., unknown, including visits to hospitals for unknown reasons

801. Caring for a sick person, including one's children, not for pay, also elderly, feeble, etc.

802. Illness (at home)

-- sick in bed
-- resting because feeling poorly
-- convalescing at home
-- other personal medical care and treatment
-- under professional care of a nurse, at home

803. Inpatient at hospital, clinic, rest home, etc.

804. Outpatient visits to hospitals, clinics, doctor's offices, etc., MD but not psychiatric services

805. Accompanying others (including one's children) to hospitals, clinics, doctor's offices, etc., MD but not psychiatric services; optometrists

806. Visiting psychologists and psychiatrists, office or clinic

807. Visiting dentists, dental clinics, orthodontists

808. Visits to non-MD, non-DDS services, such as opticians, osteopaths, orthopedists, oculists and astrologers, pharmacists for advice, etc.

809. Accompanying others (including one's children) to dental, psychiatric, or non-MD offices, clinics or services

9. (blank)

0. Miscellaneous Activities

00. Other Subsistence and unknown activities

000. Activity code for no concurrent activity

001. Unknown activities, other activities n.e.c. including "arrived" as a single activity with a duration

002. Personal care activities

-- personal washing and dressing
-- all other private activities
-- "getting up" with duration
-- "get ready for. . ." (at home)
Code "went to bed" with a duration less than ½ hour as 002--then code 016.

003. Eating in residences

-- eating meals and snacks at home and other residences

004. Drinking in residences, not with meals (coffee, cocktails, etc.)

005. Communication, unknown content

006. Eating and drinking in establishments, non-residences (code beer and cocktails as tavern, 519)
-- eating out at a restaurant, grill, etc.
-- eating at place of work
-- eating listed as concurrent with other activities
     (parties, luncheons, etc.)
-- all other eating

240

01. Sleep*

    010. Sleep, location unknown

    011. Sleep in second home, wherever located

    012. Sleep in staffed facilities (nonbusiness trip)
        -- hotels, motels, ships, etc.

    013. Sleep in unstaffed facilities (nonbusiness trips)
        -- camp, resort, cottages, etc.

    014. Sleep in the home of another person (nonbusiness trip)

    015. Sleep on a business trip, whatever facilities

    016. Sleep at home in D.C. Metropolitan Area

02. Non-travel Waiting Time

    020. Non-job waiting time (other than waiting for transportation for self--may wait with others who are seeking transport), may be a concurrent activity

        -- trying to park, waiting for someone (concurrent with 61_)
        -- waiting for other individuals, looking for them
        -- waiting for an activity to start, etc.
        -- frustrated, unsuccessful activities

    021. Out-of-home preparation

---

*When in doubt between 01 and 540, code 540 if the sleep is discretionary; if it is obligatory (part of the sleep all people must have), code 01. Usually daytime sleep will be 540. Doubt may arise if person works nights.

250

Table A-2. Key to Code Transformations in Forming 40- and 12-Code Activity Classes

40-Code System	Activity Class	3-Digit Code Groupings	12-Code System
Obligatory Activities			
01	Miscellaneous	-001, 020-021	11
02	Main Job	-131, 230, 232-233	01
03	Other income-related	-132, 200-204, 210-213, 220-223, 231 . .	11
04	Personal care	-002.	11
05	Eating	-003-004, 006	02
06	Shopping	-120-124.	03
07	Sick or utilization of medical care services	-402, 800, 802-809.	11
08	Maintenance of home, yard or car	-103-105.	04
09	Housework and child care	-110, 801	04
10	Misc. household chores, including pet care or walking the dog	-100, 106, 644.	04
11	Household business	-101-102, 125-129, 133-134, 307,612,630 .	04
12	Education	-240-246, 250	11
Discretionary Activities			
13	Child-centered activities	-111, 112, 115, 117-119	05
14	Visiting, writing letters, phoning relatives	-423-425, 430, 440, 445, 590.	05
15	Overseeing children's study, practice	-113-114, 116, 643.	05
16	Family outings or drives	-514-516, 525, 575, 656-659	05
17	Talking and visiting within family	-138, 308, 400-401, 410-414, 538.	05
18	Visiting, writing letters, phoning friends at home	-005, 420-422, 432, 442, 447, 592	06
19	Visiting in the neighborhood	-431, 441, 446, 591	06
20	Visiting outside the neighborhood	-433, 443, 448, 593	06
21	Other socializing activities	-309, 434, 501, 518-522, 524, 526	06
22	Relaxing, loafing, resting or napping	-540-543.	10
23	Reading newspapers, magazines or nonspecified material	-320, 322-323	08
24	Reading books	-321.	08
25	Cultural activities	-310-317, 330-333, 529, 551	08
26	Movies	-517.	08
27	Television	-319, 587	09
28	Radio	-318.	08
29	Crafts and hobbies	-550, 552-555	08
30	Walking and cycling	-645-646, 648-649	08
31	Driving about, sightseeing (not with family)	-650-654, 660-669	08
32	Participant sports	-560-576, 647	08
33	Spectator sports	-137, 510-513, 527-528, 580-586	08
34	Out-of-town holidays	-130, 136-139	11
35	Other recreation	-500, 523, 530-537.	08
36	Religious activities	-300-306.	07
37	Meetings of voluntary organizations	-700, 702-703, 712, 722, 730, 732-733 . .	07
38	Public affairs and service activities	-701, 710-711, 713, 720-721, 723, 731, 740-745, 750-754, 760-764.	07
39	Travel including waiting for travel	-600-642.	*
40	Sleep	-010-016.	12

*In this coding system travel is assigned to the activity for which it was incurred.

Table A-3. Activities of Heads of Households and Spouses, *Average Weekday*—Washington, 1968

Code No.	Activity Category	% Engaging in Activity (n=1,667)	Mean Hours Spent Per Participant		Mean Hours Spent Per Capita	
			Activity	Travel	Activity	Travel
Obligatory Activities						
01	Miscellaneous	.40	0.54	0.04	0.21	0.02
02	Main job	.58	7.77	0.97	4.49	0.57
03	Other income-related	.03	3.39	0.45	0.12	0.01
04	Personal care	.84	0.89	0.00	0.75	0.00
05	Eating	.96	1.63	0.11	1.56	0.11
06	Shopping	.36	1.02	0.57	0.36	0.21
07	Sick or utilization of medical care services	.06	2.03	0.34	0.12	0.02
08	Maintenance of home, yard or car	.11	1.65	0.01	0.19	0.00
09	Housework and childcare	.66	3.46	0.00	2.28	0.00
10	Misc. household chores, including pet care or walking	.06	0.76	0.05	0.05	0.00
11	Household business	.24	0.80	0.14	0.19	0.03
12	Education	.04	4.84	0.57	0.18 (10.49)	0.02 (1.00)
Discretionary Activities						
13	Child-centered activities	.10	1.12	0.08	0.10	0.01
14	Visiting, writing letters, phoning relatives	.06	1.80	0.14	0.11	0.01
15	Overseeing children's study, practice	.04	0.99	0.03	0.04	0.00
16	Family outings or drives	.01	2.26	0.11	0.03	0.00
17	Talking and visiting within family	.17	1.28	0.02	0.22	0.00
18	Visiting, writing letters, phoning friends at home	.22	1.46	0.00	0.32	0.00
19	Visiting in the neighborhood	.04	1.43	0.03	0.06	0.00
20	Visiting outside the neighborhood	.14	1.64	0.25	0.22	0.04
21	Other socializing activities	.04	1.95	0.50	0.09	0.02
22	Relaxing, loafing, resting or napping	.21	1.78	0.00	0.38	0.00
23	Reading newspapers, magazines or nonspecified material	.46	1.23	0.00	0.56	0.00
24	Reading books	.06	1.49	0.00	0.08	0.00
25	Cultural activities	.06	1.61	0.19	0.10	0.01
26	Movies	.02	2.28	0.64	0.04	0.01
27	Television	.67	2.46	0.01	1.64	0.01
28	Radio	.06	1.00	0.01	0.06	0.00
29	Crafts and hobbies	.03	1.90	0.02	0.06	0.00
30	Walking and cycling	.03	0.98	0.00	0.03	0.00
31	Driving about, sightseeing (not with family)	.01	0.90	0.00	0.01	0.00
32	Participant sports	.06	1.50	0.21	0.09	0.01
33	Spectator sports	.01	1.90	0.51	0.01	0.01
34	Out-of-town holidays	.02	7.16	0.00	0.17	0.00
35	Other recreation	.02	1.18	0.03	0.03	0.00
36	Religious activities	.04	1.66	0.26	0.07	0.01
37	Meetings of voluntary organizations	.01	1.97	0.46	0.02	0.01
38	Public affairs and service activities	.01	2.02	0.43	0.00 (4.56)	0.00 (0.16)
39	Travel including waiting for travel	.83	1.40	-	1.16	-
40	Sleep	.99	7.50	0.00	7.46	0.00

Note: Time allocated to concurrent activities is evenly split between these activities.

Table A-4. Activities of Heads of Households and Spouses, *Average Saturday*—Washington, 1968

Code No.	Activity Category	% Engaging in Activity (n=807)	Mean Hours Spent Per Participant Activity	Travel	Mean Hours Spent Per Capita Activity	Travel
Obligatory Activities						
01	Miscellaneous	.36	0.69	0.07	0.25	0.03
02	Main job	.18	6.64	0.73	1.20	0.13
03	Other income related	.02	7.86	0.41	0.17	0.01
04	Personal care	.72	0.95	0.00	0.68	0.00
05	Eating	.90	1.75	0.12	1.57	0.11
06	Shopping	.48	1.55	0.72	0.75	0.34
07	Sick or utilization of medical care services	.05	3.36	0.54	0.15	0.03
08	Maintenance of home, yard or car	.21	3.00	0.02	0.63	0.00
09	Housework and childcare	.67	3.57	0.01	2.39	0.01
10	Misc. household chores, including pet care or walking	.03	1.01	0.05	0.04	0.00
11	Household business	.21	1.00	0.20	0.21	0.04
12	Education	.01	5.77	0.57	0.07	0.01
					(8.11)	(0.71)
Discretionary Activities						
13	Child-centered activities	.09	1.50	0.10	0.14	0.01
14	Visiting, writing letters, phoning relatives	.10	2.67	0.31	0.26	0.03
15	Overseeing children's study, practice	.02	1.01	0.02	0.02	0.00
16	Family outings or drives	.02	1.62	0.38	0.03	0.01
17	Talking and visiting within family	.17	2.86	0.03	0.50	0.01
18	Visiting, writing letters, phoning friends at home	.18	2.18	0.00	0.39	0.00
19	Visiting in the neighborhood	.04	1.95	0.03	0.08	0.00
20	Visiting outside the neighborhood	.12	2.82	0.52	0.33	0.06
21	Other socializing activities	.08	2.99	0.69	0.24	0.06
22	Relaxing, loafing, resting or napping	.24	2.11	0.00	0.51	0.00
23	Reading newspapers, magazines or nonspecified material	.33	1.45	0.00	0.48	0.00
24	Reading books	.04	2.01	0.00	0.07	0.00
25	Cultural activities	.05	1.84	0.42	0.10	0.02
26	Movies	.04	2.89	0.67	0.11	0.02
27	Television	.60	2.92	0.00	1.75	0.00
28	Radio	.05	1.25	0.00	0.06	0.00
29	Crafts and hobbies	.03	2.47	0.00	0.07	0.00
30	Walking and cycling	.02	1.61	0.00	0.04	0.00
31	Driving about, sightseeing (not with family)	.01	1.18	0.00	0.02	0.00
32	Participant sports	.05	2.13	0.27	0.11	0.02
33	Spectator sports	.02	3.22	0.61	0.08	0.01
34	Out-of-town holidays	.08	10.91	0.00	0.85	0.00
35	Other recreation	.03	1.56	0.07	0.04	0.00
36	Religious activities	.05	2.16	0.21	0.12	0.01
37	Meetings of voluntary organizations	.01	1.99	0.42	0.01	0.00
38	Public affairs and service activities	.01	2.06	0.36	0.03	0.00
					(6.43)	(0.27)
39	Travel including waiting for travel	.74	1.33	–	0.98	–
40	Sleep	.99	8.26	0.00	8.16	0.00

Note: Time allocated to concurrent activities is evenly split between these activities.

Table A-5. Activities of Heads of Households and Spouses, *Average Sunday*—Washington, 1968

Code No.	Activity Category	% Engaging in Activity (n=802)	Mean Hours Spent Per Participant		Mean Hours Spent Per Capita	
			Activity	Travel	Activity	Travel
Obligatory Activities						
01	Miscellaneous	.32	0.74	0.07	0.24	0.02
02	Main job	.12	6.23	0.54	0.73	0.06
03	Other income-related	.01	6.56	0.92	0.07	0.01
04	Personal care	.76	1.01	0.00	0.77	0.00
05	Eating	.90	1.66	0.13	1.49	0.12
06	Shopping	.15	0.50	0.44	0.07	0.07
07	Sick or utilization of medical care services	.03	4.79	0.38	0.17	0.01
08	Maintenance of home, yard, car	.18	2.89	0.02	0.52	0.00
09	Housework and childcare	.62	2.71	0.01	1.67	0.01
10	Misc. household chores, including pet care and walking	.04	0.66	0.03	0.03	0.00
11	Household business	.17	1.49	0.24	0.25	0.04
12	Education	.02	3.93	0.00	0.09	0.00
					(6.09)	(0.35)
Discretionary Activities						
13	Child-centered activities	.09	1.31	0.07	0.12	0.01
14	Visiting, writing letters, phoning relatives	.16	2.67	0.30	0.44	0.05
15	Oversseing children's study, practice	.02	1.97	0.00	0.05	0.00
16	Family outings or drives	.06	1.69	0.08	0.11	0.01
17	Talking and visiting within family	.15	2.56	0.06	0.38	0.01
18	Visiting, writing letters, phoning friends at home	.20	2.01	0.00	0.40	0.00
19	Visiting in the neighborhood	.04	2.03	0.12	0.09	0.01
20	Visiting outside the neighborhood	.14	1.84	0.38	0.26	0.05
21	Other socializing activities	.05	2.36	0.75	0.13	0.04
22	Relaxing, loafing, resting or napping	.24	2.18	0.00	0.52	0.00
23	Reading newspapers, magazines or nonspecified material	.58	1.83	0.00	1.05	0.00
24	Reading books	.05	1.55	0.00	0.07	0.00
25	Cultural activities	.06	1.80	0.26	0.12	0.02
26	Movies	.01	2.93	0.75	0.03	0.01
27	Television	.67	2.98	0.18	1.99	0.00
28	Radio	.04	1.64	0.00	0.06	0.00
29	Crafts and hobbies	.04	2.07	0.01	0.09	0.00
30	Walking and cycling	.05	1.49	0.00	0.08	0.00
31	Driving about, sightseeing (not with family)	.02	2.64	0.00	0.06	0.00
32	Participant sports	.06	1.89	0.29	0.12	0.02
33	Spectator sports	.01	2.50	0.25	0.03	0.00
34	Out-of-town holidays	.10	8.81	0.00	0.89	0.00
35	Other recreation	.03	1.78	0.16	0.05	0.01
36	Religious activities	.32	1.87	0.50	0.60	0.16
37	Meetings of voluntary organizations	.00	2.84	0.12	0.01	0.00
38	Public affairs and service activities	.01	1.62	0.36	0.02	0.01
					(7.77)	(0.41)
39	Travel including waiting for travel	.67	1.14	-	0.77	-
40	Sleep	.99	8.17	0.00	8.09	0.00

Note: Time allocated to concurrent activities is evenly split between these activities.

Table A-6. Comparative Data on per Capita Weekday Durations for Activities in the 40-Code Classification System—Washington, 1968; Area A, 1969; and Area B, 1971

Code No.	Activity Category	Wash. Metro 1968 (n=1,667)[a/]	Area A (Low-Income Black) 1969 (n=399)[b/]	Area B (Low-Income White) 1971 (n=609)[b/]
Obligatory Activities				
01	Miscellaneous	.23	1.09	.18
02	Main job	5.06	2.99	4.03
03	Other income-related	.13	.20	.16
04	Personal care	.75	.66	.70
05	Eating	1.67	.96	1.39
06	Shopping	.57	.38	.61
07	Sick or utilization of medical care services	.14	.23	.22
08	Maintenance of home, yard or car	.19	.19	.56
09	Housework and childcare	2.28	2.74	2.16
10	Misc. household chores, including pet care or walking	.05	-	-
11	Household business	.22	.13	.19
12	Education	.20	.02	.07
Discretionary Activities				
13	Child-centered activities	.11	.07	.11
14	Visiting, writing letters, phoning relatives	.12	.12	.22
15	Overseeing children's study, practice	.04	.01	.01
16	Family outings or drives	.03	.06	.02
17	Talking and visiting within family	.22	.01	.03
18	Visiting, writing letters, phoning friends at home	.32	.35	.50
19	Visiting in the neighborhood	.06	.10	.27
20	Visiting outside the neighborhood	.26	.22	.39
21	Other socializing activities	.11	.08	.20
22	Relaxing, loafing, resting or napping	.38	1.72	.92
23	Reading newspapers, magazines or nonspecified material	.56	.22	.55
24	Reading books	.08	.04	.07
25	Cultural activities	.11	.05	.06
26	Movies	.05	.02	.03
27	Television	1.65	2.78	1.84
28	Radio	.06	.08	.07
29	Crafts and hobbies	.06	.07	.18
30	Walking and cycling	.03	.01	.04
31	Driving about, sightseeing (not with family)	.01	.02	.05
32	Participant sports	.10	.01	.09
33	Spectator sports	.02	.00	.04
34	Out-of-town holidays	.17	.00	.02
35	Other recreation	.03	.11	.11
36	Religious activities	.08	.05	.11
37	Meetings of voluntary organizations	.03	.02	.02
38	Public affairs and service activities	.03	.01	.06

a/ Sample size based on respondents with complete activity data and all analysis variables.

b/ Sample sizes based on respondents with complete activity data.

Note: Code 39 (Travel) is allocated to activities for which it was incurred; and Code 40 (Sleep) is omitted.

See Figure IV-1 for locations of Areas A and B.

Table A-7. Percent of Adult Sample Engaged in Various Activities at Each Particular Hour of the Day *by Race*, Weekdays—Washington, Spring 1968

	6 a.m.	7	8	9	10	11	12	1 p.m.	2	3
Main Job	1.7	4.9	21.6	42.9	47.6	48.0	31.3	36.7	45.6	45.2
W	1.2	4.3	22.5	44.4	49.4	49.4	31.1	37.1	47.1	47.0
B	3.4	7.6	20.2	39.5	43.5	45.0	33.8	36.4	42.4	41.1
Eating	2.6	9.6	11.2	5.6	3.5	2.9	20.2	13.7	4.6	2.1
W	2.3	10.7	12.3	6.1	3.6	3.1	21.6	14.8	4.4	2.1
B	3.4	5.8	7.9	3.9	3.4	1.8	16.0	10.0	5.2	2.1
Shopping	0.1	0.1	0.1	0.5	1.4	3.2	3.2	3.7	4.1	3.0
W	0.1	0.1	0.2	0.5	1.5	3.6	3.7	4.3	4.7	3.3
B	0	0	0	0.5	1.3	2.1	1.6	1.8	1.6	1.8
Homemaking	4.0	11.8	18.9	19.6	20.2	20.0	16.7	15.1	14.7	15.7
W	4.3	12.0	20.2	20.5	20.2	19.6	15.5	14.5	14.3	15.7
B	3.4	10.5	14.7	16.2	19.6	20.7	20.7	17.0	15.2	14.9
Family Activities	0	0.4	0.3	1.0	0.7	0.7	1.1	1.4	2.1	2.5
W	0	0.5	0.4	1.2	0.9	0.8	1.2	1.7	2.6	3.0
B	0	0	0	0.3	0	0	0.3	0.3	0.5	0.8
Socializing	0.1	0.4	0.6	1.2	1.6	1.7	2.5	2.4	2.5	3.2
W	0.1	0.3	0.6	1.4	1.7	1.7	2.9	2.6	2.7	3.3
B	0	0.3	0.3	0	1.1	1.6	1.3	1.3	1.3	2.6
Rest & Relaxation	0.9	2.9	3.4	2.6	2.8	2.2	1.9	4.0	5.2	5.9
W	0.9	2.9	3.7	2.3	2.8	1.7	1.7	3.1	4.5	4.7
B	0.5	2.6	2.1	3.7	2.9	3.9	2.9	7.1	7.3	10.0
Recr.-Diversions	0.4	0.4	0.9	1.6	2.6	3.0	2.5	2.5	2.7	3.4
W	0.5	0.5	0.8	1.5	2.7	3.2	2.6	2.5	2.6	3.3
B	0	0	0.8	1.6	1.6	1.8	1.6	2.4	2.6	3.4
Viewing TV	0.1	0.2	0.8	1.2	1.8	2.6	2.8	4.1	4.5	5.0
W	0	0.2	0.7	0.9	1.1	1.9	1.9	2.7	3.6	4.4
B	0.3	0.5	1.3	2.1	4.5	5.5	5.2	8.4	7.6	7.1
Church & Orgs.	0.1	0.2	0.1	0.4	1.0	1.1	0.7	0.4	0.5	0.3
W	0.1	0.2	0.1	0.5	1.2	1.3	0.8	0.5	0.6	0.3
B	0.3	0.3	0	0	0.3	0.3	0	0	0	0
Miscellaneous	15.1	24.2	13.8	8.8	6.6	5.5	5.6	4.7	4.1	5.8
W	13.9	25.7	12.8	8.8	6.7	5.8	6.3	5.2	4.1	6.0
B	19.1	19.6	16.2	8.6	6.0	5.0	3.4	3.1	4.5	5.5
Travel	1.1	7.6	12.1	5.5	4.4	4.8	8.2	8.3	6.3	4.7
W	0.9	7.7	12.5	5.3	4.3	5.3	8.6	9.0	6.7	5.0
B	1.8	7.1	11.3	6.3	4.7	2.6	6.0	5.2	4.7	3.7
Sleep	72.4	35.9	14.3	6.9	3.6	2.1	0.9	0.7	0.6	0.6
W	74.8	34.2	12.1	5.0	2.6	1.2	0.5	0.3	0.3	0.3
B	64.1	41.9	21.5	12.8	6.8	5.0	2.4	1.8	1.6	1.6

4	5	6	7	8	9	10	11	12	1 a.m.	2	3	4	5
38.2	21.4	9.3	7.0	6.2	5.4	4.2	2.8	2.4	1.8	1.3	1.2	1.2	1.3
40.3	21.4	8.1	5.8	5.6	5.0	3.9	2.6	2.1	1.2	0.9	0.7	0.7	0.9
32.7	21.7	13.9	11.5	8.6	6.5	5.0	3.4	3.7	3.7	2.9	2.9	3.1	2.9
2.1	7.6	25.6	20.5	9.4	4.8	2.7	1.8	0.1	0.1	0.1	0.2	0.1	0.7
1.3	7.4	27.2	22.3	10.7	5.0	3.3	2.1	0	0.1	0	0.2	0.1	0.6
4.7	8:1	21.2	15.2	5.8	4.2	0.8	0.5	0.3	0	0.3	0.5	0.3	1.1
2.6	2.6	1.8	2.4	2.6	1.1	0.1	0.1	0.1	0	0	0	0	0
2.7	2.9	2.1	2.9	3.1	1.2	0.1	0.1	0.1	0	0	0	0	0
2.1	1.6	0.8	1.1	0.8	0.5	0	0	0	0	0	0	0	0
18.6	23.8	19.7	16.8	13.8	9.7	5.8	3.6	0.8	0.8	0.1	0.2	0.2	0.9
18.5	24.4	19.9	17.9	13.6	10.5	6.0	3.8	0.9	0.9	0.2	0.2	0.2	0.8
18.1	22.0	18.9	12.8	13.6	6.8	5.0	2.9	0.8	0.3	0	0	0	1.6
3.1	3.6	3.2	4.5	5.2	4.5	4.1	1.9	0.2	0.2	0.1	0	0	0
3.8	4.6	3.7	5.3	6.1	5.2	5.2	2.4	0.2	0.3	0.1	0	0	0
0.8	0.5	1.6	2.1	1.8	2.1	0.8	0.5	0	0	0	0	0	0
3.3	2.9	4.0	5.3	7.6	8.2	7.6	5.3	1.4	0.7	0.4	0.1	0.1	0.2
3.5	2.6	4.2	5.8	8.6	9.1	8.9	6.1	1.7	0.8	0.4	-0.1	0.1	0.2
2.4	3.7	3.4	4.2	4.5	4.7	3.4	2.6	0	0	0	0	0	0
6.2	6.3	4.9	6.6	7.5	8.5	6.8	4.2	1.8	0.8	0.4	0.1	0.1	0.2
5.1	5.7	4.9	6.5	7.7	9.7	7.9	4.6	2.1	0.8	0.4	0.1	0.1	0.3
9.7	8.6	5.0	6.8	6.8	4.5	2.9	2.6	0.8	0.8	0.3	0	0	0
3.4	2.7	2.4	4.9	7.2	7.7	5.8	2.9	1.0	0.5	0.3	0.1	0.1	0.1
3.7	3.0	2.6	5.1	8.0	8.5	6.7	3.3	1.0	0.4	0.3	0.1	0.1	0.1
1.8	1.3	2.1	4.5	5.0	5.5	2.9	2.1	0.8	0.5	0.3	0.3	0.3	0.3
4.0	3.2	5.4	13.3	22.8	30.0	28.7	16.5	5.3	2.4	0.2	0.1	0	0
3.5	2.3	4.3	11.0	20.3	27.2	27.3	15.8	4.6	1.7	0.2	0.1	0	0
5.8	6.5	8.9	20.4	30.9	39.5	33.3	19.1	7.1	4.5	0.5	0.3	0	0
0.3	0.3	0.4	0.7	2.0	1.6	0.9	0.4	0.1	0.1	0	0	0	0
0.3	0.2	0.3	0.5	2.0	1.4	1.0	0.5	0	0	0	0	0	0
0	0.3	0.8	1.1	1.8	2.1	0.5	0	0.3	0.3	0	0	0	0
5.9	7.2	9.2	6.2	5.5	5.6	5.9	5.4	2.4	1.4	0.5	0.2	0.4	1.6
6.2	7.0	9.3	6.0	5.8	5.7	5.8	6.0	2.6	1.4	0.3	0.1	0.3	1.2
5.0	7.3	8.1	6.8	5.0	5.2	6.3	3.9	1.8	1.6	1.3	0.5	0.5	3.1
9.5	15.4	11.1	8.2	5.8	5.6	4.0	1.6	1.1	0.6	0.2	0.2	0	0.1
9.4	16.6	12.0	8.7	5.6	6.2	4.0	1.5	1.2	0.8	0.2	0.2	0	0.1
10.2	11.5	8.1	6.0	6.3	3.9	4.2	1.8	0.8	0	0.3	0	0	0.3
0.4	0.3	0.2	0.2	0.4	3.4	20.3	50.2	81.5	89.3	94.9	96.1	96.3	93.3
0.1	0.1	0	0	0.2	0.2	20.2	50.2	82.7	90.9	96.2	97.4	97.5	95.1
1.3	1.1	1.1	1.1	1.1	1.1	20.5	50.0	80.1	84.8	90.6	91.9	92.2	87.2

Table A-8. Percent of Adult Sample Engaged in Various Activities at Each Particular Hour of the Day *by Income,* Weekdays—Washington, Spring 1968

	6 a.m.	7	8	9	10	11	12	1 p.m.	2	3	4
Main Job											
L	0.8	2.5	11.9	20.1	23.8	23.0	17.2	20.1	22.1	21.3	16.0
M	2.5	6.7	23.3	39.0	43.0	44.4	32.3	33.7	40.5	41.3	31.5
H	1.7	5.0	23.8	50.0	55.2	55.5	34.8	41.8	53.4	52.6	46.1
Eating											
L	1.6	5.3	7.8	6.2	6.2	4.9	9.4	4.5	2.1	4.5	11.5
M	3.1	5.9	8.4	5.6	2.8	2.3	19.1	13.2	5.3	2.3	2.3
H	2.6	11.8	13.0	5.5	3.2	2.5	21.7	14.9	4.4	2.0	1.5
Shopping											
L	0	0	0	0	0.4	1.6	1.6	2.5	3.3	2.9	3.3
M	0	0	0	0.6	1.4	2.5	2.3	3.1	3.1	2.8	1.4
H	0.1	0.1	0.2	0.7	1.7	3.8	3.9	4.3	4.5	3.0	2.8
Homemaking											
L	5.7	14.8	20.9	22.1	29.9	31.2	30.3	25.4	23.8	24.2	29.9
M	4.2	11.5	20.2	23.9	22.8	22.5	18.3	15.7	15.7	16.0	18.8
H	3.6	11.0	18.0	17.5	16.9	16.5	13.0	12.5	12.0	13.4	15.6
Family Activities											
L	0	0.8	0.8	1.6	0.4	0.8	2.1	2.5	2.9	2.9	3.3
M	0	0.3	0.3	0.8	1.4	1.1	1.4	2.0	3.1	3.7	3.4
H	0	0.3	0.2	0.8	0.6	0.4	0.7	0.9	1.7	2.0	3.0
Socializing											
L	0	0.4	0.4	1.6	2.5	3.7	2.5	3.3	4.1	4.5	4.9
M	0.3	0.6	1.4	1.1	2.0	1.7	3.1	2.3	2.5	4.2	3.4
H	0	0.2	0.3	0.9	1.2	1.2	2.3	2.1	2.0	2.4	2.8
Rest & Relaxation											
L	1.6	2.1	2.9	4.9	4.1	4.1	5.3	11.5	12.3	14.3	12.3
M	1.4	3.4	2.0	2.0	2.5	3.1	2.5	3.1	4.2	6.5	4.5
H	0.5	2.9	3.9	2.3	2.6	1.5	1.0	2.6	3.8	3.8	5.3
Recr.-Diversions											
L	0.4	0	1.2	3.7	4.1	4.9	2.5	3.7	5.3	6.6	4.9
M	0.3	0	1.1	1.4	3.1	3.1	3.7	3.4	3.4	3.1	3.1
H	0.4	0.6	0.6	1.0	1.9	2.3	2.0	1.9	1.7	2.6	3.0
Viewing TV											
L	0.4	0.4	2.1	2.1	3.7	5.3	5.7	6.6	8.2	7.8	6.2
M	0	0.3	0.8	1.4	2.3	3.1	3.4	7.6	7.3	7.6	5.3
H	0	0.2	0.6	0.9	1.3	2.0	1.7	2.2	2.8	3.5	3.1
Church & Orgs.											
L	0	0	0	0	0.4	0.4	0.4	0	0	0	0
M	0.3	0.6	0	0	0.3	0.6	0.6	0.3	0.6	0.3	0.3
H	0.1	0.2	0.1	0.7	1.3	1.4	0.7	0.6	0.6	0.3	0.3
Miscellaneous											
L	12.7	16.0	14.3	11.9	7.8	6.6	4.9	5.7	3.7	5.7	4.5
M	14.3	20.2	14.0	7.6	7.0	6.2	5.3	6.2	5.9	4.8	6.2
H	15.9	27.5	13.3	8.5	6.0	5.2	5.9	4.0	3.7	6.2	6.1
Travel											
L	0	5.3	6.6	6.6	4.1	5.3	5.3	4.1	4.5	2.5	4.9
M	2.5	9.0	7.6	4.5	4.2	3.9	5.1	6.7	5.6	4.2	16.4
H	0.9	7.5	15.1	5.6	4.6	4.8	9.6	9.5	6.8	5.3	8.3
Sleep											
L	73.4	48.8	27.5	14.8	8.2	3.7	0.8	0.4	0	0	0
M	69.4	40.2	18.5	9.8	5.1	3.4	1.1	0.6	0.3	0.8	0.8
H	73.1	31.6	9.8	4.0	2.0	1.2	0.8	0.7	0.8	0.7	0.3

Note: L denotes low-, M, medium-, and H, high-income category. For the formation

5	6	7	8	9	10	11	12	1 a.m.	2	3	4	5
10.7	7.4	6.2	4.5	3.3	2.1	1.2	0.4	0.4	0.4	0.4	0.8	0.8
18.0	10.7	8.4	6.7	5.3	3.9	3.7	3.7	2.8	2.0	2.3	2.3	2.3
25.1	9.5	6.9	6.5	5.9	4.7	2.8	2.5	1.8	1.3	1.0	1.0	1.1
24.2	20.9	8.2	4.5	0.8	1.2	0.4	0	0	0	0.4	0	0.8
10.1	23.9	14.9	5.9	3.9	1.1	1.4	0	0	0.3	0.6	0.3	1.7
5.9	26.9	22.5	11.1	5.2	3.7	2.0	0	0.1	0	0.1	0.1	0.4
2.1	1.2	1.6	0	0	0	0	0	0	0	0	0	0
2.8	0.6	1.7	2.8	1.7	0.3	0	0	0	0	0	0	0
2.6	2.3	2.9	3.1	1.0	0	0.1	0.1	0	0	0	0	0
25.4	18.4	16.4	13.5	8.6	6.2	3.7	0.8	0.4	0	0	0	2.1
24.4	21.1	16.6	13.2	7.3	3.9	2.3	1.1	1.4	0	0.3	0.3	2.0
23.3	19.5	16.8	13.8	10.7	6.2	4.0	0.7	0.7	0.2	0.2	0.2	0.4
2.9	4.9	3.3	3.3	2.1	1.2	0.8	0.4	0.4	0.4	0	0	0
2.3	2.5	4.2	5.6	3.4	2.5	1.1	0	0	0	0	0	0
4.4	3.1	5.0	5.4	5.4	5.4	2.5	0.2	0.3	0	0	0	0
7.0	5.3	7.4	7.8	8.2	7.0	4.5	0.4	0.4	0	0	0	0.4
2.3	4.8	6.5	5.9	5.6	5.3	3.1	1.4	1.1	0.6	0	0	0
2.1	3.4	4.7	8.2	8.9	8.6	6.2	1.5	0.5	0.3	0.1	0.1	0.1
11.1	5.3	4.5	6.6	4.9	2.9	1.2	0.8	0.8	0.4	0	0.4	0.4
6.2	5.1	6.2	7.3	8.7	4.2	3.1	1.1	0.8	0.6	0	0	0.6
5.4	4.7	7.2	7.8	9.3	8.5	5.2	2.2	0.7	0.3	0.1	0	0.1
3.3	2.9	4.1	7.0	7.8	6.2	2.9	0.8	0.4	0.8	0.4	0.4	0
2.8	2.5	5.6	5.6	5.3	5.3	3.4	2.0	0.8	0.6	0	0	0
2.4	2.3	4.9	7.9	8.6	6.0	2.9	0.7	0.3	0.1	0.1	0.1	0.2
7.8	10.3	18.4	31.6	35.7	27.1	17.2	5.7	4.1	0.8	0.4	0	0
5.9	8.2	19.4	30.1	36.8	33.7	17.1	5.1	2.0	0.3	0.3	0	0
1.4	3.3	9.9	18.3	26.5	27.3	16.3	5.1	2.0	0.1	0	0	0
0.4	0.4	0.4	2.5	2.5	1.2	0.4	0	0.4	0	0	0	0
0	0.3	0.8	1.1	1.4	0.8	0.3	0	0	0	0	0	0
0.3	0.5	0.7	2.1	1.4	0.8	0.5	0.1	0	0	0	0	0
3.7	6.2	3.3	2.9	1.6	2.1	2.5	1.6	0.8	0	0	0.4	0.8
6.5	8.2	6.2	5.9	6.7	5.9	5.1	2.3	1.1	1.1	0.3	0	2.3
8.0	9.9	6.9	6.1	6.1	6.8	6.3	2.6	1.7	0.5	0.2	0.5	1.6
8.6	7.0	6.2	2.5	4.1	4.1	0.4	2.1	0.4	0.4	0	0	0.4
15.5	9.3	6.2	5.6	5.3	5.3	2.3	0.6	0.3	0.6	0	0	0
17.0	12.6	9.1	6.5	6.1	3.6	1.6	1.0	0.8	0.1	0.3	0	0.1
0	0	0	0	0	20.0	50.0	83.2	88.1	93.4	95.1	94.7	91.0
0.8	0.8	0.8	1.1	1.1	20.8	50.3	80.9	87.6	92.1	94.4	95.2	89.6
0.2	0.1	0.1	0.2	0.2	20.2	50.2	82.3	90.4	96.2	96.9	97.0	95.1

of these categories, see Figure III-3.

INDEX